Reading Middle En_g

Blackwell Introductions to Literature

This series sets out to provide concise and stimulating introductions to literary subjects. It offers books on major authors (from John Milton to James Joyce), as well as key periods and movements (from Old English literature to the contemporary). Coverage is also afforded to such specific topics as 'Arthurian Romance'. All are written by outstanding scholars as texts to inspire newcomers and others: non-specialists wishing to revisit a topic, or general readers. The prospective overall aim is to ground and prepare students and readers of whatever kind in their pursuit of wider reading.

Published

Reading Middle English Literature

Thorlac Turville-Petre

Blackwell
Publishing

© 2007 by Thorlac Turville-Petre

BLACKWELL PUBLISHING
350 Main Street, Malden, MA 02148-5020, USA
9600 Garsington Road, Oxford OX4 2DQ, UK
550 Swanston Street, Carlton, Victoria 3053, Australia

The right of Thorlac Turville-Petre to be identified
as the Author of this Work has been asserted in accordance
with the UK Copyright, Designs, and Patents Act 1988.

First published 2007 by Blackwell Publishing Ltd

1   2007

Library of Congress Cataloging-in-Publication Data

Turville-Petre, Thorlac.
Reading Middle English literature / Thorlac Turville-Petre.
p. cm.—(Blackwell introductions to literature ; 16)
Includes bibliographical references and index.
ISBN-13: 978-0-631-23171-4 (hardback : alk. paper)
ISBN-10: 0-631-23171-4 (hardback : alk. paper)
ISBN-13: 978-0-631-23172-1 (pbk. : alk. paper)
ISBN-10: 0-631-23172-2 (pbk. : alk. paper)   1. English literature—Middle
English, 1100–1500—History and criticism.   2. Civilization, Medieval,
in literature.   I. Title.   II. Series.
PR255.T87 2007
820.9'001—dc22
2005034698

A catalogue record for this title is available from the British Library.

Set in 10/13pt Meridien
by Graphicraft Limited, Hong Kong

For further information on
Blackwell Publishing, visit our website:
www.blackwellpublishing.com

Contents

Plates

Preface

Texts that are included in full in *A Book of Middle English* (*BOME*) are quoted from there. They are: *Sir Orfeo, Patience, St Erkenwald*, Trevisa's *Dialogue between a Lord and a Clerk*, selected Rawlinson, Harley and Grimestone lyrics, the York Play of the Crucifixion and Chaucer's *Parliament of Fowls*. Other texts are quoted from the editions cited in the bibliography, revised on the same principles as used in *BOME*: that is to say, the distribution of u/v and i/j has been modernized, punctuation and capitalization have been supplied or altered, and abbreviations have been expanded. The editions used are listed in the bibliography by editor, with a cross-reference from the title of the text to the edition. Bella Millett kindly supplied me with the references to her forthcoming edition of *Ancrene Wisse*.

Pages 103–8 are revised from an article published in *Studies in Late Medieval and Early Renaissance Texts in Honour of John Scattergood*, eds. Anne Marie D'Arcy and Alan J. Fletcher (Dublin, 2005), 362–74.

I am indebted to many friends, colleagues and students for their comments and discussions, and I am particularly grateful to John Burrow, Janette Dillon, Ralph Hanna and Nicola Royan for their advice so generously given.

T.T-P.

Abbreviations

ANTS	Anglo-Norman Text Society
AV	Authorized Version of the Bible
BL	British Library
BOME	*A Book of Middle English*, eds. J. A. Burrow and Thorlac Turville-Petre (3rd edn., Oxford, 2005)
CA	Gower's *Confessio Amantis*
CT	Chaucer's *Canterbury Tales*
EETS	Early English Text Society (e.s. = Extra Series; s.s. = Supplementary Series)
f.	folio
ME	Middle English
MED	*Middle English Dictionary*
OE	Old English
OED	*Oxford English Dictionary*
OF	Old French
ON	Old Norse
r	recto
v	verso

Introduction

If this book has anything so grand as an argument, it is that Middle English literature is much more accessible than many people suppose. Here I am not thinking so much of the language, for certainly there are works such as Laȝamon's *Brut* and *Pearl* that demand a good understanding of their dialect and vocabulary if a reader is to respond to them fully. I am instead referring to the culture, the ways in which texts speak in voices to which we can relate and of matters that reflect our own concerns and interests.

There are many myths about the Middle Ages that serve, and indeed may be intended to serve, to distance medieval literature from the modern reader. For example, it has been said that in the Middle Ages there was no true concept of childhood: children were seen as miniature adults, and parents were so inured to high infant mortality that they wasted no time grieving. To dispel that misconception, read a father's inconsolable grief for his baby daughter in *Pearl*. It has been said that marriage in the Middle Ages was never anything other than a business arrangement, the wife no more than a piece of property to her husband. To put paid to that error, read the tender expressions of love between husband and wife in *Sir Orfeo*. It has been said that there was no sense of England as a nation, and no concept of the nation's history. To correct such a false notion, read *St Erkenwald* with its vivid account of the early days of the English church. These and other myths can easily be shown, and have long been shown, to be quite untrue, yet they are still purveyed by those working on later periods who understandably want to present their chosen field as the age in which modern concepts of this or that began to emerge.

If our starting point is that those who lived 700 years ago were not Martians but people whose social practices and cultural attitudes were the earlier forms of the attitudes and practices of modern western societies, then we shall be in a good position to measure and analyse the differences. Some concepts have not travelled well through time: the chivalric ethos is one example, with its knightly codes of conduct, its emphasis on honour and shame, its glorification of battle. But then even medieval commentators often complained that the ideal was by their time disregarded: Christ 'showed through his chivalric behaviour that he was worthy to be loved, as knights were *once* accustomed to do', writes the author of *Ancrene Wisse* as early as the thirteenth century, and a satirical writer of the early fourteenth century complains that knights whose duty it is to fight for Holy Church 'are now lions in hall and hares in the field'. A second area of change is in religious beliefs and observances, even though many of the rituals and practices survived in recognisable form until the Second Vatican Council of the 1960s and beyond. There is change, too, in the language situation: throughout much of the Middle Ages, although the majority spoke only English, the social elite spoke and read two vernaculars and the educated knew Latin as well. In modern Britain and the United States this position is reversed, for now elite culture is monoglot while more recent immigrant populations are multilingual. All these are significant differences between the Middle Ages and today, but the change that demands the greatest stretch of our imagination is in the means of publication, which is a consequence of new technology at the end of the Middle Ages and then again in the last thirty years. Before the invention of printing, every text had to be copied individually with great effort and expense. We have to think ourselves back to a time before there were multiple, and now infinite, identical copies of each work, to a time when vernacular texts in particular would be difficult to obtain and immensely expensive to own, when two copies of the 'same' work would look quite different and might actually vary extensively in readings, dialect, punctuation, verse-order, and in short in most of the indicators that we would take to constitute the sameness of the two texts.

Another potent myth about the Middle Ages is inherent in the term 'Middle Ages'. It evokes a time between more vibrant times, the Classical Age and the Renaissance, a time when culture was static, monolithic, stagnant, unconsciously waiting for the rebirth. In presenting, as I do, the literature by themes rather than chronology, there is thus a danger of obscuring the massive cultural changes during the 400 years covered by this book. In just the fourteenth century a series of calamities had profound economic and social consequences reflected in the literature: the years of famine early in the century; the war with France from the 1340s onwards; repeated outbreaks of plague from 1348; the Peasants' Revolt of 1381. And yet the distinction between the free man and the bondman, lord and peasant, remained, perceived as a fundamental class-divider even though in reality the barriers between them had become much more permeable. During the fourteenth century, again, criticism of the church and of clerics became more vociferous, reaching the point of heresy with Wycliffe and the Lollards. But Lollardy did not in the end capture the hearts of those in power, and it remained a popular movement only. So, too, though love is always with us, ways of writing about it were powerfully influenced from the later thirteenth century by French romances and lyric poetry. Society; piety; love: these and other themes occupy the following chapters. However, the first chapter is essentially chronological, tracing the fortunes of English as a cultural medium in relationship with Latin and Anglo-Norman. This chapter will set the scene for a period of profound and pervasive change.

At the centre of this book is a close reading of a fairly small selection of texts. Though I have ranged more widely when appropriate, I have been keen to keep this study within bounds and also to avoid too many generalizations, so I have concentrated on the selection of poetry and prose in *A Book of Middle English*. These texts range in date from the mid-twelfth to the early fifteenth centuries, and cover a wide variety of subjects and genres. Furthermore, many of them will already be known to some readers, and all are easily available for those who do not know them, so that my analyses can be assessed with immediate reference to the texts. The last two chapters will offer wider discussions of longer works presented in extract in *A Book of Middle English* (*BOME*).

This book can make no claim to be comprehensive, but comprehensiveness should be the aim of the encyclopedia, not the literary history. The concentration on a selection of texts allows room for the coupling of less habitual bedfellows: to look at *Pearl* with the Prioress's

Tale, which are paired surprisingly rarely, I think: to put the *Peterborough Chronicle* side by side with *Sir Orfeo* even though the fairy king might call them 'a sory couple'.

A disadvantage of working by topic rather than by text is that each discussion inevitably focuses on one aspect of the work. When, for example, the ploughing of Piers' half-acre is analysed in a chapter about 'society', what *Piers Plowman* has to say about love is neglected; when Chaucer's *Parliament of Fowls* is discussed in a chapter on 'love', its social commentary is ignored. I have tried to compensate for this by including briefer accounts of such multi-faceted works in more than one section. I hope that this approach will show clearly how medieval writers reflected the debates and preoccupations of their culture, how they participated in them and how they shaped the forms in which to express them.

CHAPTER 1

The Use of English

Three Languages

What were the effects of the Norman Conquest upon the English language? A century and a half after the battle of Hastings, a scribe copied a celebration of the glories of Anglo-Saxon learning, the *First Worcester Fragment*, beginning 'Sanctus Beda was iboren her on Breotene mid us' – 'Saint Bede was born here among us in Britain.' The poet listed the bishops from the seventh century to the eleventh, 'by whom our people were taught in English' and who 'disseminated (*bodeden*) the Christian faith', continuing:

> Þeos lærden ure leodan on Englisc;
> Næs deorc heore liht ac hit fæire glod.
> Nu is þeo leore forleten and þet folc is forloren;
> Nu beoþ oþre leoden þeo læreþ ure folc
> And feole of þen lorþeines losiæþ and þet folc forþ mid.   (15–18)

[These taught our people in English; their light was not dark but glowed brightly. Now the learning has been abandoned and the people lost; now there are other men who teach our people, and many of the teachers are damned and the people with them.]

The scribe of this lament is known affectionately as 'the tremulous Worcester hand', and his shaky writing can be seen in several manuscripts that came from Worcester Cathedral Library, copying, glossing and interpreting the Old English that he evidently had some difficulty in understanding (Franzen 1991; Brehe 1990).

How much truth is there in this lament? The Anglo-Saxon achieve-
ments in learning and literature were undeniably distinguished, and
their passing a justified cause of regret. Such an early and substantial
tradition of vernacular writings is without parallel in Europe. The
Anglo-Saxon church had a proud history going back to the Conversion, its earliest days recorded by Bede and its later developments
charted by other historians, such as the monk Eadmer at Canterbury
shortly after the Conquest writing Latin lives of saints. Scribes were
trained to write Old English in a settled orthography based on the
West-Saxon dialect, and there was a flourishing of literary activity in
the years around 1000, with the copying of all the important codices
of Old English poetry, and the compositions of those masters of English prose, Ælfric and Wulfstan. Within a decade of the Conquest the
only English-born bishop left was – significantly – the bishop of Worcester, who had been elected in 1062; the others were all foreigners. The
majority of English lordships had been taken over by Normans. English had been replaced by Latin as the language of learning and the
language of record. Though works of prose writers such as Ælfric continued to be copied and studied, the distinctive Anglo-Saxon poetic
tradition had disappeared or, to be precise, had been replaced by a
thin stream of half-verse, half-prose, of which this Worcester lament
is a fair representative.

The writer's gloom is easy to understand, for there was a great deal
to be gloomy about. There were very obvious losses in the transition
from Anglo-Saxon to Norman. The gains were less visible, but yet the
English language survived very well in the mouths of the great majority of the people of England. There was never the remotest possibility that English would die. It was developing in ways that were to
have profound long-term effects, and this scrap of verse already records
one such development. Ironically in view of the writer's devotion to
English, its vocabulary includes loan-words: writing Bede 'unravelled
the knotty problems called *questiuns*' (4), he introduces a technical
word from Latin, perhaps via French, as a philosophical term alluding
to Bede's collections of *Quaestiones*; the last word of the poem is *feþ*,
'faith', a word introduced by the Normans in the form of their own
dialect of French. Though there were no longer scribes trained to
write according to the traditional standard based on West-Saxon, it
was a formal version of English that never represented closely the
spoken language, and later scribes instead represented English as it

developed in various regions in different ways, some dialects more conservative than others, some more influenced by the Old Norse of the Viking settlers, some more receptive to Norman French.

But why are these early developments so little visible? Part of the answer is illustrated by the Worcester lament, surviving only in a fragmentary manuscript that was cut up in the fifteenth century as scrap to be used in bindings for the books in the Worcester Cathedral Library. Manuscripts survive by chance; the losses, particularly from the early Middle English period, were enormous (Wilson 1970).

The other part of the answer is that after the Conquest English was the least prestigious of England's three main languages. Before the Conquest, English co-existed with Latin, the language of the Universal Church; after 1066 it competed with an alternative vernacular, Norman French, which in England developed its own features as Anglo-Norman. The Normans represented a relatively small proportion of the population, but since they had power in their hands their language came to have a disproportionate impact upon society. To begin with, the language situation was often simple enough: mutual incomprehension. 'The Normans say that the English are barking because they can't understand their speech', wrote Wace in his account of the battle of Hastings (Crane 1999, 36). But this situation could not last long, as Norman lords married ladies whose first language was English, employed English bailiffs with whom they needed to communicate in one language or the other if their estates were to be run effectively, and generally made themselves at home culturally as well as physically, switching from French wine to English beer, according to Reginald of Canterbury (Rigg 1992, 11). By 1176, as a result of intermarriage, Richard Fitz Neal considered it difficult to distinguish between freemen of English and Norman birth (*Dialogus de Scaccario*, ed. Johnson 1983, 53). He makes it clear, though, that he is referring to freemen, not to the majority of the population, the peasants.

The Normans traced their ancestry to Viking settlers in Normandy, who had given up Norse and adopted French manners. They showed the same ability to adapt in their new home, taking over the institutions and organizational structures of Anglo-Saxon society, and becoming bilingual, just as the English who had direct contact with them also had to do. It needs to be emphasized here that England was at some levels a multilingual community, above all in the twelfth century (Short 1991). The point is made by Walter Map's praise of

Gilbert Foliot, abbot of Gloucester, bishop of London (1163–87) and enemy of Thomas Becket, as 'a man most accomplished in the three languages, Latin, French and English, and eloquent and clear in each of them' (Bartlett 2000, 502–3).

The question of how long Anglo-Norman continued to be the first language of the conquerors cannot be answered in that form. Some Normans who intermarried must have been speaking English as a first language within a generation or two. Others who had estates across the Channel would have considered themselves as people of a Norman and Angevin realm rather than specifically English, until Normandy was lost to France in 1204, at which point they had to choose to commit themselves to one nation or the other. The aristocrats attached to the court, and those who, like a succession of English kings, took wives from the Continent, continued to speak French to some degree into the fourteenth century (Rothwell 1976).

Where English suffered long-term eclipse was as a written language. In this field it had to establish a role side by side with Latin and French. Shortly after the Conquest, royal documents ceased to be written in English and the Normans adopted Latin, probably because they neither understood English nor had their own tradition of writing documents in the vernacular. The most famous and extraordinary example of such a Latin document is Domesday Book of 1086. At first Latin was shared across a society divided by two vernaculars. Not until the mid-thirteenth century does it become at all usual to use French for official documents, and not until the early fifteenth century does English begin to make regular appearance as a language of official record (Clanchy 1993, 215–23). Neither French nor English ever entirely displaced Latin, which continued in documentary use right through the Middle Ages.

Latin had always been the language of monastic learning, particularly for writings aimed at a wider European readership. As English lost its position, so Latin increased its hold as the learned language. The range of writings in Latin is extraordinarily wide (Rigg 1992). In the reign of Henry II (1154–89), to take just one period of great activity, Latin authors, some serving as court officials or associated with the court in looser ways, achieved distinction in a variety of fields, and often influenced later writers in English (Clanchy 1983, 162–79). We must remember in this connection that the Angevin empire, ruled by the 'English' king and his queen, Eleanor of Aquitaine, included all of western France from Normandy in the north to Gascony in the south. It was a truly international and constantly peripatetic court, and many royal servants were not English in any narrow sense. Ailred of Rievaulx, however, was English, the son of an English priest (at a time when clerical marriage was not uncommon), who had started his career in the Scottish court, and joined the Cistercian order at the Yorkshire abbey of Rievaulx in 1132. His history, *Genealogia Regum Anglorum* (1152–3), was dedicated to the future Henry II, celebrating the union of the Norman and Anglo-Saxon royal lines that Henry represented, an idea Ailred expanded in the 1160s in his life of the last Anglo-Saxon king, Edward the Confessor (Clanchy 1983, 56). Ailred wrote a guide to the life of an anchoress, *De Institutione Inclusarum*, 'as seint Ailred þe abbat wrat to his suster', says the author of *Ancrene Wisse* (6.285), who drew on Ailred's book. It is a reminder that Latin was not solely the preserve of men. John of Salisbury (d. 1180), who was present at the murder of his friend Thomas Becket, served as a diplomat and later became bishop of Chartres. He wrote lives of Becket and of Anselm, the *Policraticus* on political theory, and the *Metalogicon* (1159) attacking the decline of learning. Closer to Henry II was Richard Fitz Neal, the king's treasurer and bishop of London, who wrote a guide to the exchequer in the form of a dialogue, the *Dialogus de Scaccario* (1176–7), cited above. Another royal servant was Ralph Glanvill, Henry II's chief judicial officer, who gave his name to a treatise on the laws and customs of England (1187–9). Though he was not actually its author, the work is intimately associated with the court. The *Speculum Stultorum*, 'Mirror of Fools', written in 1179–80 by Nigel Wireker, satirized the foolishness of society through the adventures of the donkey Burnellus. John Gower used it and it was cited as 'Daun Burnel the Asse' by Chaucer's smart fox in the Nun's Priest's Tale (*CT* VII.3312). In the 1180s Walter Map was the author of another satirical work, *De Nugis Curialium*, 'Courtiers' Trifles', a loosely organized collection of wild and wonderful stories, several of Celtic origin, including a version of the *Sir Orfeo* plot, a tale of the wife of a knight of 'Little Britain', that is, Brittany. A probable source of animal lore in *The Owl and the Nightingale* was Alexander Neckam (1157–1217), a considerable encyclopedist, whose *De Naturis Rerum*, 'The Nature of Things', was widely known. Finally, Joseph of Exeter wrote an epic poem on the Trojan War, the *Ylias* (c. 1185), indebted to classical and post-classical authors, in particular to the Roman poet

Statius. It was the kind of epic poem that Laȝamon must have read; Chaucer certainly knew it and drew details from it for the last book of *Troilus and Criseyde*. These learned authors of Henry II's reign wrote histories, epics, beast-fables, advice for both courtiers and recluses, lives of saints, satires, and compendia on the natural world, law and politics, philosophy and theology. In fact, the practice of composing in Latin continued long after the Middle Ages.

The range of writings in Anglo-Norman matched and overlapped those in Latin to a considerable degree (Dean 1999). In large measure the differences are to be accounted for by the nature of the reader-ship. Latin was always a language to be learned and studied in the schools and (from the thirteenth century) universities in England and on the Continent. Most of those who had received the training to become proficient in Latin at a high level were those with a clerical education, though the 'miles litteratus', the knight who read Latin, was not uncommon, as records of their books indicate (Clanchy 1993, 246–52). Furthermore, most of those with this degree of ability in Latin were men, though we have seen that women Latinists were not unknown. The 'litterati' had privileged access to a world of ancient writers as well as to the intellectual debates of the age. In the early post-Conquest period, most of those with a command of Latin would also be fluent in French, but the reverse would be less common, so that French readers would have been from a wider range, to include the laity, both male and female, from the upper echelons of society. There is secure evidence for women as patrons of Anglo-Norman in the twelfth century: Geffrei Gaimar's *L'Estoire des Engleis* was sup-ported by an aristocratic Lincolnshire lady, Constance FitzGilbert; Wace, according to Laȝamon, wrote his *Roman de Brut* for Henry II's queen Eleanor. Among women authors were Marie de France, who wrote her *Fables* and *Lais* for Henry II's court, and her contemporary Clemence, probably a nun from Barking, who wrote a life of St Catherine and perhaps also of Edward the Confessor in Anglo-Norman.

It comes as a surprise to discover that twelfth-century Anglo-Norman literature was richer and more diverse than the surviving Continental French texts of the same period, perhaps as a cultural consequence of bilingual and trilingual interaction in England. Ian Short lists:

> The first adventure narrative (or proto-romance) in French literature; the earliest example of historiographic writing in French; the first

eye-witness history of contemporary events in French; the earliest scientific texts in French; the first administrative texts in French; the first Biblical translations into French; the earliest French vernacular versions of monastic Rules; the first scholastic text to be translated into French; the earliest significant examples of French prose; the first occurrence of the French octosyllabic rhyming couplet (the standard verse-form of Medieval French narrative); the first explicit mention of secular *courtoisie* (courtly culture) in vernacular French; the first named women writers in French; the earliest named and identifiable patrons of literature in French – an impressive list of firsts by any standards, and all to be credited not to Continental French culture, but to Insular Anglo-Norman society of the twelfth century. (Short 1991, 229)

Early Anglo-Norman writers focused on narratives of the pre-Conquest past: on histories of the ancient Britons and the Anglo-Saxons, on largely mythical stories of English heroes, and on the lives of Anglo-Saxon saints, initially regarded with contempt by the settlers but soon identified as part of their newly acquired cultural heritage (Legge 1963). Through such narratives, the Normans, having redefined themselves as 'English', appropriated an identity that linked them with the land and the traditions they had inherited from a past generation of heroes and saints (Crane 1986; Thomas 2003). From their own point of view, though not necessarily from that of the conquered English, they were part of one nation. The historical ground was covered by two early verse-writers. Geffrei Gaimar supplied the history of the Anglo-Saxons in *L'Estoire des Engleis* (1136–40). Wace provided the story of the Normans in his *Roman de Rou* (1160–74); his earlier history, the *Roman de Brut* (1155), had lasting popularity as an adaptation of Geoffrey of Monmouth's *History of the Kings of Britain* (*Historia Regum Britanniae*). Geoffrey's Latin history of Arthur and the ancient Britons, completed in 1136, followed by Wace's version, had a profound influence on the way the English perceived themselves, and we shall return to their story in chapter 4. Many other Anglo-Norman histories of the British and the English were derived from Geoffrey, Wace and Gaimar, and continued the tradition of Anglo-Norman historical writing. The immensely popular Anglo-Norman prose *Brut* in its various versions followed the story into the fourteenth century, and in the early fourteenth century the Yorkshire writer Peter Langtoft of Bridlington covered the same ground in a verse chronicle. Some years later *Les Cronicles* of the Dominican friar Nicholas Trevet (or Trivet), written for Princess Mary, daughter of Edward I, grandly offered a history of the world from the Creation. Chaucer and Gower both derived the tale of Constance from Trevet (Man of Law's Tale, *CT* II.134–1162; *CA* 2.587–1598).

The Anglo-Norman romance of *Horn* (1170s) by Thomas is the first in a line of stories of exile and return set in Anglo-Saxon times. Horn is driven from his homeland, Suddene, falls in love with the daughter of the king of Brittany, is banished to Ireland, but returns in triumph to claim land and lady. The hero of *Haveloc* (c. 1200) is an exiled Danish prince who, having married the dispossessed daughter of the king of England, succeeds in regaining the thrones of Denmark and England. Such stories mirrored the Normans' own experience of moving from one homeland to another, and their own sense of the legality of their inheritance (Crane 1986). *Boeve de Haumtone* is the son of the earl of Southampton, who returns after a multitude of adventures abroad and builds a castle named after his horse Arundel. In a similar fashion, *Gui de Warewic* travels abroad for many years before returning to Warwick. Some of these poems may have been commissioned by particular Anglo-Norman families to celebrate their supposed association with ancient heroes, estates and castles. Few of the patrons can be identified, but Hugh of Roteland (Rhuddlan in Clwyd), who lived in Herefordshire, wrote two long romances, *Ipomedon* and its sequel *Protheselaus*, the latter at least for Gilbert FitzBaderon, lord of Monmouth (d. 1191), who, says the poet, possessed many books in French and Latin in his castle. The convoluted plots of both romances involve the Norman kingdom of Sicily and the struggles of Ipomedon and his son Protheselaus to regain their inheritance.

From the mid-thirteenth century onwards there are later English versions of many of these Anglo-Norman romances, *King Horn, Havelok, Bevis of Hampton, Guy of Warwick* and (from c. 1400) *Ipomadon*, which were adapted for a new and wider audience with different interests and concerns (Severs 1967). That the Anglo-Norman versions were still being transcribed into the fourteenth century shows that some of the descendants of their original audiences continued to enjoy French, yet others by now preferred English and were finding French something of a struggle. At the same time as the first English translations of the romances were appearing, Walter of Bibbesworth, a knight from Essex, compiled for 'ma dame Dyonise de Mountechensi' a treatise designed to improve the French of those whose first language was

English (ed. Rothwell 1990). The practical value as well as the social cachet of French encouraged such well-to-do families to brush up their language skills, even though English was now their mother tongue.

A manuscript from the 1280s, Bodley MS Digby 86, is an anthology of texts in three languages, and in no way unique in this respect, and for once we can identify its early and probably original owners as a Worcestershire gentry family that passed the manuscript down through several generations (Turville-Petre 2003). The household must have been trilingual, though this does not mean that every member of the family had equally good command of Latin and French. Most of the Latin items are short practical pieces in prose: prayers, devotions and charms, as well as a guide to the interpretation of dreams. Perhaps these were particularly intended for the family chaplain. It may be significant that most of the scabrously antifeminist items are in French, while those that speak most feelingly of women, such as *The Thrush and the Nightingale*, are in English. And yet the best-known English text is the wickedly funny *Dame Sirith*, in which an old crone tricks a young married woman into sleeping with a randy cleric.

Such trilingual manuscripts are most evident in the period 1280–1340. It was a period when English texts were becoming very much more numerous but French and Latin were still understood and enjoyed widely enough to be preferred for many topics. The Auchinleck manuscript of the 1330s (National Library of Scotland, Advocates' MS 19.2.1), whose contents include *Sir Orfeo*, is the first large miscellany to consist entirely of English pieces, and it points the way to the future.

The Choice of English

What space was there for English in the first two centuries after the Conquest? While English was the spoken language of the majority of the population, it had been almost elbowed out as a written language; or so it appears from the extant texts, though undoubtedly much more was lost than survives. Those who were able to read, those who had the leisure to read, those who could afford to own manuscripts, were likely to opt for the languages that had literary status: Latin and French.

An indicator of a written language's lack of status is that there is no standardized form of it. World-wide communication is so important today that written English is essentially the same everywhere, and what minor differences there are between standard American and standard British English do not seriously impede communication. In the very different circumstances of Anglo-Saxon England, a literary standard based on the dialect of the politically dominant area of the country, the West-Saxon dialect, was established. In Middle English there was no written standard, though there were sporadic attempts to develop one. This variation was a matter of concern to English writers in the later Middle Ages, not only because it was a nagging reminder of low status, but also for the much more practical reason that a text written in one part of the country could be difficult to understand in another. Versions of the Lord's Prayer illustrate the problem. One is perhaps our earliest example of the northern dialect of Middle English, from about 1250:

> Ure fadir þat hart in hevene
> Halged be þi name with giftis sevene,
> Samin cume þi kingdom,
> Þi wille in herþe als in hevene be don,
> Ure bred þat lastes ai
> Gyve it hus þis hilke dai,
> And ure misdedis þu forgyve hus
> Als we forgyve þaim þat misdon hus,
> And leod us intol na fandinge,
> Bot frels us fra alle ivele þing. Amen.   (ed. Brown 1932, 127)

On the other side of the country in 1340 Dan Michel's *Ayenbite of Inwyt* offers this prose version in the dialect of Kent:

> Vader oure þet art ine heuenes, yhalʒed by þi name, cominde þi riche, yworþe þi wil ase ine hevene and ine erþe, bread our echedayes yef ous today, and vorlet ous oure yeldinges ase and we vorleteþ oure yelderes, and ne ous led naʒt into vondinge, ac vri ous vram queade. Zuo by hit.
> (ed. Morris 1866, 262)

The northern vocabulary of the first version includes *samin*, 'all to-gether', *þaim* (ON), 'them' and *intol*, 'into'. The characteristic south-ern rounding of /a:/ to /o:/ is represented in the second version by *vondinge* as against *fandinge*, 'temptation', and the spelling also illus-trates southern voicing of initial /f/, as again in *vader* for 'father', *vri* for 'free' and *vram* for 'from'. The northern text has *gyve* (partly from ON) for 'give', while the southern text has *yef* (from OE). Very characteristic of Kent is the present participle ending of *cominde*, literally 'coming', where the north would have *comand*. These and many other differences would disconcert readers from other parts of the country, but perhaps not so much as the version from Salisbury beginning 'Hure wader þat is in evene, þyn oli name beyn olid' (Laing 1993, 152).

In the twelfth century the historian William of Malmesbury in *Gesta Pontificum* commented on the peculiarity of northern English: 'The whole language of the Northumbrians, especially in York, is so grating and uncouth that we southerners cannot understand a word of it' (trans. Bartlett 2000, 491). The idea resurfaces in Ranulph Higden's *Polychronicon*, and is turn expanded by the Cornishman John Trevisa in his wonderfully expressive translation of Higden made in 1387:

Þe contray longage ys apeyred, and som useþ strange wlaffyng, chyteryng, harryng and garryng grisbittyng. . . . Men of myddel Engelond, as hyt were parteners of þe endes, undurstondeþ betre þe syde longages, Norþeron and Souþeron, þan Norþeron and Souþeron undurstondeþ eyþer oþer. Al þe longage of the Norþhumbres, and specialych at ʒork, ys so scharp, slyttyng and frotynge and unschape, þat we Souþeron men may þat longage unneþe understonde. (Sisam 1921, XIIIB.13–15, 54–60)

[Rural speech is debased, and some use outlandish snarling, twittering, roaring and harsh gnashing . . . People of middle England, sharers, as it were, of the extremities, better understand the neighbouring languages, northern and southern, than northern and southern understand one another. All the language of those north of the Humber, and especially at York, is so sharp, piercing and grating and shapeless, that we southerners can scarcely understand that language.]

The Yorkshire author of *Cursor Mundi* wishes to incorporate a southern poem on the Assumption into his massive work, and so 'turns' it into northern English:

> In sotherin Englis was it draun,
> And turnd it have I till our aun
> Langage o northrin lede,
> Þat can nan oiþer Englis rede.   (20061–4)

[It was composed in southern English, and I've turned it into our own language of northern people who can read no other English.]

His method of proceeding is illustrated by the following lines about the angel who visits the Virgin to tell her that she will soon join her Son in heaven. In the left column is the southern original, the *Assumption of our Lady*; on the right is the northern adaptation:

Nym þis palm wiþ þi riȝt honde;	Take þis palme here in þi hand:
Hit is þi dere sones sonde.	It es þi dere sunes sand.
The þinkeþ long hym to se;	Þe thinck ful lang þi sun to sene,
Ne schaltu her no lenger beo.	Here mai þu nu na langer bene.
He wile senden after þe	He sal send efter þe ful sone,
Fram hevene adun of his meigne,	Ne sal þu noght here lang hone.
And fecche þe into his blisse	þu sal be broght til heven blis
Þat evre schal leste wiþute misse.	þar þu sal neuer of mirthes mis.
(*Assumption*, 105–12)	(*Cursor Mundi*, 20161–8)

In the northern 'translation' the Old Norse loan *take* replaces the synonym from Old English, *nym*, and the penultimate couplet is re-written, presumably to avoid the French loan *meigne*, 'retinue', instead creating a rhyme on the northern word *hone*, 'wait'. The variation between the southern form *þinkeþ*, 'it seems', and northern *thinck* demands the addition of *ful* to make up for the lost syllable.

For William of Malmesbury the dialectal variation was a matter for wry and perhaps exaggerated comment; for the author of *Cursor Mundi* it was a problem that could be resolved with a bit of rephrasing; for Chaucer, however, it was an issue of real concern:

> And for ther is so gret diversité
> In Englissh and in writyng of oure tonge,
> So prey I God that non myswrite the,
> Ne the mysmetre for defaute of tonge. (*Troilus* 5.1793–6)

[*Ne . . . tonge* Nor spoil your metre as a result of a deficiency in their spoken language]

A poem that pays obeisance to the authors of classical Rome (*Troilus* 5.1791–2) cannot be altered or adapted without detriment. Chaucer is not the first English author to comment on linguistic diversity, but he is the first to express concern about it.

Standardization also puts a brake on chronological change, so that any English speaker in the world today can read a poem by Byron with little sense that it is separated from us by a distance of two centuries. Chaucer, in contrast, would have had a considerable struggle with Laȝamon. Once language is required to communicate across space and time, it must establish a standard variety. In the thirteenth century there was no such standard, although a group of texts that includes *Ancrene Wisse* and other south-west Midland treatises for women show that a number of scribes were trained to write in a homogeneous representation of the Herefordshire dialect (Tolkien 1929). The first steps in establishing a national standard were based on London English from the mid-fourteenth century onwards. That this was not yet a universally recognized standard is expressed clearly enough by Chaucer, but the development of this variety during the fifteenth century led to what is known as Chancery Standard, initially used in royal documents from the 1430s, and gradually adopted for texts both literary and non-literary from anywhere in the country (Smith 1996, 68–78). Now English was increasingly the language of legal documents, invading territories from which it had once been excluded. As early as 1362 it was ordained that legal proceedings should be conducted in English rather than French, since defendants 'have no knowledge nor understanding of that which is said for them or against them' (trans. Baugh and Cable 2002, 149), and in the same year Parliament was first opened in English. In practice, French continued to dominate the business of both institutions into the fifteenth century.

In the twelfth and thirteenth centuries the status of English as a literary language was much less assured. English was not the most obvious choice for an author envisaging a wide circulation, and so there appear to be special factors motivating that preference in many of the works that survive. For example, the *Peterborough Chronicle* began as an early twelfth-century copy of the *Anglo-Saxon Chronicle*, so it was natural enough for the monks of Peterborough to add their continuations in English. And yet they had the option of continuing in French or Latin, as is demonstrated physically by the short Anglo-Norman chronicle added a century later in the margins around the English text near the end of the manuscript (see plate 1). Writing in English

1 *Peterborough Chronicle*

The margins of the *Peterborough Chronicle* have been used a century later for a short Anglo-Norman chronicle of England. See Dean (1999, no. 13). Photograph: Bodleian Library, University of Oxford, MS Laud. Misc. 636, fol. 89v.

perhaps encouraged the chroniclers to express anti-Norman sentiments, an opportunity seized in the entry for 1137. Here the cruelty
of the lords is described in horrific detail, together with their French
tax called *tenserie*, their lack of *justice* and their *prisun* in which the
'wrecce men of þis land' are tortured so savagely. The wretched people of the country are innocently caught up in the struggles of the
Norman lords, losing their lands and lives to political forces that have
nothing to offer them or to do with them, and the social cleft is
powerfully figured in the linguistic divide represented by the chronicler's vocabulary.

Laȝamon, adapting Wace's Anglo-Norman poem in turn adapting
Geoffrey of Monmouth's Latin history, fashions an English epic, drawing (through whatever channels) on Anglo-Saxon traditions and styles.
His technique is to offer Arthur as an English hero, no straightforward
task since Geoffrey presents him as a Celtic warrior-king beating back
the savage and duplicitous Saxons. Laȝamon's style recalls the vocabulary and metrical features of the poetry of those very Saxons,
leading to the point at which Laȝamon can say without jarring incongruity that 'an Arthur will one day come to help the English' (14297),
at the point where with more obvious logic Geoffrey and Wace refer
to the Britons. The Englishing of Arthur provides Laȝamon with a
powerful motive for writing in English, as we shall see further in
chapter 4, where we shall analyse Laȝamon's epic style and its literary effects.

Ancrene Wisse is one of a group of devotional texts written in English for female recluses early in the thirteenth century. Such women
entered the enclosed life from a wide spectrum of social and educa-
tional backgrounds, and only some of them trained first as nuns. The
three women to whom the original version of *Ancrene Wisse* was specifically addressed were well-born (*gentile*) sisters who have 'in the
blossom of your youth given up all worldly joys and become
anchoresses' (ed. Day 1952, 85, ll. 26–7). It is likely that they were
taught at home to read the vernacular, perhaps both French and
English. The author also envisages his work reaching a wider female
audience of differing abilities, referring both to well-educated women
(*clergesse*) and to those unable to follow all but the most familiar Latin
texts. Those who could understand Latin would be in a position to
appreciate the frequent Latin quotations (often from the Bible)
throughout the text, but less educated readers would not lose the

thread of the argument since the author generally translates or para-phrases the Latin into English. Not translated are the well-known devotions such as the Lord's Prayer and the Psalms, which were daily recited by the anchoresses in Latin, though the author advises them to read further in English or French as their hearts incline them. By composing his treatise in English, the author opens the work to the widest range of female readers, for most of whom English would have been by this date the first language, and for some the only language (Millett 1996; Robertson 2003).

The Owl and the Nightingale must be situated even more firmly within a multilingual context, to such an extent that it would be easy to think of it as undermining the foregoing argument that special factors are involved in the choice of English at this early date. It belongs, first of all, to a European tradition of debate poems, some learned, some frivolous, often witty, many in Latin and others in French. The debate may be between summer and winter, the lily and the rose, the body and soul, water and wine. The earliest Latin example dates from the eighth century. The two closely related manuscripts in which the poem survives (BL Cotton Caligula A.IX and Jesus College, Oxford, 29) are from the second half of the thirteenth century, and the poem could possibly be as late as that, though it is usually dated soon after 1189 (Cartlidge 2001, xv). The manuscripts are miscellanies of Eng-lish and Anglo-Norman, perhaps for households or monasteries in the south-west midlands, and both include *Le Petit Plet*, 'the Little Debate', in Anglo-Norman. Both *The Owl and the Nightingale* and *Le Petit Plet* are written in octosyllabic couplets, a measure that English learnt from Anglo-Norman. The two poems proclaim their Englishness, but in significantly different ways. The Anglo-Norman is overtly national-istic, roundly asserting the superiority of English women over French, and the greater beauty of 'England covered with flowers like a beau-tiful meadow. England surpasses all the realms there are, and do you know in what? In all pleasure and in nobility (*franchise*)' (*Le Petit Plet*, 1261–5). The setting of the debate reflects this idealized view: an orchard with a clear spring purling softly over the gravel, little flowers, tall trees to offer shade from the heat, birds singing sweetly. In con-trast, *The Owl and the Nightingale* describes a much more familiar Eng-lish scene: a secluded spot in a summer valley, where the Nightingale hides in an impenetrable thick hedge mixed with reeds and green sedge-grass:

In ore vaste þicke hegge
Imeind mid spire and grene segge   (17–18)

and the Owl, true to its nature, sits on an old ivy-covered stump 'mid ivi al bigrowe' (27). Still more down to earth is the Nightingale's singing station (according to the Owl):

I mai þe vinde ate rumhuse
Among þe wode, among þe netle;
Þu sittest and singst bihinde þe setle.   (592–4)

[I can find you at the privy among the weeds, among the nettles; you sit and sing behind the seat.]

In both poems the arguments are supported on the authority of proverbs. These formulas of traditional wisdom can have a literary (and, of course, biblical) heritage, or by contrast can be an evocation of popular wisdom passed down orally from generation to generation. In *Le Petit Plet* many of them are drawn from Seneca and from a standard Latin school-text, the *Distichs of Cato*, quoted by name (154–6) (Merrilees 1970, 74–5). In *The Owl and the Nightingale*, on the other hand, the multitude of proverbs, whatever their actual origin, are frequently ascribed to King Alfred, thus presenting them as the wise sayings inherited from a great figure from the Anglo-Saxon past:

Vor soþ hit is þat seide Alvred:
'Ne mai no strengþe aȝen red.'   (761–2)

[For it is true as Alfred said: 'Might can do nothing against cleverness.']

In fact another text from the Jesus College manuscript, the *Proverbs of Alfred*, ascribes its collection of sensible rules of life to the same figure (Rouse 2005):

Þus queþ Alvred:
'If þu havest seorewe
Ne seye þu hit nought þan arewe;
Seye hit þine sadelbowe and ryd þe singinde forþ.'   (150–3)

[Thus says Alfred: 'If you have sorrow, don't tell it to your enemy; tell it to your saddle-bow and ride away singing.']

The best critic of *The Owl and the Nightingale* writes that 'its "English-ness" is of that international brand we have had cause to trace in both the art and the literature of the twelfth and thirteenth centuries' (Salter 1988, 39). This leaves unanswered the question of why it was written in English rather than Anglo-Norman. Whatever the date of the poem, by the time it was composed Anglo-Norman was for most of its potential audience a language that had to be learnt, and there

2 The owl, MS Harley 4751, f. 47.
An illustrated bestiary from about 1230, much the same date as *The Owl and the Nightingale*. The owl is mobbed by other birds, including a magpie, as described in the poem (ll. 65–70). Morgan (1982, no. 76). Photograph © British Library, London.

was strong motivation for the poet to choose what was now the mother tongue.

The Owl and the Nightingale is, above all, funny, even though serious and weighty issues are debated. The comic effect lies in our awareness of the poem's incongruities: the insults, bad temper and shrill invective of the debaters can scarcely be contained within the formal and legalistic structure of the debate genre. Even more incongruously, the debaters are birds. Human birds and animals are a common motif for gargoyles, for misericords and in the grotesqueries pictured in the margins of medieval manuscripts (e.g. plate 5), and owls in nature have a somewhat human face which artists are happy to exaggerate (plate 2). It is the same joke that the poet so skilfully exploits. He collapses the distinction between human and animal, so that the birds are fully birdlike and fully human. They are capable of *speche, fayre worde* and *tale*. At the same time they *singe*; the Nightingale tells the Owl 'þu schrichest and ʒollest' (223), to which the retort is that the Nightingale *croweþ* (335). The sounds of *ʒoʒelinge, writelinge, pipinge* and *chokeringe* ring out in the accusations of the two. When it is the priests that *singeþ* (733) while the Nightingale is told that 'þu chaterest so doþ on Irish prost' (322) – 'you chatter like an Irish priest' – the distinction between bird and human has dissolved. It comes, then, as a salutary reminder of the incongruity of that fusion when the poet comments daftly that the Nightingale 'would have fought with sword and spear-point if she had been a man' (1068–9).

A leading element of the comedy of the human birds is that their verbal exchanges are in language that imitates speech. The poet calls our attention to the nature of everyday exchanges when he refers to shepherds' *schitworde* (286), and occasionally the language of the birds is no better than that: 'A tort ne ʒive ich for ow alle' (1686) – 'I don't give a turd for any of you', says the Owl. Often the exchanges are strikingly colloquial:

> Lat þine tunge habbe spale!
> Þu wenest þat þes dai bo þin oʒe.
> Lat me nu habbe mine þroʒe!
> Bo nu stille and lat me speke! (258–61)

[Give your tongue a rest! You think the day is yours. Let me have my turn now! Be quiet now and let me speak!]

Anglo-Norman literature is quite capable of low repartee, as evidenced in some very obscene fabliaux, but by the thirteenth century a provincial audience would be peering at it through the veil of a second language rather than associating its vocabulary with the English sounds all around them.

In 1354 Henry, duke of Lancaster, wrote his devotional *Livre de Seyntz Medicines*, modestly pointing out that 'if the French is not good, I ought to be excused because I am English and have not practised French much' (Arnould 1940, 239, ll. 25–7). By the end of the fourteenth century English had become the norm for literary expression and reading at all social levels, so that Chaucer sees no incongruity in writing of Richard II as 'the king that is lord of this langage' (*Astrolabe*, Prologue 56–7). Even so, in 1387 John Trevisa implied that some justification was still needed for translating a Latin history into English for his learned patron, Lord Berkeley, for in the *Dialogue between a Lord and a Clerk*, prefaced to his translation of Higden's *Polychronicon*, Trevisa imagines himself as *Clericus* saying to the lord:

> Ʒe cunneþ speke and rede and understonde Latyn. Þanne hyt nedeþ noʒt to have such an Englysch translacion. (*BOME* 12.44–5)

To which the lord replies:

> Y denye þys argument; for þey I cunne speke and rede and understonde Latyn, þer ys moche Latyn in þeus bokes of cronyks ['chronicles'] þat y can noʒt understonde. (*BOME* 12.46–8)

The 'clerical' attitude is that translation is potentially dangerous, since it opens up privileged texts to the unlearned, who may misuse them (Dillon 1998, 12–14). *Clericus* says:

> A gret del of þeuse bokes stondeþ moche by ['draw heavily upon'] holy wryt, by holy doctors and by philosofy. Þanne þeuse bokes scholde noʒt be translated ynto Englysch. (*BOME* 12.108–10)

With the Lollards now translating the Bible to make it available to all, these issues of language and power became increasingly sensitive.

By this date John Gower had begun *Confessio Amantis*, where he still represents the choice of English as far from inevitable:

> And for that fewe men endite
> In oure Englissh, I thenke make
> A boke for king Richardes sake.   (Prologue 22–4)

He is presumably thinking narrowly of the poets within the courtly circle. In the court of Edward III (d. 1377) were several French poets, some associated with Queen Philippa of Hainault, such as Jean Froissart, who served as her 'clerk de chambre' during the 1360s, and Oton de Granson, who was at court from 1368 until 1387, and then again in the 1390s (Pearsall 1992, 68–73). Gower's earlier works were in French and Latin, the French *Mirour de l'Omme* from the 1370s, and the Latin *Vox Clamantis* after 1381. It has been suggested that Gower's choice of language was influenced by the events of the war with France, the preferences of the three monarchs in whose reigns Gower wrote, and the dark cloud of Lollardy that hung over English writings at the end of his career (Yeager 2000). This argument cannot be conclusively demonstrated, but it reveals the range of factors and political ramifications that might have been involved in language-choice at this time. In this context it seems somewhat surprising that all Chaucer's surviving works are in English. His earliest compositions 'in the floures of his youthe . . . Of ditees and of songes glade', as Gower refers to them (*CA* 8.2943*-5*), may have been in French, but already by 1368 he was writing a major English poem, *The Book of the Duchess*. Perhaps he was leading fashion rather than following it. After Chaucer there are no major English poets who choose to write in French.

Social Register

The two birds in the *Owl and the Nightingale* speak the same kind of English, using the same everyday vocabulary and colloquial expressions, and exchanging proverbs in identical fashion. There is no attempt to distinguish between them on the basis of language. It is quite different in Chaucer's dream-debate, the *Parliament of Fowls*, where the birds are characterized by their language. Chaucer's joke is not simply that the birds speak like humans, but that they speak like humans of different social classes. The three male eagles (tercels) vying for the female eagle (formel) are at pains to demonstrate their courtly eloquence, as the royal tercel does, saying:

> And yf I be founde to hir untrewe,
> Dysobeysaunt, or wilful negligent,
> Avauntour, or in processe love a newe,
> I pray to yow thys be my jugement,
> That with these foules y be al torent,
> That ylke day that ever she me fynde
> To hir untrewe or in my gylte unkynde.   (428–34)

This provides the earliest example of the adjective *dysobeysaunt*, 'disobedient', and the related verb and noun are no earlier, so that it is likely that this word-cluster came across as refined Frenchification. Equally important, the very concept expresses an attitude to sexual relationships that is held to typify *gentilesse* (224), the finer feeling of the nobility: the lover offers the beloved *servise* (470), which demands his obedience to her every command and his commitment to be *trewe*, 'loyal', to her. Other words in this stanza such as *negligent*, and *avauntour*, 'a boaster', are also recent French acquisitions from the same cultural orbit, and they, too, contribute to the perceived elevation of the royal eagle's speech. This impression of refinement is built up further by the rather complex structure of a sentence that runs right through the stanza.

At the opposite end of the social scale are the vulgar water-fowl, who regard this lengthy display of courtly refinement as so much poppycock, and are impatient to get on with picking their own mates. The duck pours scorn on the turtle-dove's notion that a lover should *serve* his lady unto death with no expectation of response:

> 'Wel bourded', quod the duk, 'by my hatte!   *bourded* joked
> That men shulden alwey loven causeles,
> Who kan a reson fynde or wytte in that?
> Daunceth he murye that ys murtheles?
> Who shulde rechche of that ys rechcheles?'
>
> > > [*Who . . . rechcheles* Who should care about
> > > anyone who doesn't care for himself]
>
> 'Ye quek' quod the goos 'ful wel and faire,
> There ben moo sterres, God woot, than a paire!'
>
> > > > [*moo* more; *woot* knows]
> > > > (589–95)

The birds' vulgarity is underlined by the colloquial interjection 'by my hatte' and the triumphant use of a homely proverb ('there are many more stars in the sky') to clinch the argument, so reminiscent of the interchanges between the Owl and the Nightingale. The syntax is simple, with a series of abrupt questions expressing plebeian opinions.

For the author of the *Owl and the Nightingale* it would have been much more difficult, perhaps impossible, to express social difference through language. The verbal signals to express such difference were as yet undeveloped, and in any case the courtly language was still French. By Chaucer's time the literary language had acquired means of indicating social status, recognized in the word *termes*, which we shall explore a little further on.

The Harley Lyrics, preserved in BL MS Harley 2253 of about 1340, offer further suggestions that elegant conversation and refined manners were not comfortably expressed in English until later. In these poems the protestations of courtly love are often wittily undercut, so that the inflated passions of the lovers are revealed. In 'When þe nyhtegale singes' (*BOME* 14k) the lover is gored by love's spear and begs for a kiss to heal his wound; he knows no girl more lovely in any of the villages between Lincoln and Lindsey, between Northampton and Lound. These small-town amorists ape the sentiments of their courtly betters, either in a desperate attempt to convince the beloved of their passion, or in a cynical ploy to lead her to bed. The lover in 'My deþ y love' (*BOME* 14j) is significantly not a courtier but a *clerc* and a wide boy whose verbal dexterity covers his sexual demands with a thin veneer of refinement. He has learnt all the gifts of the gab, the trite similes, the rhetorical devices such as the yoking together of opposites:

> My deþ y love, my lyf ich hate,
>   For a levedy shene;
> Heo is brith so daies liht,
>   Þat is on me wel sene;
> Al y falewe so doþ þe lef
>   In somer when hit is grene;
> Ȝef mi þoht helpeþ me noht
>   To wham shal y me mene?   (1–8)

[My death I love, my life I hate, for a lovely lady; she is bright as light of day, that's very evident in me; I fade like the leaf when it is green in summer; if my thoughts don't help me, to whom shall I complain?]

The adored object has no illusions, telling him bluntly to 'Be stille, þou fol!' (33). A cold, courtly mistress would make him wait for evermore, but a warm-blooded girl has sexual needs, and she ends up submitting to his clerkly persuasiveness 'to don al þi wille' (72).

Not available to earlier writers in English were certain indicators of polite speech and social difference that were borrowed from French. These included not only a range of vocabulary, but also, and most telling of all, the use of *ye* to address a single individual. In early Middle English usage, *ye* and *you* were plural pronouns as in Old English; an individual was addressed as *þou* and *þe*. During the thirteenth century the practice of using the plural pronoun as a mark of deference began to be copied from French usage. Since modern English no longer makes the distinction, it is easy for speakers of English today to miss the significance of this. It becomes a wonderfully useful way for a medieval writer to indicate in shorthand both the social awareness of the speaker and the relationship between the speaker and the person addressed. A peasant would not know the distinction; a noble would understand its social complexities and would display deference where it was due. Among the social factors that come into play are context, rank, age, gender and familiarity (Burnley 1989, 19–21).

The earliest sustained example of the practice is from a surprising source, the story of *Havelok* composed around 1300. The hero is an exiled Danish prince who arrives penniless at Grimsby on the Lincolnshire coast. In order to earn some money, he goes barefoot to Lincoln to see if he can pick up a job at the castle, and there the earl's cook spots him

> And seyde 'Wiltu ben wit me?
> Gladlike wile ich feden þe.
> Wel is set þe mete þu etes,
> And þe hire þat þu getes.' (906–9)

[And said 'Wilt thou be with me? I will gladly feed thee. The food thou shalt eat and the wages thou shalt get shall be well spent.']

To which Havelok answers:

> 'Goddot!' quoth he, 'leve sire,
> Bidde ich you non oþer hire,
> But yeveþ me inow to ete.

> Fir and water y wile you fete,
> Þe fir blowe an ful wel maken;
> Stickes kan ich breken and kraken,
> And kindlen ful wel a fyr,
> And maken it to brennen shir.   (910–17)

['By God!' he said, 'dear sir, I don't ask you for any other wages; just give me enough to eat. I'll fetch fire and water for you, blow the fire and make it up well; I can break and crack sticks and kindle a fire very well and make it burn bright.']

In this context it pays to be deferential, even if you are a prince in disguise speaking to a cook. What is surprising at this date is that a provincial writer should pay attention to the convention and expect his audience to observe the irony of the situation. Certainly it is not standard in English writings until much later. There is no sign of the polite *ye* in the Harley Lyrics, and in *Sir Orfeo*, where the courtly setting as well as the London audience for the poem might have encouraged its consistent use, it is found just once, at the very significant moment when the court acknowledges Orfeo as the king they had believed dead: 'Ȝe beþ our lord, sir, and our king!' (582).

Chaucer and Gower fully exploit the convention, as is to be expected. In the *Parliament of Fowls* Nature and the formel eagle address one another as *ye* (448, 633, 640), and the second male eagle similarly addresses his superior, the royal eagle (451). The lower birds are individually addressed by the aristocratic hawks as *thou* (598, 612), fittingly since the eagle calls the goose a *cherl* (596). The subtle use that is made of the complex practice throughout *Troilus and Criseyde* and the *Canterbury Tales* is worth attention since it tells us much about the status of the speaker and his or her attitude to those addressed, as well as the sophistication of Chaucer's audience.

If *ye* as a singular pronoun acts as a marker of polite speech, what constitutes impolite English? We think at once of those 'Anglo-Saxon monosyllables', *piss*, *shit* and *swive* (*fuck* is not recorded until the sixteenth century). In fact *piss* is of French origin, and it is not in itself a vulgarism in Middle English, for it is found in contexts where we would use *urine* and *urinate*, already beginning to replace *piss* as a medical term: 'purgacioun of uryne' says the Wife of Bath grandly (*CT* III.120–1). *MED pisse* records legal use, 'Cast no pysse into the high weye', and quotes medical advice, 'Take þyn ouwyn pisse and drynke hit.' Chaucer's Canon's Yeoman lists dung and piss among the many substances his master uses in his search for the philosopher's stone (*CT* VIII.807), and even the pious Parson uses the verb when he likens an old lecher to a dog that lifts its leg when it can't piss (*CT* X.855–60). Of course Waster's advice to Piers Plowman to 'go pisse with his plogh' (C.8.151) is as aggressive and as insulting as it would be today. So the context is important: the word can be neutral in its literal sense, but it can be used as an insult by crude people.

Nor can *shit* automatically be classed as a vulgar word. It finds appropriate use in a particularly violent Old Testament passage in the Wycliffite Bible of 1382: one of the graphic punishments the Lord will inflict on sinners will be itching and worse in 'þe parte of þe body by þe whiche tordys been shetyn out' (Deut. 28.27), a passage toned down in the revised version. Chaucer refers to a corrupt priest as 'a shiten shepherde' (*CT* I.504). We have seen the abusive term *schitworde* in *The Owl and the Nightingale*, and the verb is used later in a revealing passage in the morality play *Mankind*. Here the cleric Mercy speaks with a grandiloquent Latinate vocabulary and is mocked by the world-lings for his 'Englysche Laten'. The shallow gadabout Nowadays sets Mercy a test:

> I prey yow hertyly, worschypfull clerke
> To have þis Englysch mad in Laten:
> 'I have etun a dyschfull of curdys,
> Ande I have schetun yowr mowth full of turdys.'
> Now opyn yowr sachell wyth Laten wordys
> Ande sey me þis in clerycall manere!   (129–34)

This exchange dramatizes the gap between the clerical style and 'honest English', and there can be no mistaking the meaning of the contemptuous insult 'shitted your mouth full of turds' (Dillon 1998, 54–69).

The one Chaucerian word that seems to be truly obscene is *swive*. Though it descends from an Old English verb with a different sense, 'to sweep about', it is rarely found before Chaucer in the sense 'fuck'. Chaucer uses it seven times in the *Canterbury Tales*, always in the fabliaux and low-life tales. In four of these instances its expression comes at the denouement of the plot. It is surely no accident that the Cook's Tale breaks off with its promise of debauchery, 'and swyved for hir sustenance' (*CT* I.4422). The Merchant cannot at first bring himself to describe what January saw his wife May doing in a pear tree:

> And saugh that Damyan his wyf had dressed
> In swich manere it may nat been expressed
> But if I wolde speke uncurteisly.   (*CT* IV.2361–3)

May then finds the fine euphemism, *strugle*, but the sharp-sighted January will have none of it, and eventually calls a spade a spade:

> 'Strugle?' quod he, 'Ye, algate in it wente!
> God yeve yow bothe on shames deth to dyen!
> He swyved thee; I saugh it with myne yen.'   (*CT* IV.2376–8)

['Struggle?', he said, 'yes, but it went in! God bring both of you to a shameful death! He *fucked* you – I saw it with my own eyes.']

That *swive* is a taboo word is confirmed in the Hengwrt manuscript (National Library of Wales MS Peniarth 392D) where the scribe jokingly replaced it with 'etcetera' (*CT* IX.256), though the rhyme makes the missing word obvious and the scribe copies it elsewhere (Burnley 2000, 241). The Miller's final triumphant use of the word in humiliation of a carpenter – 'Thus swyved was this carpenteris wyf' (*CT* I.3850) – is the last straw for the carpenter-Reeve, who vows to get his own back on the Miller 'right in his cherles termes' (*CT* I.3917). Here *termes* refer to social register, the language particular to a social group. Lydgate uses the word contrastively at the end of *The Churl and the Bird*, where he reckons it madness to try 'to teche a cherl termys of gentilness' (343). In line with the traditional division of society into three estates, the knights, the clergy and the peasants, there is the vocabulary appropriate to each: the Frenchified 'termys of gentilness' as used by the eagles in the *Parliament of Fowls*, the technical and Latinate 'termes clergial' enumerated by the Canon's Yeoman (*CT* VIII.752) and mocked in *Mankind*, and the Reeve's 'cherles termes'.

In this way the inhabitants of Chaucer's fabliaux are characterized as much by the churlish language as by their limited horizons and base activities. In the Reeve's Tale Chaucer takes a further step and for the first time in English literature imitates speech through dialect to signify the status of non-standard speakers (Tolkien 1934). His two feckless student heroes come from 'Strother / Fer in the north, I kan nat telle where' (*CT* I.4014–15), and their speech includes a number of striking northernisms. The most immediately distinctive feature of northern English today is short /a/ in words like *grass* and *laugh* for long /a:/ south of the Trent. In Chaucer's time the equivalent was the northern retention of long /a:/ in words such as *na, banes, twa*, rounded in the south to *no, bones, two*, and so the students' use of the former set immediately places them in the north. Furthermore, in their speech the third person singular form in the present tense of verbs ends in *-(e)s* ('the corn *gas* in', 4037, 'he *brynges*', 4130), whereas Chaucer's usual form ends in *-(e)th*: *goth, bryngeth*. In the plural verb, where Chaucer has *-e* or *-en*, the students again have *-(e)s*: *fares* (4023), *werkes* (4030). The form *is* serves throughout the present singular: *is I* (4031), *thou is* (4089). Northern lexis such as *til and fra*, 'to and fro' (4039), and *il-hayl*, 'bad luck to you' (4089), gives additional regional flavour. Chaucer even has a dialectal pun at the expense of the students, who use *hope* in the northern sense of 'expect', and thus to a Londoner seem to be saying the opposite of what they intend: 'Oure manciple, I hope he wil be deed' (4029) – 'I fear/hope our steward will die.' In the rich interplay of social pretensions in the Reeve's Tale, explored in chapter 3, these northernisms characterize their speakers as country loons. Students they may be, and so, like all students, totally impractical, but they are actually not very bright. The miller – arrogant, violent, contemptuous and quite absurdly snobbish – is set on making a good marriage for his daughter, and so he is utterly humiliated by these two daffy northerners who get the better of him and in the process fuck both his wife and his daughter (three times). Says the Reeve with satisfaction:

> Thus is the proude millere wel ybete,   *ybete* beaten
> And hath ylost the gryndynge of the whete,
> And payed for the soper everideel   *everideel* entirely
> Of Aleyn and of John, that bette hym weel.   *bette* beat
> His wyf is swyved, and his doghter als.
> Lo, swich it is a millere to be fals!   *swich* thus
> (4313–18)

Evidently a London dialect could be regarded as superior to a northern one, and we have seen the long tradition behind this, starting with William of Malmesbury, recycled by Higden and in turn Trevisa with his snooty comments on 'þe contray longage'. As a matter of fact those in the north and other non-metropolitan areas had their own traditions of distinguished poetry expressed appropriately in their own dialects. *Sir Gawain and the Green Knight* demonstrates something very significant, for the plot turns upon Gawain's reputation as a master of what Lydgate calls 'termes of gentilness', and the *Gawain*-poet refers to as 'termes of talkyng noble' (917), yet these *termes* are expressed in a distinctive north-west midlands dialect. In this text, then, we can observe both regional and social registers: a basic northern vocabulary enriched with the diction of north-western alliterative verse, and over-lying this the language of courtly society. When the hero arrives at the castle in the north-west, his reputation for courtliness has pre-ceded him, and the courtiers congratulate themselves on having taken into their midst the 'fyne fader of nurture' (919) – the 'exquisite master of good manners'. The audience of the poem has been pre-pared for this aspect of Gawain's reputation by his opening words, characterized by elaborate politeness: an address to Arthur using the deferential plural, a piling up of conditional clauses ('Wolde 3e, worþilych lorde' ... 'Þa3 3e 3ourself ...'), and a syntax that advances sinuously throughout the stanza (343–61). The task for Gawain when dealing with the lady's attempted seduction is whether he can disen-tangle the complex of ideals and assumptions that constitute courtly behaviour; whether he can maintain his reputation for graceful lan-guage and refined manners and yet avoid the offence of humiliating the amorous lady. In chapter 6 we shall follow in detail the issues that confront Gawain in the first exchange between them. In the second meeting the lady reproves Gawain for forgetting the lesson in courtly convention that she had taught him on the previous day: that a knight should respond to a glance of encouragement by offering a kiss. Gawain is both mystified and mortified at the reproof, and yet has to find a graceful way of not accepting the lady's invitation:

> '3et I kende yow of kyssyng', quoþ þe clere þenne,
> 'Quere-so countenaunce is couþe, quikly to clayme;
> Þat bicumes uche a kny3t þat cortaysy uses.'
> 'Do way', quoþ þat derf mon, 'my dere, þat speche,
> For þat durst I not do, lest I devayed were;
> If I were werned, I were wrang, iwysse, 3if I profered.'

'Ma fay', quoþ þe meré wyf, 'ȝe may not be werned.
ȝe ar stif innoghe to constrayne wyth strenkþe ȝif yow lykez,
ȝif any were so vilanous þat yow devaye wolde.'   (1489–97)

['But I taught you about kissing', said the fair lady then, 'to claim a kiss
quickly wherever a favourable glance is shown. That's proper behaviour
for every knight who follows the rules of courtesy.' 'My dear', said the
valiant man, 'put that talk aside, for I wouldn't dare do that in case I
were refused. If I were turned down, I'd have been absolutely wrong to
have made the offer.' 'On my word,' said the lovely woman, 'you couldn't
be refused – you're strong enough to exert your strength if you choose,
if anyone should be so discourteous as to wish to turn you down.']

A London audience (if there had been one) would have been very
conscious of the northernisms here: the form *uche* for London *eche*,
'each', the words *derf*, 'valiant' (not found in the south), and *wrang*
(ON) for 'wrong'; the third person verb forms *bicumes, uses* and *lykez*;
the form *ar* for London *ben*; the practice common to alliterative poetry of using an adjective as a noun, as in *þe clere* for 'the lovely lady'.
At the same time the conversation is rich in courtly *termes* of French
origin: *countenaunce, cortaysy, profered, constrayne, vilanous*, twice the
unique verb *devaye*, and the purely French exclamation *ma fay*. All of
this contributes to the courtly atmosphere of *Sir Gawain and the Green
Knight*, and to what the poet actually describes as the French manners, *Frenkysch fare* (1116), of this court beyond the Wirral.

If fashionable Londoners could represent those from anywhere
vaguely north as boorish and rustic, honest-to-goodness northerners
got their own back by portraying southerners as effete dandies. In the
Towneley *Second Shepherds' Play* the rascally Mak tries to make himself out to be better than the shepherds, and so uses southern forms
such as *ich be, goyth*, 'goes', and *ye doth* to distinguish his speech from
their Yorkshire dialect (Cawley 1958, 131). He even falls into the trap
of hypercorrecting to *some* for 'same' on the analogy of *bone* for *bane*
(just as some northerners today say 'put' with a short vowel on the
analogy of southern pronunciation of 'but'). The shepherds have brisk
instruction for Mak:

> Now take outt that Sothren tothe
> And sett it in a torde!   (215–16)

CHAPTER 2

Texts and Manuscripts

Information from Manuscripts

The manuscripts are of course a prime source of contextual information about medieval works; in many cases, indeed, they are the only source. For not only do they transmit the texts themselves, but they also provide much if not all of the evidence for what we now know about those texts: their dates, their dissemination through the country, their authorship, and indications about how readers perceived and appreciated them. A startling example is that of the four great alliterative poems that might as well never have been written had one small manuscript, Cotton Nero A.X, now in the British Library, been destroyed in the catastrophic fire at the Cotton Library in 1731. Upon its solitary survival rests a critical industry that has established *Pearl*, *Cleanness*, *Patience* and *Sir Gawain and the Green Knight* as poems of a quality and importance to equal any other medieval English works. From this particular manuscript the information we can glean is comparatively meagre, and yet we shall see it provides us with a few fundamental facts that underpin our understanding of the four poems.

Of all the information a manuscript can give us, the least significant is usually evidence about authorship. This may seem a surprising comment. It is true that one of the two manuscripts of the *Brut*, BL MS Cotton Caligula A.IX, not only gives the author's name in the first line – 'A priest among the people was called Laȝamon' – but inside that capital 'A' shows a miniature picture of a tonsured priest sitting bent over a book with a pen in his right hand (plate 3). Laȝamon writing the *Brut*, of course, as the text there confirms:

3 Laȝamon's *Brut*, MS Cotton Caligula A.IX, f. 1r.
The opening of the *Brut*. Inside the capital 'A' of 'An preost' is a cleric writing. The poem itself is written out as prose, with punctuation to indicate the verse-lines. Photograph © British Library, London.

Feþeren he nom mid fingren and fiede on boc-felle. (26)

[He took a quill in his fingers and wrote on the parchment.]

Yet the fact that he is writing in a book gives the game away, since an author composing his work would be accustomed to write on reusable wax tablets or on loose sheets of parchment before handing the work to a scribe to make a fair copy, and that too would be written out before the volume was assembled and bound. These portraits of the writer or scribe with an open book are traditional illustrations not intended to be realistic but conventional signals that you are reading the book that the scribe or author wrote. Not author portraits at all, then, but authenticating portraits, establishing from the outset the relationship between writer, text and reader.

No doubt this illustrator knew no more about Laȝamon than we can learn from the opening lines of the work: that he was a priest living at a fine Worcestershire church at Areley Kings near Redstone. In the majority of cases we have not even this information. With a few exceptions, authors had nothing to do with the production of the manuscripts in which their works were disseminated, and we can well leave authors out of our consideration until we have examined the way manuscripts were produced and circulated.

Scribes and their Manuscripts

Scribes wrote on parchment or paper, the former being much more usual until the end of the Middle Ages. Parchment is what Laȝamon calls *boc-felle*, 'book-skin', the hide of sheep or calf that has been prepared for writing by soaking it in lye, stretching it on a frame, removing the flesh and hair, bleaching it and smoothing and whitening the surface (de Hamel 1992, 8–11). The author of *A Meditacioun of þe Fyve Woundes* likens Christ's Passion to this process:

> Streyned ['stretched'] on the harde cros moore dispitously ['cruelly']
> and grevously þan ever was schepys skyn streyned on the wal or upon
> þe parchemyn-makeris harowe ['frame'] ayens þe sonne to drye.

The quality of the finished product depended upon many factors, including the age and health of the animal: it is common to see in manuscripts of even quite high quality that tics and other parasites have left holes and blemishes in the skin which the scribe had to skirt round.

Paper was much cheaper than parchment and became increasingly so as the trade expanded, though it had to be imported until the end of the fifteenth century. It was made of rags or linen, and has lasted a lot better than modern paper will. Even so, it was scarcely used for English manuscripts before 1380 and was not common until the mid-fifteenth century. Paper usually has watermarks, and these give evidence about the age and source of the paper stock (Lyall 1989).

The sheets of parchment or paper were folded once for a large folio volume, twice for a quarto or three times for an octavo, to make two, four or eight leaves when cut. A number of these folded sheets were gathered into a quire, typically of eight or twelve leaves, nesting in one another, so that in a quire of eight, for example, leaves 1 and 8, 2 and 7, 3 and 6, and 4 and 5 were each a single sheet (a 'bifolium'). The sheets were generally prepared for writing by ruling them in lead pencil or some other material, first using a device for pricking the outer leaves at regular intervals for the marks to act as guides so that the lines could be ruled neatly. When the scribes had finished their work, the individual quires were gathered together for binding (de Hamel 1992, 17–19, 41).

Materials were expensive, and so an important consideration was not to waste space by leaving blank parchment, though if you really wanted to show that money was no object the wide margins of your manuscript would do precisely that. The manuscripts of Laȝamon's *Brut* are not extravagant productions of this sort, and in both the verse is written out as prose with two columns to a page. The resulting page is attractive and clear, and the scribe manages to fit many more long alliterative lines onto a side than if he had written it out as verse. So rigid is the post-medieval tradition that verse must look like verse that even with today's book prices no one would imagine printing a book with verse set out as prose to save cost.

What signals Laȝamon's text as verse is not the layout but the punctuation (see plate 3). Every full line ends with a dot (known as a *punctus*); since alliterative lines are divided into half-lines, these are indicated by another punctuation mark looking like an upside-down semi-colon, known as a *punctus elevatus* (Parkes 1992, 306). This again is quite at odds with more recent practice, but it is the essential nature of medieval punctuation of verse that it has more to do with metrics and rhythm than with syntax and meaning. Many medieval texts have no punctuation at all or very little, especially when they are set out in verse-lines where metrical punctuation is unnecessary. The only punctuation in the *Gawain* manuscript is a series of marks in the margins indicating the stanza divisions of *Pearl* and *Sir Gawain and the Green Knight* and the arrangement of four-line groups in *Cleanness* and *Patience*. How different this is from the way that medieval poetry appears on the printed page! In any modern edition the stanzas of *Pearl* and *Sir Gawain and the Green Knight* are separated by a space, and the text is punctuated according to modern conventions of syntax and sentence structure, with speeches indicated by quotation marks. The experience of reading is significantly different. Adding modern punctuation is a slyly unobtrusive branch of editing, since the editor has decided (sometimes questionably) what the passage means. There are many cases of genuine doubt, where editors will quite reasonably disagree, as on the interpretation and hence punctuation of the opening lines of *Sir Gawain and the Green Knight* (*BOME*, p. 64). Similarly, at the end of *Patience*, there is no boundary between God's reproof to Jonah and the poet's concluding advice to his audience. To appreciate the effect of this we need to listen to these lines being read aloud and be prepared to allow the merging of voices that the poet intends, but the hapless editor is obliged to mark the end of one speech and the beginning of another, and so the effect is destroyed.

Editors also add titles where, as often, there are none in the manuscript. The titles *Pearl* and *Patience*, though both supplied by nineteenth-century editors, seem entirely appropriate since these are the first words of those poems as well as the focus of their action. On the other hand, we should be aware that *Sir Gawain and the Green Knight* is a modern title, since it gives prominence to a reticent hero who makes a first hesitant intervention in line 343 and steps back into the shadows of the court at the end of the poem. It would better represent the poet's strategy to allow the reader to discover what the poem is about, but if we are wedded to a title then we might take it from l. 29 of the poem, and call it *An Outtrage Awenture of Arthurez Wonderez*.

Without the intervention of the modern editor, the relationship between the text and its reader is more fluid, the process of reading slower and more demanding, requiring more attention and reflection. To the medieval reader it was a different experience, and surely a more rewarding one? For the page is not just a series of symbols conveying meaning, but a physical space full of activity: letters shaped by hand, and colours, the brown or black of the ink on the cream or yellow of the parchment, the red and blue of coloured initial letters, the blue, green and red of paragraph markers, in rarer instances brilliant illustrations ranging from matchbox-size miniatures to full-page pictures. How perverse that a modern editor should remove all that is colourful and attractive to replace it with commas and exclamation marks! And yet how we should grumble if that were not done!

'The archaeology of the book' is a phrase coined to emphasize the ways in which experts in the construction of manuscripts (codicologists) and in medieval handwriting (palaeographers) can set about an exploration of the book's history and significance, rather as an archaeologist can unearth the secrets of a historic site. Handwriting can be dated within limits of a century or so even by non-experts, and experts – though they are not always to be trusted – offer dates accurate to within a quarter of a century or less. In general, though this is counter-intuitive, the older the medieval text, the easier it is to read (Parkes 1979). The regularity and precision of the work of the twelfth-century monks who copied the *Peterborough Chronicle* into Bodley MS Laud Misc. 636 can be read as easily as print once a few unaccustomed letter-forms become familiar (see chapter 1, plate 1). There are few abbreviations apart from the line ('macron') over final vowels to represent 'm' (l. 1 heo*m*). The careful professional scribe from about 1400 who wrote Bodley MS Fairfax 3 of Gower's *Confessio Amantis* has rather more swirls and sweeps, but they are soon interpreted (illustrated in *BOME*, p. 245). The copy of *St Erkenwald* made in 1477 (BL MS Harley 2250) is written with speed and economy in mind: the letter-shapes and the layout are much less regular, and abbreviations are frequent (illustrated in *BOME*, p. 62). From about the same date is the text of the York Plays, BL MS Add. 35290, still quite legible to a practised reader, but written by a scribe who wanted to make an official record as quickly as possible with no thought of pleasing the eye of a patron or purchaser. From here the path to the head-splitting documents of the late sixteenth century goes downhill all the way.

There are many kinds of scribe, and their books reflect a great variety of occupation, experience, training, skill or lack of it. Most of the early scribes, and indeed many of the later, were monastic, such as the Benedictine monks who compiled and wrote the chronicle from Peterborough Abbey. The Corpus manuscript of *Ancrene Wisse*, Corpus Christi College, Cambridge, MS 402, was closely associated with the Augustinian abbey at Wigmore where it ended up in about 1300 (Laing 1993, 24). Other scribes were clerics serving in households of the gentry and nobility, not just as priests celebrating mass in the chapel as they do in the description of the New Year festivities in *Sir Gawain and the Green Knight* (62–5), but as penmen, carrying out a range of other functions that demanded literacy and Latin: record-keepers, accountants, and 'clerical' workers in the modern sense. A rather grand example is John Trevisa, chaplain at Berkeley Castle in Gloucestershire, who indicates in his *Dialogue*, no doubt self-servingly, the high regard in which Lord Berkeley held him as a Latinist.

At this time, towards the end of the fourteenth century, the evidence for professional scribes becomes more abundant. Many of them did not devote themselves full time to transcribing, but it was a significant part of their activities and a major source of their income. An earlier example is well documented and instructive, for it shows a scribe spending most of his time over a period of 35 years making copies of legal records, but also accepting commissions to copy literary texts. This is the scribe of the Harley Lyrics in BL MS Harley 2253, whose distinctive hand has been traced in two other literary manuscripts and also in a series of 41 local documents from the Ludlow region in Herefordshire from 1314 to 1349 (Revard 2000). MS Harley 2253 has the characteristics expected of such a scribe; the hand is neat and practised, with nothing more than some red penwork as decoration, a local not a metropolitan product.

If we turn to London in the early years of the fifteenth century, we come across scribes employed in the offices of government using their training for a spot of moonlighting. One such was Thomas Hoccleve, working at the Privy Seal, a poet himself who claimed to be a friend and admirer of Chaucer. Hoccleve's hand has been identified as one of a number of scribes contributing to a copy of Gower's *Confessio Amantis* at a date after 1408 (Doyle and Parkes 1978). The manuscript demonstrates that at this time, perhaps because of greatly increased demand for good texts of Gower, Chaucer and Langland, scribes would work in loose co-operation. London was, after all, a small town by our standards, with perhaps 50,000 inhabitants. A scribe who was commissioned to produce a copy of the *Confessio Amantis* would know whom he could trust to help him out, which scribes were skilled in the appropriate styles, where to find the artist to paint the borders and provide the illustrations, who could make a smart job of the binding and so on.

Confessio Amantis was quite frequently illustrated or illuminated (Scott 1996, 2.65–6, 109–10, 323–5). Illumination strictly meant the application of glittering silver or gold to a picture. It raised the status of a manuscript but it was very expensive, and particularly so to employ a top illuminator (the medieval term was a *limnour*) such as John Siferwas or Herman Scheerre, both working as artists in the early fifteenth century for royal and noble patrons (Scott 1996, 2.54–5, 86–8). Plate 10 below (chapter 6) is a miniature by Sheerre for *Confessio Amantis*.

Until late in the period, manuscripts were generally produced to order rather than as a speculative venture. It was too risky to do the work in the hope that someone might want it, since manuscripts were extremely expensive. In 1397 the warden of Winchester commissioned a 'legend', a collection of saints' lives (Schramm 1933, 141). It was nothing very special, but the bill was considerably more than the stipend customarily paid to a parish curate for a year's work:

> Parchment 51 shillings
> Writing 72 shillings
> Illumination and binding 30 shillings
> Total £7 13 shillings

A monastery might want a copy of the *Anglo-Saxon Chronicle*, as Peterborough Abbey did after the fire that destroyed its library in 1116. Through their contacts with other religious houses, especially those of their own order, the monks could borrow a text of the *Chronicle* and make a copy for their own use, keeping the record up to date in subsequent years. Sir William Clopton, a Warwickshire gentleman, wanted a smart copy of *Piers Plowman* and other fashionable works, and in 1408 he approached a professional scribe, probably in Westminster or London, which he had to visit as MP for Worcestershire (Turville-Petre 1990, 35–8). When Clopton took home to Wixford the completed book, for which he must have paid considerably more than the warden of Winchester's £7 13 shillings, he was the proud possessor of an object of beauty that had employed the skills of a team of specialists, including an illuminator who had painted handsome capital letters and borders in blue, red and gold in the latest style. As a permanent mark of his ownership, Clopton wanted his shield and those of his relatives painted at the foot of the first page, which was done rather clumsily and inaccurately, perhaps by a local artist.

In this way texts travelled around the country to and from the metropolis and from region to region, and they themselves became the source of further copies. The most popular texts were transcribed over and over again: some 250 copies survive of the Wycliffite Bible in whole or in part, over 170 copies of the English version of the *Anglo-Norman Brut*, over 50 complete copies of the *Canterbury Tales*, *Confessio Amantis* and *Piers Plowman*. At a conservative guess one might reckon that one manuscript in twenty has survived to this day, giving some indication of the multiplication of copies of English works, especially from the fifteenth century.

Audiences

Texts were modified to suit the needs and tastes of the audience. Works written in a distant dialect could be difficult to understand, and we have seen in the previous chapter how the author of *Cursor Mundi* 'translated' a southern work into the northern dialect of his parishioners. Involving less wholesale alterations, there are texts of the *Canterbury Tales* in the dialect of the north-east midlands, of *Piers Plowman* (originally from Worcestershire) in the dialect of Durham, and of *The Owl and the Nightingale* (perhaps from Surrey) in that of Herefordshire. More drastic steps could be taken, *pace* the author, to modify a text that was difficult or displeasing, or did not satisfy the particular needs of the 'editor' of a volume or the demands of a patron. The text of Laȝamon's *Brut* in MS BL Cotton Otho C.XIII has been substantially revised, its archaic vocabulary replaced by more current diction (see chapter 4). Several of the romances in the huge Auchinleck manuscript have been adapted in order to shape the volume, presumably in accord with the wishes of the person for whom it was intended.

The purchaser of a volume was able to exercise a strong influence upon its contents, structure and scale, and to issue precise instructions to the scribes on the kinds of works to include and the level of decoration to adorn them with. The Auchinleck manuscript, National Library of Scotland, Advocates' MS 19.2.1, contained over 50 works before the volume was damaged; its range of contents suggests a secular owner, with many romances and political items as well as pious and instructive poems. Whoever commissioned it in the 1330s must have been wealthy, for the production is of professional quality with some 40 small illustrations to mark the beginning of the items, all but five since cut out. A considerable team was employed on its construction. In common with many large manuscripts, it is made up of originally independent booklets, in this case 12, which were finally bound as one volume (Schonk 1985; Hanna 2000). Some three-quarters of the surviving texts are written by the chief scribe, who brought in a number of his fellows to help him speed up and complete the major undertaking. The artist who then added the miniatures at the head of the poems can be associated with a group of illuminators working on legal texts in London; pictures are unusual in manuscripts of English works at such an early date. This range of expertise would be most readily available in London, and other features of the book, including the dialect of the scribes, confirm that this is a metropolitan construction. The miniatures, though attractive and unusual, are not particularly ambitious and are presumably in part intended to help readers find their way around the volume. One of the best that remains is a pretty scene set on a diamond-patterned gold background on f. 167r, with the hero and his companion and horse arriving at a castle, to mark the opening of the romance of *Reinbrun, Son of Guy of Warwick*. The commissioner of the Auchinleck manuscript was not so much interested in the illustrations as in the contents, with a weakness for popular romances and a strong interest in national prestige, revealed rather desperately in *Sir Orfeo* where the Thracian king is transmuted to 'a kinge in Inglond' (39–40) and the action set in Winchester. Presumably the patron worked closely with the 'editor' of the volume, picking items that interested him and arranging for many texts to be adapted and reworked, perhaps even commissioning translations of French works.

As is usually the case, we do not know for whom the Auchinleck manuscript was written, so that the only guide is our assessment of the character of its contents. BL MS Cotton Nero A.X, the *Gawain* manuscript, is as mysterious in this respect as in all others. What sort of person would have collected these four extremely sophisticated poems with such difficult vocabulary and highly wrought poetic forms, written in the distinctive dialect of Cheshire/Staffordshire? It could not be described as a de-luxe manuscript, yet it has the unusual feature of 11 full-page and one half-page pictures to illustrate the chief events of the poem, not very skilfully and sometimes inaccurately (Edwards 1997, 202–19). It looks as though these illustrations, grouped on blank leaves at the beginning and end and between the texts, were added later to give more distinction to the volume.

By the fifteenth century it became commoner to grace English works with more professional illustrations and floral borders. One such, MS Digby 233, contains another of Trevisa's translations made at the behest of his patron Lord Berkeley, which has two large pictures of royal courtiers dressed in fashionable costume. This volume may have been made for Berkeley's son-in-law, the earl of Warwick, or perhaps Prince Henry (Scott 1996, 2.123–5). Such books were for display at least as much as for reading, like the richly illuminated psalters and liturgical books with which aristocratic households proclaimed both their piety and their prestige. Many lovely copies of the works of Chaucer, Gower and Lydgate were produced in the fifteenth century for rich, often noble, buyers as these authors became highly fashionable (Doyle 1983, 169–75).

As families lower down the social scale had more opportunities to see or hear texts that appealed to them, and acquired the skill to make copies for their own entertainment, so book ownership became more widespread. The household miscellany or commonplace book, put together by the amateur anthologist from attractive pieces that could be borrowed from friends or neighbours, is a feature of the fifteenth century and later, but was not unknown earlier. A very early example, probably copied by the owner or by a scribe working for his household, is MS Digby 86, compiled towards the end of the thirteenth century for the Grimhill family in Worcestershire. It has a wide range of contents in Latin, French and English. *Dame Sirith*, often described as the earliest fabliau in English, is marked for four voices including a narrator. *The Fox and the Wolf* is an amusing and lively beast-fable. The fox, finding himself stuck at the bottom of a well, invites his friend the wolf to jump into the bucket at the top:

> Þe wolf gon sinke, þe vox arise –
> Þo gon þe wolf sore agrise!
> Þo he com amidde þe putte
> Þe wolf þene vox opward mette.

'Gossip,' quod þe wolf, 'wat nou?
Wat havest þou imunt – weder wolt þou?'
'Weder ich wille?' þe vox sede.
'Ich wille oup, so God me rede!'   (239–46)

[The wolf began to sink, the fox to rise – then the wolf got very frightened. When he reached the middle of the shaft the wolf met the fox going upwards. 'Dear chap,' said the wolf, 'what now? What's the idea? Where are you off to?' 'Where am I off to?' replied the fox. 'God bless me, I'm going up.']

Side by side with the many literary pieces is a range of other material: medical remedies and charms, for example, on getting rid of mice from a barn, tricks for how to make it look as if there is a river running inside the house or to make a dead bird sing, lists of unlucky days, a treatise on the care of hawks, and a range of experiments using eggs, quicksilver and candles. Here, too, is the character-telling game of Ragman's Roll, in which the stanzas would be copied out onto a roll with a string attached to each, and each player would draw a stanza describing him or her, with often embarrassing results. It is a surprisingly early example of an anthology put together to instruct and amuse the family (Turville-Petre 2003).

A century and a half later (c. 1425–50) Robert Thornton, a gentleman of East Newton in Yorkshire, copied for his own use two large volumes containing religious and instructive works, medical texts and romances, as well as unique copies of several alliterative poems including *Morte Arthure* and *Winner and Waster* (BL MS Add. 31042 and Lincoln Cath. Lib. MS 91). He writes in a rather untidy but legible and practised hand, not taking much trouble to beautify his manuscripts, although there is some simple decorative penwork such as ornamental scrolls and grotesque faces (Thompson 1987, 56–63). Books such as Thornton's, where compiler and owner are one and the same, allow us to visualize with particular clarity the owner of the manuscript reading to himself in private or reading aloud to his household and friends, instructing them or entertaining them. In this case it makes little sense to distinguish between 'reader' and 'listener', since a member of the household might on one occasion want to look up a medical recipe, on another spend the evening listening to a romance or participating in a quasi-dramatic performance. What is most obviously true of these household books may equally well be true of any manuscript. We tend to have somewhat rigid ideas about how medieval texts were communicated and for the most part we envisage a listening audience. This perception is enhanced by the famous frontispiece in Corpus Christi College, Cambridge, MS 61, which is often taken to be an idealized portrait of Chaucer reading *Troilus and Criseyde* to the court (Scott 1996, 1 pl. 242; 2 no. 58), and by the conventional tendency of medieval writers to set their works in an oral context: over 30 Middle English poems actually begin with the word 'Listen . . .', just as the author of *Sir Gawain and the Green Knight* tells us to 'lysten þis laye bot on littel quile' (30). There is also the problem that we have no single word to mean reader/listener, so that we generally plump for 'audience', although this word is equally loaded. There are plenty of counter-examples to confirm the picture of non-professional readers, literate women just as much as men. At the beginning of the thirteenth century the author of *Ancrene Wisse* instructs his anchoresses to read their Latin devotions just as they have them written down (1.86) and to read aloud to their maids every week. He tells them also:

> Of þis boc redeð hwen ȝe beoð eise euche dei leasse oðer mare. Ich hopie þet hit schal beon ow, ȝef ȝe hit redeð ofte, swiðe biheve, þurh Godes muchele grace; elles ich hefde uvele bitohe mi muchele hwile. (ed. Millett, 8.336–9)

> [Read more or less of this book every day when you are free. If you read it often, I hope it will be very useful to you, through the great grace of God; otherwise I have misused a great deal of my time.]

Brother Simon Wynter gives a nicely circumstantial account of how he wishes his *Life of St Jerome*, written for the duchess of Clarence, to be communicated:

> Wherfore I desire þat hit schulde lyke ȝoure ladyshype first to rede hit and to doo copye hit ['have it copied'] for ȝoureself and syth to latte other rede hit and copye hit whoso wyl. (quoted Doyle 1989, 116)

An inscription in a fifteenth-century London manuscript of mystical writings and Lollard tracts defines itself as a 'common profit' book:

> This booke was made of þe goodis of John Collopp for a comyn profite, . . . and so be it delyvered and committed fro persoone to

persoone, man or womman, as longe as þe booke endureth. (Scase 1992, 261)

Many texts remained popular over a surprisingly long time, and works were recopied for new generations of readers. At the end of the fourteenth century *Ancrene Wisse* was copied into the largest of all collections of English works, the Vernon manuscript (Bodley MS Eng. Poet. a.1), weighing in at 22 kilos (which would count as excess baggage on a plane). It shares a place in Vernon with a copy of *Piers Plowman*, and there are manuscript copies of *Piers Plowman* well into the sixteenth century, a century and a half after Langland's time. It is often the case that no manuscript contemporary with the author survives, so that it is difficult to be sure when a work was composed. BL MS Cotton Caligula A.IX containing Laȝamon's *Brut* and *The Owl and the Nightingale* used to be dated early in the thirteenth century; this dating has been revised and the manuscript is now thought to have been copied towards the end of the century, and so it is possible that both works were composed some time after the date of c. 1200 usually assigned to them. The only copy of *St Erkenwald* is in BL MS Harley 2250, a paper manuscript, dated 1477 by its scribe, which is supported by the dating of its watermarks; on grounds of style and subject matter the poem is usually dated almost a century earlier, but this is fragile evidence. BL MS Harley 2253 with the Harley Lyrics includes an up-to-the-moment political lyric that cannot have been composed before 1340, but the scribe has also included poems about Simon de Montfort, presumably contemporary with the events of 1264–5 that they describe.

Other indications of texts being read with interest many years after their composition are given by the comments in the margins scribbled by later readers, who were prone to write their names as proof of ownership of their prized manuscripts in such form as 'Adam Smith owns this book; he that steals it shall be hanged on a hook.' Just as frequent are annotations such as 'John Clerk owes Adam Smith vij d.', or 'For the palsy, take . . .', as well as direct comments on the text. *Piers Plowman* attracted particular interest in the years of religious turmoil, as the Tudor reformers found plenty in it to demonstrate to their own satisfaction the corruptions of the medieval church, so that several manuscripts of the poem have extensive political/religious comments added in the first half of the sixteenth century.

Authors

What did these later readers know about the authors of the works they were reading? A few authors such as Laʒamon reveal their names; Nicholas of Guildford, parish priest of Portesham in Dorset, is named in the *Owl and the Nightingale* (191, 1746–74) as a wise man whose virtues have been shamefully overlooked by his superiors, and it is therefore likely that he was the author looking for recognition. William Langland conceals/reveals his name in a line in the B-Text only: '"I have lyved in *londe*;" quod I, "my name is *Longe Wille*"' (*Piers Plowman* B.15.152), a clue recognized by some early readers, such as one who writes in the margin 'the name of th'auctor'. The only information about Langland not provided by the poem itself comes from an early fifteenth-century note, accurate or not, added to a manuscript of *Piers Plowman*, that William Langland was the son of Stacy de Rokayle from Shipton-under-Wychwood in Oxfordshire. Most contemporary readers of the poem would not even have known that. A few writers such as Chaucer and Gower attracted sufficient attention that their careers were known in more detail. Commonly, though, later readers knew nothing whatsoever about the author of the work they were reading, not even the name; perhaps more surprisingly, it is likely that even contemporaries and near-contemporaries knew nothing either. The texts that reached their readers by various routes were generally quite anonymous, and there is no evidence that readers had much interest in the matter, strange as that must seem to our age, which is obsessed by authors' lives and much less concerned about their writings. For authors in most religious orders, writing required special permission from the prior of their house, and self-promotion was contrary to all that their order stood for. The writer of the *Cloud of Unknowing* would have been disconcerted by the vain efforts made to uncover his well-concealed identity.

Only in exceptional cases do we have texts copied by the authors themselves. The most noteworthy example is Thomas Hoccleve, three of whose holograph manuscripts containing his poems survive from the 1420s. As he tells us himself in his autobiographical writings, Hoccleve's whole career was spent as a clerk in the Privy Seal, where formal documents were drafted and written on behalf of the king and Council (Burrow 1994). Another manuscript in his hand is the *Formulary*, a collection of documents, all in French or Latin, to be used as models. We have already observed that he also did some freelance work, probably like many such clerks. So he was a professional scribe as well as a poet, and it is therefore not so surprising that he should produce his own copies of his poems. At least it cut out a great source of error, the scribe, although even the author himself inevitably made copying errors.

A few other authors seem to have exercised a certain degree of control over the immediate copies of their works. Many of the early manuscripts of *Confessio Amantis* are so accurate and in such similar format that it is probable that Gower himself took an interest in their production. Had Chaucer lived, he would presumably have overseen the production of copies of the *Canterbury Tales*, as he evidently did in the case of the two works of whose inaccuracy he complains to his scribe in *Chaucer's Wordes unto Adam his Owne Scriveyn*:

> Adam scriveyn, if ever it thee bifalle
> *Boece* or *Troylus* for to wryten newe,
> Under thy long lokkes thou most have the scalle,
> But after my makyng thow wryte more trewe;
> So ofte adaye I mot thy werk renewe,
> It to correcte and eke to rubbe and scrape,
> And al is thorugh thy negligence and rape.

[Scribe Adam, if you ever come to write out *Boece* or *Troilus* again, I hope you get scab under your long locks if you don't copy more faithfully according to what I have composed. So many times a day I have to redo your work, to correct it and also to rub and scrape, and all because of your carelessness and haste.]

The arrangement described here is that Chaucer handed over to Adam the final drafts of *Boece* and *Troilus and Criseyde*, and took them back together with the fair copies Adam had made so that he could correct them himself, scraping the parchment with a small knife to erase the numerous errors. But the *Canterbury Tales* was unfinished at Chaucer's death in 1400, and it was left to the poet's literary executors to present it in some sort of order. This turned out to be an impossible job, since Chaucer's work was in disarray, individual tales or groups of tales in separate booklets, with no final order established, old links now obsolete, new links not written, some tales reassigned to different tellers but not yet revised. Nevertheless, the work was in great demand among wealthy readers, for already versions of a number of tales had circulated, at least among a coterie, with or without Chaucer's permission. It was therefore an urgent matter to assemble the whole work, and the Hengwrt manuscript (National Library of Wales MS Peniarth 392D) was produced with evident signs of haste, lacking certain parts of the work, with spaces where there were hopes that another section might turn up. Perhaps once the immediate pressure was off the executors had the leisure, and presumably the commission from a wealthy patron as well, to organize a much fancier volume: the magnificent Ellesmere manuscript (Huntington Library MS El. 26.C.9), famous for its little portraits of the individual tellers of tales as they ride on their pilgrimage. This was copied by the same scribe, who has now been identified as Adam Pinkhurst (Mooney 2006), with much more splendid layout and opulent decoration than the earlier volume, including many beautiful floral borders. Considerable trouble had been taken to put the text in better order and to smooth over the cracks. It was the best that could be done, imposing a final order on what Chaucer himself never finalized (Pearsall 1985, 8–23).

In the end, however much the author scolded Adam – appropriately named as the archetypal scribe – and scraped and emended his slapdash work, the text would become the exemplar used by a second scribe and that in turn would be copied by a third and, as if by a series of Chinese whispers, the work would become increasingly corrupted. Once the copy had left the author's grasp, he no longer had any control over its fortunes.

In the unlikely event that all the copies had survived, the modern editor could follow Adam's archetypal text down its family tree of manuscripts, noting where the corruptions originated. If only a proportion, but enough, of the copies survived, and Adam's text was lost, it should theoretically be possible to trace the direction of descent, which manuscript was copied from which, by identifying the errors, and so work back up the family tree established in this process. But things are never that simple. Scribes tend to make the same kinds of mistakes as one another, perhaps skipping a word or two or even a line or two, substituting an easier word for a more difficult, copying what they imagine to be there rather than what actually is there; worse still, the scribes themselves are all too aware that their exemplar is likely to be full of error, and so they are keen to correct it to what they think it ought to read, sometimes by referring to another copy of the work, which of course may be even more inaccurate than their first copy. After all, the scribe is not a xerox machine but an interpreter of the text in front of him. And so, as often as not, it turns out to be impossible to establish the family tree with any certainty.

Piers Plowman is notorious as the text that presents the most horribly complex problems for the editor. Three authorial versions can be distinguished, one consisting of a Prologue and 11 completed passus or chapters (the A-Text); a second, which is the version most commonly read today, extending the poem to 20 passus (the B-Text); and a third that makes extensive revisions and additions (the C-Text). Yet this is a tidy account of the actual situation, in which there is considerable leakage between versions, some manuscripts presenting copies conflating A and B, or A and C, or indeed all three versions (Hanna 1993, 37–42; Hanna 1996, 203–43). To make matters worse, there are two distinct traditions of the B-Text, one of which may represent the poet's partial revision prior to the full-scale revision into the C-Text. Worst of all, every surviving manuscript of the B-Text descends from a lost copy, the B-Archetype, which had already become considerably corrupted. We may take a single example to demonstrate this. In the C-Text Glutton and his friends are sitting in the pub drunkenly bartering their clothes for a drink and quarrelling over their value, until they ask Robin the ropemaker to get up and act as umpire:

> Til Robyn the ropere aryse they bisouhte.   (C.6.387)

Comparison of the readings of the manuscripts of the B-Text shows that the B-Archetype misread the last word with this nonsensical result:

> Til Robyn the ropere aroos by þe southe.   (B.5.330)

If Langland had ever overseen and corrected a copy of the B-Text of his poem, that copy must have been soon destroyed or lost, for when he came to compose his final C revision he was evidently obliged to rely on a corrupt copy of B, doing his best to repair or rewrite the damaged lines (as with the example quoted) at the same time as he made the larger revisions.

What were the rewards for a writer for his labours of composition? In the final revision of his poem, Langland added a passage describing the life of his alter ego Will and, though we must be cautious about assuming the description is autobiographical, nevertheless we may be sure that it expresses some of Langland's deepest concerns. Will's is a life that is neither secure nor well rewarded. Like the London layabouts among whom he lives, he is not engaged in productive labour, and Reason rebukes him sternly for his idleness. Can Will say mass, he asks, or work in the fields? Will is not a priest in full orders, since he has a wife Kytte and a daughter Calote, but it was possible for those in minor orders, on the bottom rung of ecclesiastical office, to be married. It fits the description well to see Will as a cleric in minor orders, because he identifies himself as a *clerc* and talks of his schooling and his fitness to wear 'this longe clothes' of a cleric. He explains unconvincingly that he is too tall to manage agricultural labour, so his work, as he describes it, is to travel through London and beyond, earning his living by saying prayers for those who provide for him:

> The lomes þat y labore with and lyflode deserve
> Is *pater noster* and my prymer, *placebo* and *dirige*,
> And my sauter som tyme, and my sevene psalmes.
> This y segge for here soules of suche as me helpeth.   (C.5.45–8)

[The tools I work with and earn my living by are the Our Father and my prayer-book, the Office for the Dead, the Psalter sometimes and my Seven Penitential Psalms. I say these for the souls of those who support me.]

This may in fact be a literal description of Langland's 'day job', but it can also be taken as a metaphor for the life of a poet dependent upon the favour of those who will listen to him. There survive several fine manuscripts of *Piers Plowman*, though probably none from Langland's lifetime, so he was not the one to be rewarded for them. Perhaps he had a rich patron or hoped by writing to attract one; perhaps there was a coterie of well-placed Londoners who offered Langland some approach to the sources of power and influence; through the prestige attached to writing *Piers Plowman* might come preferment. There might also be dangers in writing material that was politically and religiously sensitive, and it was no bad idea to have a powerful protector. It may be that Langland lived his life in expectation, or it may be – nothing is impossible – that he was more or less content with his work of saying prayers in exchange for bread.

It is Hoccleve, again, who gives us the clearest view of the life of one writer in London, and for this we can draw upon his autobiographical poems as well as a few official documents that mention him (Burrow 1994). Like other civil servants he was granted an annuity (at first £10) for his work at the Privy Seal, and like other clerks he frequently had to wait a long time for payment. All his life he was in fear of poverty, for 'paiement is hard to gete adayes' (*The Regiment of Princes* 829). Unlike his colleagues who could only write begging letters, Hoccleve had the talent to write piteous and witty poems addressed to the chancellor and the under-treasurer to draw attention to his poverty, and the documents suggest that such poems were sometimes effective in speeding up payment. In a *balade* to the under-treasurer Henry Somer that elegantly plays on the concept of Somer's name, Hoccleve begs that the delayed annuity should be paid to him and his fellow clerks (who no doubt had to offer a cut for the mention):

> We your servantes, Hoccleve and Baillay,
> Hethe and Offorde, yow byseeche and preye,
> Haastith our hervest as soone as yee may;
>> [*hervest* harvest, i.e. reward]
> For fere of stormes our wit is aweye.
> Wer our seed inned, wel we mighten pleye   *inned* gathered in
> And us desporte and synge and make game.
>> [*us desporte* enjoy ourselves]
> And yit this rowndel shul we synge and seye
> In trust of yow and honour of your name.
>> (*Balade to H. Somer* 25–32)

The huge success of his long poem, *The Regiment of Princes*, surviving in 43 manuscripts, evidently did not bring Hoccleve riches. The poet describes in the introduction how, musing on his poverty, he met a poor old man and told him in detail of his financial worries:

> Sixe marc ȝeerly, and no more þan þat,
> Fadir, to me me thynkyth is ful lyte.   (974–5)

[Six marks a year and no more than that, father, seems very little to me.]

Like Will in *Piers Plowman*, he is no good at agricultural work:

With plow can I nat medlen, ne with harwe,
>   [*medlen* go to work; *harwe* harrow]
Ne wot nat what lond good is for what corne;
>   [*Ne wot nat* Nor do I know]
And for to lade a cart or fille a barwe   *lade* load
To whiche I never used was toforne –   *toforne* previously
My bak unbuxum hath swich thyng forsworne.
>   [*unbuxum* unwilling; *forsworne* renounced]
>   (981–5)

Writing is not generally regarded as a proper job:

Many men, fadir, wenen þat writynge   *wenen* believe
No travaile ys, þey hold hit but a game.
Art hath no foo but swich folk unkonyng.
>   [*foo* enemy; *unkonyng* ignorant]
>   (988–90)

The beggar suggests to Hoccleve the idea of writing a work to advise Prince Hal, the future Henry V, as a way of confirming the prince's favour and securing the poet a more settled future. The copy in BL MS Arundel 38 has a very fine picture by a follower of Herman Scheerre showing a young man on his knees presenting his book to Prince Hal. After Henry came to the throne in 1413 Hoccleve continued to write begging poems and continued to court the great: the king himself, his brothers the dukes of Bedford and Gloucester, his aunt the countess of Westmorland, the duke of York, writing also at the command of the king's grandmother the countess of Hereford. The most that can be said is that Hoccleve went on receiving his annuity until his death in 1426. No writer could more assiduously have employed his pen in the service of the powerful, but there is no evidence of direct financial reward for writing, despite the survival of nearly 70 financial documents mentioning his name.

Though Hoccleve may have been exaggerating his financial difficulties, it seems that even the best-placed court poets could not expect to live by writing. The most they could hope for was preferment on the basis of some other activity. John Trevisa's position as chaplain at Berkeley Castle allowed him to engage in large-scale translations of

Latin works for his master, and Lord Berkeley would have gained considerable prestige within his own circle as the patron of such major enterprises (Hanna 1989). Once the text escaped into the public world, neither author nor patron had any control over it (Hanna 1996, 66–71). The monastic author who wrote at the command of his superior was in a similar situation; the Gilbertine canon Robert Manning compiled his *Chronicle* in 1338 on the orders of Canon Robert of Malton for the benefit of his fellow Gilbertines. The Gilbertines gained prestige, and Manning had the security of life within his monastic community.

We have seen that although there were many kinds of manuscript, all were expensive, so that a gentry family interested in books would be proud to own one or two quite ordinary miscellanies, though they would probably feel obliged to spend the money first on a book for the chapel and another for private devotion. Copying a large book was a laborious process; it has been calculated that the Vernon manuscript must have occupied the scribe for a good four years, though of course this is an exceptionally large volume. As texts were copied and recopied, they grew increasingly distant from the authors' originals, each copy different from every other, in large or in small ways, and with no possibility of getting together the range of variant texts for comparison and correction. Indeed, scribes' attempts at correction usually made matters worse.

That is one way of looking at it: a downward slope into error and confusion. A more positive approach is to see every manuscript as a work of art rather than comparing it to a modern book. Every manuscript is an individual, not one of a multitude of identical copies. Every one is the work of a group of craftsmen. Some are attractive and pleasing to the eye, others are incompetent. A few are, in the most literal sense, works of art, with their illuminations brilliantly preserved between their sheltering covers away from the damaging effects of light and dust. Today we are lucky enough to be able to reproduce facsimiles of these sometimes beautiful objects, but, as with facsimiles of any other work of art, there is always some loss. To feel the parchment, to look at the colours of the inks, to spot where the scribe has recovered from a mistake, got tired or drunk or cold, to observe where a later reader has added an approving comment or exploded in anger – all these are ideally a part of the experience of reading a medieval text. And it is more than a pleasure, because details of this sort give us information about the nature of the text, the trustworthiness of the scribe, the readership for whom the manuscript was intended and the reactions of those who read it.

Note on facsimiles

Facsimiles of many of the manuscripts discussed here have been published. I list them in approximate order of the date of the manuscript:

The Peterborough Chronicle, ed. Dorothy Whitelock (Copenhagen, 1954)

The Owl and the Nightingale, intro. N. R. Ker, EETS 251 (1963)

Facsimile of Oxford, Bodleian Library, MS Digby 86, intro. Judith Tschann and M. B. Parkes, EETS s.s. 16 (1996)

Facsimile of British Museum MS. Harley 2253, intro. N. R. Ker, EETS 255 (1965)

The Auchinleck Manuscript, intro. Derek Pearsall and I. C. Cunningham (London, 1979)

The Vernon Manuscript: A Facsimile of Bodleian Library, Oxford, MS Eng. Poet.a.1, intro. A. I. Doyle (Cambridge, 1987)

Pearl, Cleanness, Patience and Sir Gawain, with an introduction by I. Gollancz, EETS 162 (1923)

The Canterbury Tales: A Facsimile and Transcription of the Hengwrt Manuscript, ed. Paul G. Ruggiers (Norman, OK, 1979)

The Ellesmere Manuscript of Chaucer's Canterbury Tales: A Working Facsimile, intro. Ralph Hanna III (Cambridge, 1989)

A Facsimile of Corpus Christi College Cambridge MS 61, intro. M. B. Parkes and Elizabeth Salter (Cambridge, 1978)

Thomas Hoccleve: A Facsimile of the Autograph Verse Manuscripts, intro. J. A. Burrow and A. I. Doyle, EETS s.s. 19 (2002)

The Thornton Manuscript: Lincoln Cathedral Library MS 91, intro. D. S. Brewer and A. E. B. Owen, 2nd edn (London, 1978)

The York Play, intro. Richard Beadle and Peter Meredith (Leeds, 1983)

High-quality colour facsimiles are now available on the web and on CDs. For example:

The Auchinleck Manuscript on the National Library of Scotland website: www.nls.uk/auchinleck.

The Hengwrt Chaucer Digital Facsimile on CD-ROM, ed. Ceridwen Lloyd-Morgan (Cambridge, 2003)

The Piers Plowman Electronic Archive (documentary editions of *Piers Plowman* manuscripts on CD): vol. 1: *Corpus Christi College, Oxford MS 201 (F)*, eds.

Robert Adams, Hoyt N. Duggan, Eric Eliason, Ralph Hanna III, John Price-Wilkin and Thorlac Turville-Petre (Ann Arbor, 2000); vol. 2: *Cambridge, Trinity College, MS B.15.17 (W)*, eds. Hoyt N. Duggan and Thorlac Turville-Petre (Ann Arbor, 2000); vol. 3: *Oxford, Oriel College MS 79 (O)*, eds. Hoyt N. Duggan and Katherine Heinrichs (Cambridge, 2004); vol. 4: *Oxford, Bodleian Library MS Laud 581 (L)*, eds. Hoyt N. Duggan and Ralph Hanna (Cambridge, 2004); vol. 5: *London, BL MS Add. 35287 (M)* (Cambridge, 2005), eds. Eric Eliason, Hoyt N. Duggan and Thorlac Turville-Petre.

CHAPTER 3

Literature and Society

Bond and Free

By the middle of the fifteenth century the Pastons had become a family of great consequence in Norfolk, and were desperate to conceal the fact that they had risen in status with unseemly rapidity. Their enemies, and they had many, were equally keen to make it public. In an attack with the sarcastic title 'A Remembraunce of the wurshypfull Kyn and Auncetrye of Paston', the writer pointed out that Clement, father of William Paston (1378–1444) who established the family's position, 'was a good pleyn husbond', that is, a simple farmer, and gave this detailed account of his circumstances:

> The seyd Clement yede att on Plowe ['went plowing'] both wynter and sommer, and he rodd to mylle on the bar horsbak wyth hys corn under hym, and brought hom mele ageyn ['back'] under hym. And also drove hys carte with dyvers cornys to Wynterton to selle, as a good husbond ought to do. Also he had in Paston a fyve skore or a six skore acrys of lond at the most, and myche þerof bonde lond to Gemyngham-halle with a lytyll pore watyr-mylle rennynge by a lytylle ryver þere . . . And he weddyd Geffrey of Somerton (qwhos ['whose'] trew surnome ys Goneld) Sister qwhych ['who'] was a bond womanne. (*Paston Letters* I, xli–xlii)

The matter was of such concern to the Pastons that in 1466 they obtained a royal declaration that stated that the family had produced 'divers great evidences', court rolls and 'a great multitude of old deeds' to show that from the time of Henry III they had been lords of Paston, where they had a chaplain, and that they had made grants to religious houses, and they 'made open by evident proofe how they and their ancetors came linealy descended of right noble and worshipfull blood and of great lords sometime liveing in this our realme of Ingland'. Going still further back, they produced a family tree to show that 'their first ancetor Wulstan came out of France' (*Paston Letters* II, 551–2). We should be wrong to put these inventions down to snobbery. The *Paston Letters* recorded the constant struggles of the family, like so many others in this turbulent period, to defend their possessions from their rivals who were prepared to lay claim to the Paston lands on the argument that, being of servile origin, the family had no right to them (see Richmond 1990, 1–22).

The accusation in the 'Remembraunce' is that Clement held bondland and that his wife was a bondwoman, that is to say that they were *villeins*, legally the property of their lord, working on his estates as his serfs, forbidden to leave his lands, and obliged to perform a range of fixed services and to yield to him annually a part of their produce. When a *villein* married he had to pay the lord a *merchet* (called a *mariage* in English), when he died he paid a *heriot*, and he handed over a *talliage* whenever the lord chose to demand it. The distinction between a bondman and a freeman was fundamental to medieval society and was constantly confirmed and enforced in the courts. Clement appears to have been an unusually prosperous peasant, holding up to 120 acres with a little mill. Perhaps he had done well out of the Black Death, for when so many died, those who survived had opportunities to take over vacated lands. The accusation about the origins of the Pastons was not that Clement was destitute, but that, however prosperous, he was a *villein*.

Though a legal term, *villein* is very much more than that. Its associations spread into the language and culture of the Middle Ages. John Lydgate expresses the standard view succinctly in the *Fall of Princes*:

> Gentil blood, of his roial nature,
> Is ever enclyned to merci and pité,
> Wher of custum thes vileyns do ther cure
> Bi ther usurpid and extort fals pousté
> To be vengable bi mortal cruelté
> Thoruh hasti fumys of furious corage,
> Folwyng the techchis of ther vileyn lynage.   (4.2955–61)

[*Gentil* blood, from its noble nature, is always inclined towards mercy and compassion, while as a matter of habit these *villeins* make it their business by their presumptuous and falsely exercised power to be vengeful by deadly cruelty, through hot-tempered bursts of intemperate rashness, resulting from the nature of their *villein* ancestry.]

From *villein* derive our words 'villainy' and 'villainous', which have already acquired their derogatory meanings in Middle English. Lechers, writes the author of *Ancrene Wisse*, are so shameless that they seek out ways of performing acts of *vilainie* (4.545). The term 'peasant' is found very late in Middle English; the technical words apart from *villein* are *bondman* and (mainly in early use) *thrall*. *Cherle*, which survives as the basis for our disparaging adjective 'churlish', does not necessarily imply unfree status, but is often used in opposition to *gentil*. In the *Parliament of Fowls* the eagle rebukes the goose for his down-to-earth proverb:

> 'Now fye, cherle!' quod the gentil tercelet,
> 'Out of the dunghille come that word ful ryght.' (596–7)

The abusive term *cherle* is precisely chosen by the *gentil* eagle to characterize the goose's sentiments as those to be expected of a peasant: vulgar, inelegant, utilitarian and narrow-minded.

On the better side of the social divide are the *gentil man* and the *fre man*. *Gentil* is ultimately derived from Latin *gentilis*, 'of a good *gens* or family', and so it means both 'well born' and also 'elevated, refined, sophisticated' and so on. 'Free' in modern English has lost its association with character and conduct, so its use in Middle English can trap the unwary. Arthur's knights in *Sir Gawain and the Green Knight* are his *fre meny* (101), retainers who are both 'nobly born' and 'of courtly behaviour'. In a Grimestone Lyric the loving husband (who is Christ) begs his dear spouse (mankind) to unlock the door to him as he stands outside covered with the blood he, her *make*, 'husband', has shed for her:

> Undo þi dore, my spuse dere;
> Allas! wy stond I loken out here?
> Fre am I, þi make.
> Loke mi lokkes an ek myn heved

An al my bodi with blod beweved
For þi sake.   (*BOME* 14r/1–6)

[Undo the door, my dear spouse; Alas, why do I stand here locked out?
I, your husband, am noble. See my hair and my head too, and all my
body covered in blood for your sake.]

Only someone of such high birth could accomplish such selfless actions that demonstrate to his beloved that he is *fre*.

The word *franklin* is based on the medieval Latin adjective *francus*,
'free', and the term takes on a more specific sense of someone who
is free but not a member of the nobility, a country gentleman (as
Chaucer's Franklin). A *yeoman* is further down the scale, but still on
the free side of the divide. Like Chaucer's Yeoman, he is often a paid
servant, but not a bondman.

In reality, of course, the divide was not nearly as clear cut as the-
orists wished it to be. Increasingly peasants found the resources to
acquire their own land and to pay cash to remit their servile duties,
even to buy their freedom. Classic peasant society relied on a subsistence economy, but in the fourteenth century peasants were involved
more and more in a market economy, selling their produce or exchanging it for other goods. Clement Paston is called a *husbond*, which,
unlike *bondman*, is ambiguous. Though Clement Paston held bond-
land, the implication of the 'Remembraunce' may be that he also had
free land of his own. Certainly he had sources of income and was able
to borrow money to train his son William as a lawyer:

> Also the seyd Clement had a sone William qwhych þat ['whom'] he
> sett to scole, and oftyn he borowyd mony to fynd hym to scole: and
> after þat he yede ['went'] to Courte wyth þe helpe of Geffrey Somerton
> hese uncle and lerned the lawe, and þere bygatte ['acquired'] he myche
> good and þanne he was made a Serjaunt ['barrister'], and afterward
> made a Justice ['judge'], and a ryght connyng ['knowledgeable'] mane
> in þe lawe. (*Paston Letters* I, xlii)

To be trained in the law was a classic route to freedom and status,
though only wealthy peasants could take it. As the more prosperous
of them acquired property and used it to alleviate the burdens of
servitude and even to buy their way out of it altogether, so the
practical distinctions between bond and free became muddied. The

Pastons are a prime example of the social mobility that was possible even within an apparently rigid system. Will in his 'autobiography' in *Piers Plowman* supports the traditional position that those going for ordination had to be of free blood and born in wedlock:

> Hit bycometh for clerkes Crist for to serve,
> And knaves uncrounede to carte and to worche.
> For should no clerke be crouned but yf he come were
> Of frankeleynes and fre men and of folke ywedded.
> Bondemen and bastardus and beggares children,
> Thyse bylongeth to labory, and lordes kyn to serve
> God and good men, as here degré asketh.   (C.5.61–7)

[It is fitting for clerics to serve Christ, and for lads without the tonsure to cart and work manually. No one should be a tonsured cleric unless he is descended from franklins and freemen and married people. It is for bondmen and bastards and beggars' children to labour, and for the kindred of lords to serve God and good men as their status demands.]

Yet it was possible (if expensive) to be granted freedom, and possible also to obtain a dispensation for bastardy and so open the way to an attractive career, especially for the son of a priest (Swanson 1989, 37–40). The result of all this is social disintegration, says Will,

> sythe bondemen barnes haen ben mad bisshopes
> And barnes bastardus haen be erchedekenes.   (C.5.70–1)

[since bondmen's children have been made bishops, and those children's bastards have become archdeacons.]

Like William Paston, Will the dreamer had been helped through his schooling by his father and his relatives (C.5.36), but unlike his namesake, his education has done nothing for him except make him unfit for agricultural labour. No wonder he is bitter about those who have climbed through the clerical hierarchy to become bishops and archdeacons.

Social Tensions in the Reeve's Tale

Chaucer describes both the Reeve and the Miller as 'churls':

The Millere is a cherl; ye knowe wel this.
So was the Reve eek and othere mo,   *eek* also
And harlotrie they tolden bothe two.   *harlotrie* filth
(CT I.3182–4)

The role of a reeve in village society was a difficult one. Though a peasant, he was appointed by the lord as a condition of his tenure to oversee the work of his fellow peasants and to present the annual accounts to his lord:

His lordes sheep, his neet, his dayerye,
[*neet* cattle; *dayerye* dairy cows]
His swyn, his hors, his stoor, and his pultrye   *stoor* livestock
Was hoolly in this Reves governynge.   *hoolly* wholly
(CT I.597–9)

It was not a position that was likely to win many friends. A reeve was obliged to ensure that his fellow peasants fulfilled their servile duties and to spot if they attempted to cheat; as a result 'they were adrad of hym as of the deeth' (*CT* I.605). Yet the lord's accountants, no better friends, were always on the lookout for any trickery or failure, so he had to be careful that 'ther was noon auditor koude on him wynne' (*CT* I.594). Village society exhibited all the self-interests, rivalries and tensions at work in any small community, and a reeve's position, constituted by both power and servility, was likely to earn him distrust and resentment from all quarters.

For this reason it is understandable that Chaucer's Reeve should be peculiarly attuned to the issue of status within the village community, and that his tale should focus upon it. It is set in Trumpington, a village on the river a couple of miles from Cambridge (Bennett 1974, 110–14). The village characters are a clan on the way up; a swaggering miller who has done well for himself, married to the illegitimate daughter of the village priest. Though we never meet the priest, his social ambition is the trigger for the action and the key to the family's shaming. We are not told whether he himself was born 'of frankeleynes and fre men' but, as the parson, he has authority and status within the community, and he has sources of income that allow him to buy social advancement for his family. The villagers are obliged to pay tithes to support the church, which the parson diverts to other ends. As the Reeve explains in lines of sustained irony:

For hooly chirches good moot been despended
On hooly chirches blood that is descended.
Therfore he wolde his hooly blood honoure,
Though that he hooly chirche sholde devoure.   (*CT* I.3983–6)

[For Holy Church's wealth must be spent on the blood that descends
from Holy Church. Therefore he wanted to honour his holy blood even
though he should swallow up Holy Church.]

To establish the family fortunes, the parson has paid a dowry of 'ful
many a panne of bras' (*CT* I.3944) to marry off his daughter to the
miller Symkyn, who is a good catch since he has built up a thriving
business with plenty of opportunity for enrichment through theft.
Symkyn is described as a 'market-betere', someone who frequents
markets, underlining his involvement in the market economy. He has
established 'greet sokene' (*CT* I.3987), that is to say that he has acquired exclusive rights to grind the corn in the neighbourhood. The
parson's daughter is a suitable match for him, not only because she
and her children stand to inherit her father's 'catel and his mesuage'
(*CT* I.3979), his property and his house, but also because she has been
educated in a nunnery where she has acquired the airs and graces of
a lady. The nuns have furthermore ensured that she has remained a
mayde. Haughty (*deynous*) Symkyn, as his neighbours call him, is determined to maintain his yeoman status, 'to saven his estaat of yomanrye'
(*CT* I.3949); positioned at the bottom of the ladder of freemen, owning
a small (*streit*, *CT* I.4122) house, he is ambitious to climb higher, and
he and his wife therefore insist on recognition of their status within
the village:

> A ful fair sighte was it upon hem two;
> On halydayes biforn hire wolde he go
> With his typet wounde aboute his heed,   *typet* hood-tip
> And she cam after in a gyte of reed;   *gyte of reed* red dress
> And Symkyn hadde hosen of the same.   *hosen* stockings
> Ther dorste no wight clepen hir but 'dame'.
> > [*clepen hir but* call her anything but]
> > (*CT* I.3951–6)

The wives of the five guildsmen in the General Prologue also considered it 'ful fair to been ycleped madame' (*CT* I.376), though they had

more right to the title than Symkyn's wife, who has a grand notion of herself as a lady:

> Hir thoughte that a lady sholde hire spare,
> What for hire kynrede and hir nortelrie
> That she hadde lerned in the nonnerie. (*CT* I.3966–8)

[She considered that a lady should keep herself at a distance, because of her family connections and the manners that she'd learnt in the nunnery.]

The parson intends even further social elevation for his granddaughter Malyn, from yeoman's daughter into the ranks of the aristocracy:

> And straunge he made it of hir mariage.
> His purpos was for to bistowe hire hye
> Into som worthy blood of auncetrye. (*CT* I.3980–2)

[He made difficulties over her marriage. His aim was to give her away grandly into some worthy aristocratic stock.]

As the Paston family recognized, even though wealth is a necessary condition for social prestige, money alone cannot buy the respect of others.

Into this nasty little world of pretension ride 'yonge povre scolers two' (*CT* I.4002). The crucial point is that they cannot be slotted in to any social position; they are *povre* in the same way that all students are poor, whether or not they are literally as hard up as the Clerk of Oxenford in the General Prologue. That is to say that they are, for the time being, outside the economy, and therefore outside the world of financial deals of all sorts, including marriage settlements. It is still more evident that they have no place within Trumpington society: every word they utter in their outlandish northern dialect marks them as aliens. This is underlined by the Reeve's supercilious remark that they come from 'fer in the north; I kan nat telle where' (*CT* I.4015). However, they are temporarily attached to a society of a different sort, the Cambridge college Soler Hall. A college is an enclosed society of those chosen to be partners (Lat. *con-* + *legere*, 'to choose together'), with its own rules, conventions and privileges. Even such a self-contained society needs occasionally to venture beyond the walls into the world outside; the scholars need to eat, which is what brings Aleyn and John to Trumpington. Pretending great interest in the workings of the mill, the students plan to catch Symkyn out in his cheating, since he has been defrauding the college outrageously. But the wily miller sees through them at once, and contemptuously says to himself 'The gretteste clerkes been noght wisest men' (4054). Having released their horse to run after the wild mares, Symkyn has ample opportunity, while the students chase their horse around the Cambridgeshire fens, to remove half a bushel of their flour for his wife to bake a cake. The students return weary and wet, and too late to get back to college that night, so are obliged to take lodgings in the miller's little one-bedroom cottage and pay for supper for everyone.

While the family snore and fart, Aleyn demonstrates that he has not been wasting his time at Soler Hall. He is evidently studying law (shades of William Paston), and reminds John of a legal maxim:

> Som esement has lawe yshapen us,
> For, John, ther is a lawe that says thus:
> That gif a man in a point be agreved,
> That in another he sal be releved.
> Our corn is stoln, sothly, it is na nay,
> And we han had an il fit al this day,
> And syn I sal have neen amendement
> Agayn my los, I will have esement.   (4179–86)

[The law has provided us with some 'easement', because, John, there's a law that says this: that if someone is injured in one particular, he shall be redressed in another. Our corn has been stolen, truly there's no denying it, and we've had a bad time the whole day, and since I shan't get compensation for my loss, I want to have 'easement'.]

The word *esement* has the general sense 'bodily comforts', and the legal sense 'the right to use what is not your own'. Both are relevant here, since Aleyn claims that because he cannot obtain compensation for his bad day and the loss of the corn, he will take his *esement* with the miller's daughter.

So Aleyn is *aton*, 'at one', with Malyn before she is awake enough to cry out; John tricks the miller's wife into his own bed and she is amazed at the unaccustomed prowess of the man she takes to be her husband. As day dawns, Aleyn pays mock homage to his noble paramour with an *aubade*, a courtly song of farewell at daybreak, and she, having slipped the confinement of her grandfather, however briefly and in however seamy circumstances, is sufficiently moved (almost to tears) to tell him where to find the cake that she helped steal. Unfortunately Aleyn returns to the wrong bed, and whispers of his conquest to the miller.

Symkyn's reaction to the deflowering of his daughter is extraordinary:

> Who dorste be so boold to disparage
> My doghter that is come of swich lynage?   (4271–2)

His outrage is caused by the thought that Malyn has been degraded and her value on the marriage market consequently diminished; no longer a *mayde*, she has lost her virginity to someone of no standing, a northern *clerk*. Presumably he picked up the technical word *disparage* in discussions with his more educated father-in-law. Its precise sense is illustrated in John Audelay's lines on modern marriage:

> Bot now a lady wil take a page
> Fore no love bot fleschelé lust,
> And so here blod is disparage;
> Þus lordus and lordchip al day ben lost.
> (ed. Whiting 1931, 49.27–32)

It means 'to make an alliance that degrades a family's status'. The careful planning for the family's step-by-step ascent of the social ladder has been cut away at a stroke. For the same reason the Pastons did all they could to prevent their wayward daughter Margery from marrying their bailiff Richard Calle, for fear, as her brother writes, that she should be reduced to selling candles and mustard in Framlingham, but she outwitted them with great spirit. 'Three generations to make a gentleman' is an expression both Symkyn and the Pastons would have taken to their hearts. Truly the Reeve got his revenge on his hated fellow pilgrim, the Miller.

Ploughing Piers' Half Acre

In passus 8 of the C-Text of *Piers Plowman* (passus 6 in the B-Text) we see a characteristic example of Langlandian allegory, setting issues of timeless concern in a specific context of late fourteenth-century rural society. It is the scene that introduces us to Piers Plowman. The sinners' search for salvation is represented by their work in Piers Plowman's half acre; his scheme for this tiny plot of land represents his vision of social organization. Here I concentrate on the way in which Langland's evocation of rural life relates to the contemporary scene, though the fact that this is an allegory with broader signification needs to be kept in mind.

It is an aspect of this allegorical level that the ploughman is the leader of the work in the field, since Piers stands for the virtuous layman enacting his faith through everyday labour. His vision is that all who work in the half acre will similarly express their faith under his leadership in a co-operative endeavour for the common good. In terms of this allegory, Piers can direct all classes of society, not just his labourers, but the aristocratic women with their long fingers who are to sew fine vestments for the clergy, and the knight himself. This allows for the comedy of the reversal of social positions as the knight asks Piers if he can join in. He acknowledges that he has never driven a plough-team, but what fun it might be to try!

> 'By Crist,' quod a knyhte tho, 'a kenneth us þe beste,
> Ac on þe teme treuely ytauhte was y nevere.
> Y wolde y couthe,' quod the knyhte, 'by Crist and his moder;
> Y wolde assaie som tyme, for solace as hit were.'   (8.19–22)

['By Christ,' said a knight then, 'he gives us the best instructions, but I was never taught to handle a plough-team. I wish I could,' said the knight, 'by Christ and his mother; I'd have a go sometime, for fun as it were.']

Piers has a more useful role for him, assigning him the traditional knightly occupations of exercising his legal authority over 'wastores and wikked men' through his manor court, and of hunting and hawking to protect the crops from marauding animals and birds.

Piers then instructs the knight more broadly in his social duties: he is to treat his bondmen and the poor with justice, to impose taxes mercifully and not to accept bribes. In this way Piers sets out his programme for a model society established on traditional feudal lines, with women of different classes contributing in ways appropriate to their station, with the knight fulfilling his obligation to keep order on his manor and maintain his bondmen fairly, and with Piers' own family submitting to authority, his daughter obeying her mother for fear of a beating, his son bowing to established leadership. This traditional model of society is represented by the earlier pictures of the lord and his peasants in plates 4 and 5, yet it was very far from the actual social relationships of the late fourteenth century. As we have seen, many peasants were not bondmen at all but worked for wages; others held both free land and bond-land on which their servile duties were increasingly commuted for cash payments. It is just this mixed economic arrangement that Langland proceeds to represent in the scene as it develops.

Piers himself serves a lord called Truth (7.182–94), yet is quite prosperous, owning freehold land ('my croft, my corn', 8.31) a plough and a plough-team (Dyer 1994), and he hires the workmen he needs for his half acre:

> Now is Perkyn and þis pilgrimes to þe plouh faren.
> To erien this half aker holpen hym monye,
> Dikares and delvares digged up þe balkes.
> Therwith was Perkyn apayed, and payede wel hem here huyre.
>
> (8.112–15)

[Now Piers and these pilgrims begin ploughing. Many helped him to plough this half acre; ditchers and diggers dug up the ridges. Piers was pleased with that and paid them their wages.]

Since they are not his bondmen, they have no feudal obligation to contribute their labour; they work for wages. Piers plans to rehire the best of them when harvest time arrives (120–1). Their perspective on the work is therefore very different from the idealistic vision Piers had at the start, and some of them, after a few beers, contribute solely by singing 'hey trollilolly!' In a fury, Piers threatens that those who won't work will starve, to which they respond by feigning to be blind and lame. As their contribution, they offer prayers for Piers and his enterprise. This prompts Piers to distinguish between these *wastours* who devour what society produces, and those genuinely unable to work, who alone will receive the support of the community. It is a problematic distinction, as every society recognizes. The wasters are not at all daunted by this threat, but threaten Piers in their turn, 'and

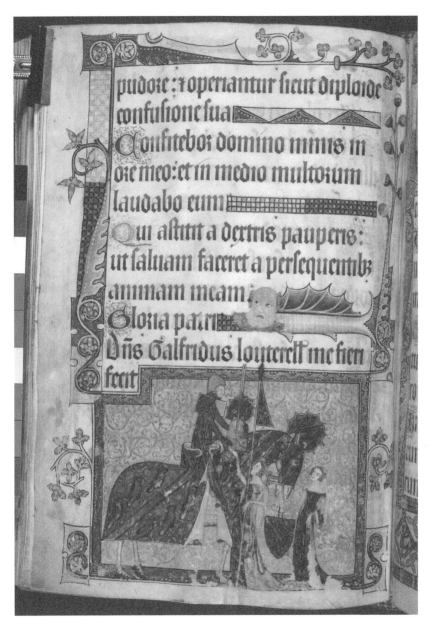

4 Sir Geoffrey Luttrell, MS Add. 42130, f. 202v (Luttrell Psalter).
This extraordinary manuscript was prepared for Sir Geoffrey Luttrell (1276–1345), who is pictured here preparing for battle, attended by his wife and his daughter-in-law. Sandler (1986, no. 107). Photograph © British Library, London.

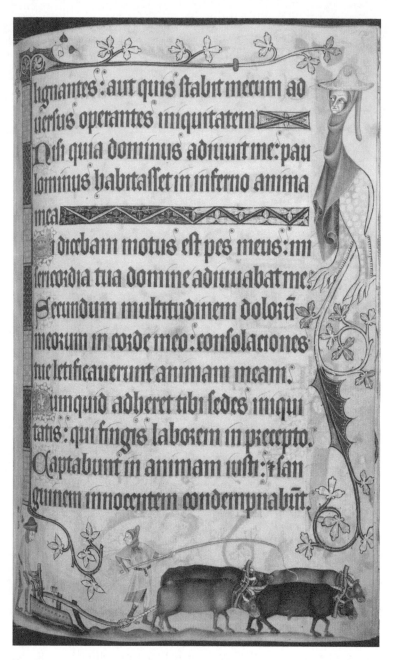

5 Ploughing: Luttrell Psalter, MS Add. 42130, f. 170 (with hybrid monster). One of a series of marginal scenes depicting work on the Luttrell estate. In the right margin is a hybrid woman-monster. See Camille (1987) on the significance of plates 4 and 5. Photograph © British Library, London.

bad hym go pisse with his plogh' (8.151), so Piers calls upon the knight to fulfil his agreement by dealing with these disrupters. The knight, acting in character, is courteous but ineffectual:

Courteisliche the knyhte thenne, as his kynde wolde,
Warnede Wastour and wissede hym betere,
'Or y shal bete the by the lawe and brynge þe in stokkes.'   (8.161–3)

[The knight then, as was his nature, courteously admonished Waster and advised him to improve, 'or I shall beat you in accordance with the law, and put you in the stocks.']

This is an empty threat:

'I was nat woned to worche,' quod Wastour, 'and now wol
    y nat bygynne!'
And leet lyhte of þe lawe and lasse of the knyhte.   (8.164–5)

['I wasn't accustomed to work,' said Waster 'and I won't begin now!' and took little notice of the law, and less of the knight.]

The issues presented in these exchanges were very familiar to a late fourteenth-century audience. In 1348 England had been struck by an epidemic of bubonic plague so severe that within a year or so about half of the population had died. A further 10 per cent died in subsequent outbreaks (Schofield 2003, 92; Dyer 2002, 271–5). Langland describes the horrors of:

                                        feveres and fluxes,
        Cowhes and cardiacles, crampes and toeth-aches,
        Reumes and radegoundes and roynouse scabbes,
        Byles and boches and brennynge aguwes.   (C.22.81–4)

[fevers and discharges, coughs and heart-attacks, cramps and toothaches, colds and running sores and scurfy scabs, boils and tumours and burning agues.]

It is astonishing that, despite a disaster on such an unimaginable scale, social organizations continued to function reasonably well. Of course, the long-term effects of the Black Death were profound. With a surplus of land and a desperate shortage of labour to work on it, the move away from serfdom accelerated. Not content to work as the lord's bondmen, peasants left the manor to hire themselves out as labourers elsewhere. Rather than tie themselves to long-term contracts, they worked by the month or by the day, moving from place to place for better pay. Those who stayed on the manor might negotiate what was effectively freedom, substituting cash payments for servile duties, and reducing these payments as the economic conditions allowed (Dyer 2002, 330–62).

These developments caused deep concern, to moralists as well as employers. 'Sithe þis pestelence tyme' (C.Prol.82) it seemed that the ties that bound the ranks of society in mutual obligation and benefit had been torn apart. The lords faced a situation where land was cheaper because it was plentiful, and where the value of produce was static or declining because there was less consumption, and yet labour costs rose because there were fewer to work in the fields. In an attempt to maintain their economic position, the lords responded by introducing labour legislation.

In the immediate aftermath of the Black Death, the Ordinance and the Statute of Labourers (1349 and 1351) attempted to hold prices and wages at pre-plague levels and to restrict the movement of workers in search of higher wages (Aers 1988, 20–72; Dyer 2002, 282–5). Those who were able to work were ordered to do so and no charity was to be given to them. The legislation was extended to place particular emphasis on controlling the movement of labourers by the Statute of Cambridge of 1388, passed at around the time that Langland was completing his final revisions of *Piers Plowman* (Middleton 1997). These laws seem to have been widely evaded by labourers seeking higher pay and employers seeking labour, and the continuing issue of able-bodied beggars is reflected throughout *Piers Plowman*.

Frustrated by the breakdown of his model society, Piers does something deeply troubling. He summons Hunger:

> And houped aftur Hunger, þat herde hym at the furste.
> 'Y preye the,' quod Perus tho, 'pur charité, sire Hunger,
> Awreke me of this wastors, for þe knyhte wil nat.' (8.168–70)

[And shouted for Hunger, who heard him right away. 'I beg you,' Piers said then, 'for God's sake, sir Hunger, avenge me on these wasters, because the knight won't.']

Hunger sets to work immediately, squeezing Waster by the stomach until his eyes water. The labourers resume work with alacrity:

> Tho were faytours afered and flowen into Peres bernes
> And flapton on with flales fro morwen til even,
> That Hunger was not hardy on hem for to loke.
> For a potte ful of potage þat Peres wyf made
> An heep of eremytes henten hem spades,
> Sputeden and spradden donge in dispit of Hunger.   (8.179–84)

[Then shammers were afraid and fled into Piers' barns and lashed with their flails from morning till evening, so that Hunger didn't dare look at them. For a pot of soup that Piers' wife made, a great mass of hermits took up spades, dug and spread dung in defiance of Hunger.]

The apparently blind and the lame are cured, and the hungry people eat food prepared for horses. Every worker promises to obey Piers faithfully in return for the basic essentials of life. Piers is delighted that the show is back on the road:

> Tho was Peres proude and potte hem alle a-werke
> In daubynge and in delvynge, in donge afeld berynge,
> In threschynge, in thekynge, in thwytinge of pynnes.   (8.197–9)

[Then Piers was proud and put them all to work plastering and digging, carrying dung to the field, threshing, thatching and whittling pegs.]

The contemporary reader would have had a sharper appreciation of Hunger than ours. Since many peasants lived close to the breadline, famine might always be just round the corner and a series of bad harvests was disastrous. 'The worst famine in recorded history' (Dyer 2002, 233) began with poor harvests in 1314–16, followed by an outbreak of murrain (a cattle epidemic) in 1319–21, events that would have been within the experience of the older members of Langland's audience. Up to this point, Piers has come across as idealistic and perhaps rather naive, so it is shocking that he should now rely on hunger to drive the community back to work.

Hunger – again this is typical of Langland's allegory – is a complex figure not simply representing the driving force of famine (Hanna 2005, 279–83). He comes to life in surprising ways, so that he can put forward his own opinions on social control. In his dialogue with Piers he reflects the legislators' views about the justice of withholding charity from able-bodied beggars, and curiously goes on to pose as an expert on food, giving Piers dietary advice culled from contemporary textbooks. Now that Hunger has given the enterprise a fresh start, Piers begins to worry about the moral implications of starving workers into submission, so he asks Hunger to leave. He questions him on the best way to deal with beggars, knowing full well that they are working for fear of starvation and 'nat for love' (8.214), yet recognizing that they are his blood-brothers in Christ whom it is his Christian duty to support. Hunger maintains that it is entirely proper to distinguish between beggars who are capable of work and the genuinely disabled who deserve charity, and he cites biblical texts to demonstrate the necessity of labouring for food, supplying this harsh rendering of the parable of the talents in Matthew 25.14–30:

> He þat hath shal have and helpe þer hym liketh,
> And he þat nauht hath shal nauht have and no man ȝut
>   helpen hym,
> And þat he weneth wel to have y wol hit hym bireve.   (8.256–8)

[He who has shall have, and be given help where he wants, and he who has nothing shall have nothing, and no one shall help him even so, and I shall deprive him of what he fully expects to have.]

Much encouraged, Piers promised to pass these texts on to the shirkers, and then asks Hunger what he and his workers should do to ease their stomach-ache. Hunger supposes – quite implausibly in the circumstances – that their pain is due to overeating, and so gives platitudinous prescriptions on good dietary habits. Politely Piers thanks him for his advice, and again invites him to leave as soon as he chooses. Of course Hunger, true to character, cannot so easily be dismissed when there is a prospect of food, but it is still winter and food is in short supply:

> 'Y have no peny', quod Peres, 'polettes for to begge,
> Ne noþer goos ne gries, but two grene cheses
> And a fewe croddes and craym and a cake of otes
> And bred for my barnes of benes and of peses.'   (8.303–6)

['I haven't a penny', said Piers 'to buy chickens, or geese or pigs either, only two green cheeses and a few curds and cream and oatcakes, and bread for my children made of beans and peas.']

As harvest time approaches, the people find better provisions for their insatiable guest and send him to sleep with good ale. At once, inevitably, Waster downs tools and begins to 'wandren about', beggars call on their best French to insist on *haute cuisine*, and subsistence labourers spurn what they had previously eaten:

> May no peny-ale hem pay ne no pece of bacoun
> But hit be fresh flesch or fisch yfried or ybake,
> And þat *chaut* and *pluchaut* for chillyng of his mawe.   (8.332–4)

[No cheap ale nor any piece of bacon can please them, just fresh meat or fried or baked fish, and that has to be *chaud* and *plus chaud* for fear of a chill on the stomach.]

They demand higher wages, lament the time that they ever became labourers, and curse the king and his justices for enacting the laws that afflict them. Langland remarks pointedly that no one ever dares to contravene *Hunger's* laws (341–2), and the passus ends with a prophecy warning the workers that Hunger will return and 'famyne shal aryse'.

These complaints and demands are no doubt perennial, but they had a particular resonance in Langland's time. Grievances against the lords and their exactions came to a head in 1381 in the Peasants' Revolt, and although the pressures that led to this had been building up for a long time, the Revolt itself seems to have come as a surprise and was regarded by contemporaries with fear and wonder (Dyer 2002, 286–93; Dobson 1983, e.g. 132). The wealthier peasants especially, with their expectations heightened as a result of their raised economic status, became increasingly restive at the financial burdens imposed by the lords and the government, and at the levels of taxation and the legislation restricting their wages and limiting their freedom. The rebels marched unopposed on London under their leaders Wat Tyler and Jack Straw, murdered archbishop Sudbury, the treasurer Robert Hales, and others whom they regarded as their oppressors, burnt legal records, destroyed John of Gaunt's fine palace of the Savoy and sacked the Tower. They arranged an audience with the 14-year-old king at which they demanded that 'there should be no more villeins in England, and no serfdom nor villeinage but that all men should be free and of one condition' (quoted Dobson 1983, 165). When Richard II diplomatically promised them charters of liberty, many of them dispersed. Tyler was killed and the rebellion swiftly put down. Contemporaries were horrified by this impudent assault on the social fabric, and John Gower wrote his long Latin poem *Vox Clamantis* to express his condemnation of the animals who had attacked his 'New Troy' (London) and imperilled the established faith and good order.

The B-Text of *Piers Plowman* was evidently available to the leaders of the Revolt. In phraseology reminiscent of Langland's poem, the renegade priest John Ball wrote to his fellow rebel leaders that he 'biddeþ Peres plouȝman go to his werke and chastise wel Hobbe þe Robbere . . . and do wel and bettre'. Jak Carter is reported to have written: 'Lat Peres þe plowman my broþur duelle at home and dyȝt us corne and I wil go wiþ ȝowe and helpe þat y may to dyȝte ȝoure mete and ȝoure drynke' (Justice 1994, 13–15). With an understandable literal-mindedness, these rebels interpreted Piers himself as a peasant leader (Dyer 1994, 171–2). It has been reasonably supposed that Langland was disturbed by the appropriation of his creation for the Revolt, and that some of the C-Text revisions are an attempt to distance the arguments of the poem from the rhetoric of the peasant leaders. One small addition to passus 8 of the C-Text is interesting in this respect, since in it Piers sets out for his son the need for obedience to established authority:

> Maystres as þe mayres is, and grete menne, senatours,
> What þei comaunde as by þe kyng countreplede hit nevere;
> Al þat they hoten, y hote, heiliche thow soffre hem,
> And aftur here warnynge and wordynge worche þou þeraftur.
> (8.87–90)

[Masters such as mayors are, and great men such as aldermen, whatever they command in the king's name never argue against it. Scrupulously agree to all that they command, I order you, and act according to their spoken and written commands.]

The leaders of the revolt misinterpreted Piers in order to appropriate him as a figurehead for their revolutionary movement, but the frequent modern description of Langland as a conservative is an even greater misunderstanding. Many of the speakers in Langland's poem, including Will the dreamer in the 'autobiographical' addition in the C-Text (6.1–105), express their despair at the corrupt state of contemporary society, but that need not be a conservative point of view. In setting up his model society, Piers looked back to a mythical age of simple morality and good order, but the attempt to establish society on such principles ends in disruption and bitterness when it inevitably proves to be impossible. The only way is forward, and in his third dream Will sets off in search of the meanings of Dowel, Dobet and Dobest. It is a long while before he again encounters Piers.

At the Court of King Arthur

The chronicler of chivalry Jean Froissart (b.1337) wrote this account of Edward III's foundation of the Order of the Garter:

> King Edward of England conceived the idea of altering and rebuilding the great castle of Windsor, originally built by King Arthur, and where had first been established the noble Round Table, from which so many fine men and brave knights had gone forth and performed great deeds throughout the world. King Edward's intention was to found an order of knights, made up of himself and his sons and the bravest and noblest in England and other countries too. There would be forty of them in all and they would be called the Knights of the Blue Garter and their feast was to be held every year at Windsor on St George's Day. (trans. Brereton 1968, 66)

Following the precedent of his grandfather, Edward III adopted Arthur as an emblem of kingship, and modelled his chivalric display upon stories of Arthur and his knights of the Round Table (Vale 1982, 57–75). As elsewhere in Europe, English kings summoned knights to assemblies known as round tables for jousting, dancing, feasting and dressing up as Arthurian characters. By such assemblies they very effectively unified their powerful nobility and encouraged them in their support for the wars with Scotland and France. In 1344 Edward III called all his nobles to Windsor Castle for three days of music and feasting and, magnificent in his royal regalia, made a solemn announcement that 'he would institute the Round Table, in the same form and condition in which Arthur, once king of England, left it, namely to the number of 300 knights' (Adam of Murimuth, trans. Juliet Vale 2001, 192). Froissart conflates two stages in the development of Edward's grand design, for the original plans were scaled down and given a new focus four years later, in 1348, when Edward instituted the Order of the Garter, restricted to 26 knights, to celebrate the great victory over the French at Crécy (Collins 2000, 6–33). The first knights of the Garter were those who had been involved in that battle. The knights of the Order had to be of noble blood, and were pledged to fellowship and loyalty, and to support one another in all dangers. The patron of the Order was the soldier-saint George. Yet the association with Arthur that Froissart noted is a feature of the Garter that is maintained into the fifteenth century, as shown by a challenge sent to Henry IV in 1408 by Jean Werchin, seneschal of Hainault (Collins 2000, 242–3):

> I have read and heard that in the time when the noble and mighty Arthur reigned over that lordship where you now reign, that there was established an order to which a number of knights belonged, who called themselves the knights of the Round Table . . . and now I have heard that certain kings of your kingdom in recollection of that order have instituted that which is called the Garter. (trans. Keen 1990, 142)

This notion of the Order of the Garter as a recreation of the noble brotherhood established by Arthur is signalled at the end of *Sir Gawain and the Green Knight* where a scribe has written: *HONY SOYT QUI MAL PENCE*, 'Shamed be he who thinks ill', the motto of the Order. Whether or not this reference goes back to the author, it acknowledges a number of fairly obvious similarities between the last part of the story and the establishment of the Order. The green *lace, silke, gordel* or *belt* that the lady unbuckles from her waist is worn by Gawain as a badge of shame, but is then adopted by Arthur and his court to wear as a symbol of honour and a mark of their brotherhood. There is a romantic tale, first recorded in the fifteenth century, about the origins of the Garter symbol, relating that a lady of the court dropped her blue garter, which Edward picked up and adopted as the emblem of his chivalric order, uttering the words that became the motto (Collins 2000, 12). However that may be, the Garter is generally depicted as a miniature knight's belt (plate 6).

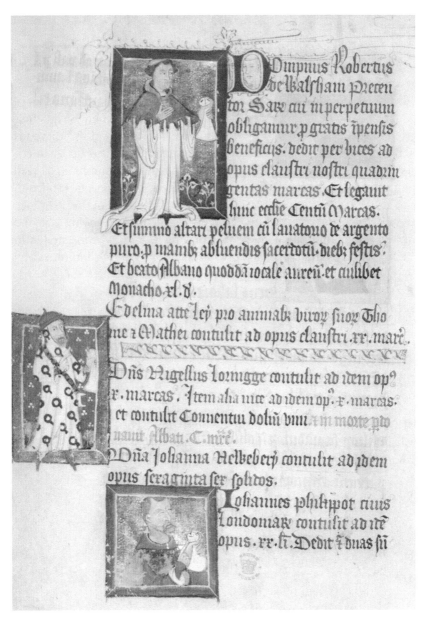

6 Sir Neil Loring in Garter robe, MS Cotton Nero D.VII, f. 105v.
Loring was one of the founder members of the Order of the Garter. He is
pictured here (centre) in about 1380 as one of the benefactors of St Alban's
Abbey. He wears a white tunic decorated with dark garters. Above him is
Fr Robert de Walsham, the Black Prince's confessor. Sandler (1986, no. 158).
Photograph © British Library, London.

Sir Gawain and the Green Knight is a celebration of the chivalric life as exemplified historically by Arthur and in the contemporary world by the royal courts throughout Europe and not least by the courts of Edward III, his son Edward, the Black Prince, and his grandson Richard II. The poet's descriptions of court life can be matched in all their essentials with accounts by writers such as Froissart and the Chandos Herald who wrote the *Life of the Black Prince*, and backed up by documents recording expenditure on clothes, furnishings and food, as well as by illustrations of court scenes in de-luxe manuscripts (Malcolm Vale 2001, 165–294). In 1388 Froissart travelled to southern France to visit the court of Gaston Phoebus, count of Foix, who was the author of an influential book on hunting that was translated into English by Edward, duke of York. Froissart was much impressed by his host:

> Though I have seen many knights, kings, princes and others in my life, I have never seen one who was so finely built, with better-proportioned limbs and body or so handsome a face, cheerful and smiling, with eyes which sparkled amiably when he was pleased to look at anyone. He was so accomplished in every way that it would be impossible to praise him too highly. (trans. Brereton 1968, 264)

This is the ideal chivalric leader whose prototype was Arthur, described with equal admiration at the opening of *Sir Gawain and the Green Knight*:

> With all þe wele of þe worlde þay woned þer samen,
> Þe most kyd knyȝtez under Krystes selven
> And þe lovelokkest ladies þat ever lif haden,
> And he þe comlokest kyng þat þe court haldes;
> For al watz þis fayre folk in her first age
>   On sille;
> Þe hapnest under heven,
> Kyng hyȝest mon of wylle;
> Hit were now gret nye to neven
> So hardy a here on hille.   (50–9)

[They lived there together with all the joys of the world, the most famous knights on earth and the loveliest ladies who ever lived, and the ruler of the court the most handsome king; for all this fair company in the hall were in the prime of life. The most fortunate under heaven, their king a man pre-eminent in courage; it would now be very difficult to name so bold a company on a castle-hill.]

After mentioning the count's passion for hunting and his pleasure in arms and love, Froissart describes the protocol followed at dinner:

When he came out of his room at midnight to sup in his hall, twelve lighted torches were carried before him by twelve serving-men, and these twelve torches were held up in front of his table, giving a bright light in the hall, which was full of knights and squires and always contained plenty of tables laid for supper for any who wanted it. No one spoke to him at his own table unless he first asked him to. He usually ate much poultry – but only the wings and the legs – and drank little. He took great pleasure in minstrelsy, of which he had an excellent knowledge. He liked his clerks to sing songs, rondeaux and virelays to him. He would remain at table for about two hours, and he also enjoyed having travelling entertainers to perform between the courses. After he had watched them, he sent them round the tables of the knights and squires. (trans. Brereton 1968, 265)

In similar vein the *Gawain*-poet describes how Arthur entered the hall for his New Year feast:

Fro þe kyng watz cummen with knyȝtes into þe halle,
Þe chauntré of þe chapel cheved to an ende,
Loude crye watz þer kest of clerkez and oþer.　(62–4)

[When the king had come into the hall with his knights and the singing of the chapel had reached an end, a loud cry was raised up by the clergy and the others.]

First Arthur's noble companions are seated at the high table and served,

And siþen mony siker segge at þe sidbordez.
Þen þe first cors come with crakkyng of trumpes,
Wyth mony baner ful bryȝt þat þerbi henged,
Nwe nakryn noyse with þe noble pipes.　(115–18)

[and then many trusty knights at the side-tables. Then the first course came with the sounding of trumpets that had many bright banners hanging from them, and another noise of kettledrums accompanied by fine pipes.]

Descriptions of court life such as those in Froissart and *Sir Gawain and the Green Knight* are paralleled in the French chivalric romances with which both writers were very familiar (Putter 1995, 51–99). Froissart was himself the author of a long chivalric romance, *Méliador*, set in the court of a young King Arthur. The *Gawain*-poet must certainly have known the seminal description of an Arthurian banquet in Wace's *Roman de Brut* (ll. 10197–620). Here Arthur celebrates his Pentecostal feast at Caerleon on Usk, at which he is crowned. Geoffrey of Monmouth provided the germ of the account, but Wace expanded it into a representation of chivalric magnificence. After solemn mass with the singing and playing of the clergy (cf. *Gawain* 63), the court proceeds to the palace and the knights are seated in the hall, not at a round table but according to their rank (cf. *Gawain* 109–15). After a lavish feast, at which wine is served in golden goblets, the knights go out to joust, to throw javelins and to wrestle (cf. *Gawain* 40–2). Minstrels sing and play a multitude of instruments:

> Fiddle music, lays with melodies, lays on fiddles, lays on rotes, lays on harps, lays on flutes, lyres, drums and shawms, bagpipes, psalteries, monochords, tambourines and choruns. There were plenty of conjurors, dancers and jugglers. (trans. Weiss 2002, ll. 10547–54)

Some courtiers tell stories, some play chess or dice, some win, some lose (cf. *Gawain* 69–70). As the festivities draw to a close after three days, Arthur hands gifts to the departing guests.

All over Europe kings and princes replicated such scenes to celebrate the noble life, holding 'round tables' at which there would be tournaments, dancing, games and of course feasting, and where knights and ladies dressed up as figures from the romances to enact scenes of a more glorious age as imagined by the poets. By such spectacles the very rich displayed their wealth and confirmed their elite status through their exclusive knowledge of courtly codes and rituals. Edward III was especially keen on such events. He participated at a tournament in Dunstable in 1334 dressed as the Round Table knight Lionel (after whom he named his son) (Collins 2000). A few surviving financial accounts offer a glimpse into the celebrations, such as the accounts

for the king's Christmas feasts in 1347 and 1348, which list the pur-
chase of masks and disguises, including heads of peacocks and swans,
bats, elephants and *wodwoses* ('wildmen', cf. *Gawain* 721) and tunics
painted with peacock eyes and gold and silver stars (Vale 1982, 175).
Edward's son, the Black Prince, and grandson, Richard II, continued
the tradition of acting out episodes from the courtly romances. In
1378, for example, a knight disguised as a damsel brought the young
King Richard a challenge to a joust as he banqueted at Windsor
Castle, replaying the classic opening scene of countless romances
(Barker 1986, 92).

Froissart describes Charles VI's great banquet in Paris in 1389, at
which interludes (*entremets*) were performed in the hall (Froissart,
transl. Brereton 1968, 357–8). The theme of these interludes was the
siege of Troy, and the mechanisms were exceedingly ingenious, including a castle with Trojan flags, a ship, and an assault tower with
Greek arms, all moving on hidden wheels. Unfortunately, such was
the crush of excited spectators that the king had to put a stop to the
performance for fear that the queen and her ladies would collapse in
a faint. It is this sort of scene that is recalled in *Gawain* when Arthur
turns to reassure Queen Guenevere, whose condition after witnessing
the beheading of the Green Knight we are left to imagine. Whether
fainting or not, she certainly needs reassurance, which Arthur offers
her by likening the terrifying spectacle to 'laykyng of enterludez'
(472) – 'acting out interludes'. In this way the huge Green Knight can
be incorporated into the established and expected court entertainment, no more than a disguising, a Christmas game (283).

By observing the protocols of courtly society, Arthur and Edward
III are subscribing to a set of values referred to collectively as 'courtesy' (Burnley 1998). Thus when the challenger bursts into Arthur's
hall he tells the company that he is visiting them on account of their
great reputation and because 'here is kydde cortaysye' (263) – 'here
courtesy is displayed'. The qualities of that courtesy are what the
Green Knight proposes to challenge. In contrast to several of the
earlier versions of the story, this challenger is not an uncouth churl
but is himself part of the same knightly world as the court, with a
shared understanding of what is at issue. So the Green Knight himself
sets out some of the defining characteristics of the courtly ethos. Skill
at fighting is a fundamental accomplishment, and the knights of the
Round Table, he reminds them, are reputed to be 'stifest under

stel-gere' (260) – 'the most resolute in armour'. Edward III depended upon his Garter knights as leaders in the French fields of battle, and a criticism levelled against Richard II's courtiers was that they had become 'knights of Venus rather than of Bellona: more effective in the bedchamber than the field' (Walsingham, *Chronicon Anglie*, quoted Saul 1997, 333). Despite their supposed martial prowess, Arthur's knights seem afraid to accept the Green Knight's challenge, leaving them open to the grave charge of cowardice (315).

In courtly society great emphasis is placed upon courtliness in speech, as we shall see further in chapter 6. Gawain's opening words (343–61), in which he asks for permission to take on the challenger, are characterized by a marked formality and elevation, in terms of both diction and syntax, and a refinement of sensibility, as he expresses his deference to his worthy lord, to his liege lady, and to the brotherhood of knights, and emphasizes his own utter worthlessness: 'I am þe wakkest, I wot, and of wyt feblest' (354). Courtly speech was an important element because it was the outward expression of the loyalty and respect that a knight felt for his superiors and his fellows. In the 1390s the vocabulary used to address Richard II became increasingly formal and deferential as an expression of Richard's emphasis on the prestige of royalty (Saul 1997, 340–2). For those to whom the art of elegant behaviour did not come naturally, there existed a number of instructive 'courtesy books' (Nicholls 1985).

The relationship between outward show and inner virtue is exemplified by the concept of *largesse*, 'generosity'. The most visible aspect of *largesse* is the conspicuous display of the knight's wealth: the costly robes and jewellery he wears, the hall tapestries of Tharsian silk 'enbrawded and beten wyth þe best gemmes' (*Gawain* 78), the rich feasts, the lavish gifts for his guests. These are signs and markers of the *largesse* that lies in the knight's heart, the 'larges and lewté þat longez to knyȝtez' (2381), expressed by an open-heartedness towards others, by the *fraunchyse*, 'magnanimity', and *felaȝschyp*, 'comradeship', that Gawain professes (*Gawain* 652). The opposite of *largesse* is *covetyse* (2380), the grasping love of material objects that, in Gawain's view, leads to his own downfall.

Gawain is also set up as a model of faith in Christ and devotion to the Virgin Mary (642–7). The indivisibility of religious and secular aspects of courtliness is perfectly captured by the remark that to encourage himself in battle Gawain would gaze at the image of the Virgin painted on the inside of his shield (648–50). We should re- member that the patron of the Order of the Garter is St George, a model of both martial valour and fidelity to Christ. Even without the inscription recording the Garter motto at the end of the poem, con- temporaries would surely have spotted the echoes of that most fa- mous Order in the poet's celebration of *cortaysye*. How does this effect our interpretation of the poem? It means that we can hardly suppose that the poet directs criticism at the ethos of chivalry represented by Arthur's court, with all its manifestations of luxury and display. How- ever alien it is to us, we must accept that this is the genuine expres- sion of an ideal, in literature and in life, to encourage brotherhood, religious devotion, self-sacrifice, generosity, and a willingness to risk all in loyalty to the king and for the love of Christ. Within this context of general admiration it is the more startling that Arthur is described as *childgered* (86), whether this means 'childishly behaved' or something rather more like 'with youthful manners'. That immat- urity, demonstrated by the exuberance and impulsiveness of Arthur's knights, leaves the Round Table vulnerable to the Green Knight's challenge, so that we realize that failure is always a possibility: 'þenk wel, Sir Gawan' (487), warns the poet. At the end of the poem Arthur's chivalric impulse to take over Gawain's green badge of shame as a symbol of their brotherhood is a declaration that, whatever Gawain's personal sense of failure, his adventure has confirmed 'þe renoun of þe Rounde Table' (2519). Shamed be anyone who thinks ill of him.

In Criseyde's Palace

The mythical Camelot is no place at all, unlike Caerleon in Glamor- gan, in Wace's story, where Arthur holds his coronation feast amid the crowds, churches and splendid palaces of the town. There are no towns in *Sir Gawain and the Green Knight*: the hero rides his solitary way from Camelot along the coast of north Wales and through the 'wyldrenesse of Wyrale' (701), over cliffs and through a forest until he comes across Hautdesert, a magnificent castle that appears through the trees. This rural setting in the north-west presumably reflects the experience of the poet's audience, familiar with this landscape of a few little country towns, the largest of which was Chester, but dominated by the monasteries and the rural manor houses of the gentry.

In contrast, Chaucer's primary audience was a metropolitan one, and his own life brought him into daily contact with courtiers, administrators and city officials. His early experience was as a servant in a royal court. The first references to 'Galfrido Chaucer Londonie' are in household accounts from 1357 of Elizabeth, countess of Ulster, wife of Edward III's young son Lionel (Pearsall 1992, 34–42). Chaucer was then apparently a pageboy. He advanced in service to the rank of *valettus*, 'esquire', in Edward III's court during the 1360s. Much of Chaucer's time there was probably spent at Westminster Palace, the court's administrative centre, but the king was constantly on the move between his palaces outside London, at Eltham in Kent, which he refurbished quite lavishly, at Kings Langley in Hertfordshire, and at Sheen (now Richmond, Surrey) (Mathew 1968, 32–7). John of Gaunt, the grieving knight of *The Book of the Duchess*, was often at court, and also had his own palace of the Savoy, which, as we have seen, was burnt down by the rebels in 1381.

To fourteenth-century Londoners, Chaucer's description of Troy, its streets and its palaces, would have seemed familiar in many ways, the connection strengthened by the idea originating with Geoffrey of Monmouth that London was a refoundation of Troy, a belief reflected in the opening lines of *St Erkenwald*: 'Now þat London is nevenyd hatte þe New Troie' (25) – 'what was then called the New Troy is now named London'. The city is ever-present throughout the love story of *Troilus and Criseyde*, right from the opening lines recording the Greeks' 10-year siege of Troy (1.59–60). Criseyde's comfort and security within the walls of her palace are undercut by her realization of the city's precarious situation: 'I am of Grekes so fered that I deye' (2.124), she says to her uncle Pandarus. She is reminded of these hostilities later that day as she looks out of her window down into the street where Troilus is riding back magnificently bloody from battle with the Greeks, so that her first softening of emotion for him is coloured by its martial context. It is city politics that precipitates the tragedy, and Chaucer creates a scene where parliament demands the exchange of Criseyde for the hero (later traitor) Antenor who had been captured by the Greeks. Perhaps there is an allusion to the recent sacking of London by Jack Straw and other leaders of the

Peasants' Revolt when Chaucer writes of the citizens' reaction to Hector's protest that 'We usen here no wommen for to selle' (4.182):

> The noyse of peple up stirte thanne at ones
> As breme as blase of strawe iset on fire. (4.183–4)

In this volatile situation, Criseyde's position is a fragile one (Aers 1979). She needs supporters, since she is a widow whose father Calkas has fled as a traitor to the enemy camp. The Trojan citizens vow to take vengeance on Calkas' family:

> Gret rumour gan, whan it was first aspied
> Thorugh al the town, and generaly was spoken,
> That Calkas traitour fled was and allied
> With hem of Grece, and casten to be wroken
> On hym that falsly hadde his feith so broken,
> And seyden he and al his kyn at-ones
> Ben worthi for to brennen, fel and bones. (1.85–91)

[A great uproar began when it was first realized through the whole town and spoken of everywhere that Calkas had fled as a traitor and made alliance with the Greeks, and the people planned to take vengeance on him who had treacherously broken faith, and they said that he and all his family ought to be burnt at once, skin and bones.]

In fear of her life, Criseyde goes to plead with Hector for her safety:

> This lady which that alday herd at ere
> Hire fadres shame, his falsnesse and tresoun,
> Wel neigh out of hir wit for sorwe and fere,
> In widewes habit large of samyt broun,
> On knees she fil biforn Ector adown,
> With pitous vois, and tendrely wepynge
> His mercy bad, hirselven excusynge. (1.106–12)

[This lady who heard her father's disgrace, treachery and treason spoken of all the time, almost at her wits' end for sorrow and fear, wearing ample widow's weeds of brown silk, fell to her knees before Hector, and with a piteous voice, weeping pitifully, asked for his mercy, exonerating herself.]

Hector graciously assures her of his protection. Inevitably, though, Criseyde is aware of the constant threat to her circumstances, understandably 'the ferfulleste wight / That myghte be' (2.450–1). In her anxious reflections on the pros and cons of a relationship with Hector's brother Troilus, one of the first considerations that occurs to her is that it might be impolitic to turn him down:

> Ek wel woot I my kynges sone is he,
> And sith he hath to se me swich delit,
> If I wolde outreliche his sighte flee,
> Peraunter he myghte have me in dispit,
> Thorugh whicch I myghte stonde in worse plit.   (2.708–12)

[Also I know well that he is my king's son, and since he has such desire to see me, if I were to flee entirely from his sight, perhaps he would hold a grudge against me, as a result of which I might be in a worse situation.]

Once the relationship has begun, she finds Troilus 'a wal / Of stiel and sheld from every displesaunce' (3.479–80). Her position depends ultimately on the good graces of the Trojan leaders, and her constant concern for her *honour*, her reputation, is an expression of her well-founded insecurity. Her abiding thought is 'what men wolde of hit deme' (2.461), and this issue comes to a head when Troilus vainly urges her to run away with him:

> What trowe ye the peple ek al aboute
> Wolde of it seye? It is ful light t'arede.
> They wolden seye, and swere it out of doute,
> That love ne drof yow naught to don this dede,
> But lust voluptuous and coward drede.
> Thus were al lost, ywys, myn herte deere,
> Youre honour which that now shyneth so clere.
>
> And also thynketh on myn honesté
> That floureth yet, how foule I sholde it shende,
> And with what filthe it spotted sholde be
> If in this forme I sholde with yow wende.
> Ne though I lyved unto the werldes ende,
> My name sholde I nevere ayeynward wynne;
> Thus were I lost, and that were routhe and synne.   (4.1569–82)

[What do you think the people all around would say about it? It's easy to guess. They would say, and vouch it for a fact, that it wasn't love that drove you to do this, but sensual lust and cowardly fear. So, my dear heart, all your reputation, which now shines so brightly, would be lost. And also think about my reputation which still flourishes, how shamefully I'd damage it, and with what filth it would be stained if I went with you in this way. Even if I lived until the end of time, I'd never win my name back again. So I'd be lost, and that would be a miserable and wicked outcome.]

We can easily understand that Criseyde's widowhood leaves her vulnerable to social pressures and dependent upon male support, particularly in a city at war where male values are more than ever prominent. What is less obvious to us, though it would have been clear enough to medieval readers, is that her widowhood at the same time gives her a certain measure of independence. In the eyes of the law, a wife was financially dependent upon her husband, but her position changed entirely on her husband's death. At that point she took control of a considerable proportion of the estate, even if there were children of the marriage, and she held that property for life (Ward 1992, 34). Until she remarried, she was legally independent and responsible for the management of the estate. There are examples of rich widows, often married as teenagers, living on for half a century or more after the death of their husbands, much to the frustration of their heirs. Elizabeth de Burgh, granddaughter of Edward I, was widowed for the third time at the age of 26, in the process becoming fabulously rich, living as a widow from 1322 until her death in 1360 (Ward 1992, 6). A wealthy widow was a good catch, but she might well choose instead to preserve her independence. If she remarried and her husband died, she would then add a proportion of his estate to what she already held; marrying three elderly men seemed to the Wife of Bath a reasonable gamble.

Chaucer tells us nothing at all about Criseyde's husband; he says he does not know her age or whether she had children (5.826, 1.132–3). We learn immediately, though, that she is well off, and had considerable standing in Troy until her father fled (1.99–105). Her status is fully confirmed by the view we are given of her sitting in her 'paved parlour' (2.82) when her uncle Pandarus comes to call at her palace to speak to her of his friend Troilus. Here we see a fine picture of the elegant life of a great lady and her relationships with friends and relatives. Pandarus finds Criseyde with her two companions listening to a girl reading to them from a *romaunce* of the Siege of Thebes, a long historical poem which contemporary readers would know from the Latin *Thebaid* (c. AD 90) by Statius and the twelfth-century French *Roman de Thèbes*. (Lydgate completed his English version in 1422.) Pandarus tells Criseyde to put the book aside and dance in celebration of the month of May. In her shocked reaction to this suggestion, she falls back on a concept of widowhood as a life of contemplation and prayer, withdrawn from the world: 'in a cave / To bidde and rede on holy seyntes lyves' (2.117–18). This was an option which a pious widow could take, as a 'vowess' making a formal pledge to devote the remainder of her life to God. Rather than dancing, she chats with her uncle as friends do about this and that, about the progress of the war and about Hector, at which point Pandarus slyly praises Hector's brother Troilus, hinting that there is more that he dare not tell her about. Criseyde detains him as he prepares to leave, saying she wants to consult him privately 'of hire estat and of hire governaunce' (2.219), that is, her financial situation and the running of her affairs. The experienced Pandarus can give useful advice on the day-to-day matters involved in managing a large estate, and also on the particular threats that every rich widow had to guard against, as the envious eyed up her assets. She has had trouble with one such, 'false Poliphete', and it is a simple if heartless ruse for Pandarus to tell her that Poliphete is planning to bring renewed legal action to claim her possessions (2.1419, 1467–9). Pandarus then easily persuades her of the necessity of seeking support in person from Troilus and his brothers, leading to the lovers' first meeting.

Pandarus' adept manipulation of his niece therefore plays upon her justifiable insecurities, and he mercilessly exploits the precariousness of her situation in Trojan society. Having built up her anxieties with a long preamble about her need to seize her good fortune, he tells her that the king's son, the noble Troilus, loves her to the point of death, and if she lets him die, Pandarus will cut his own throat 'with this knyf' (2.325). Criseyde cunningly asks what he suggests she should do about it, and he incautiously tells her that she should love Troilus in return; she breaks into tears, accusing him of advising her to have an affair, when he of all people, her uncle and closest supporter, should have prohibited her from a liaison (2.408–13). He angrily threatens to leave, accusing her of having no care for his life or Troilus', at which Criseyde relents sorrowfully, saying:

> 'Ah, Lord! What me is tid a sory chaunce!
> For myn estat lith in a jupartie,
> And ek myn emes lif is in balaunce.
> But natheles, with Goddes governaunce,
> I shal so doon, myn honour shal I kepe
> And ek his lif' – and stynte for to wepe.   (2.464–9)

['Ah, Lord, what a miserable fate has struck me! For my position is at risk, and also my uncle's life is in the balance. Nevertheless, with the help of God I shall manage to preserve my reputation and also his life' – and she stopped weeping.]

As she sees it, her position in Troy is under threat, and yet to secure that position she must endanger her reputation. Thus, while she cannot promise to love Troilus, she concedes that she can, 'myn honour sauf, plese hym fro day to day' (2.480). Her choices now seem very limited.

When she is alone, she reflects at length on her situation. In favour of the proposed relationship is the fact that a man so excellent as Troilus is in love with her, and since she is an independent woman there is no reason why she should not enjoy such a liaison:

> I am myn owene womman, wel at ese,
> I thank it God, as after myn estat,
> Right yong, and stonde unteyd in lusty leese,
> Withouten jalousie or swich debat.
> Shal noon housbonde seyn to me 'Chek mat!'   (2.750–4)

[I am my own woman, very comfortable in terms of my position, I thank God for it; very young, in a pleasant situation without ties, with no jealousy or any contention of that sort. No husband will say 'checkmate!' to me.]

On the other hand, that very independence can so easily be lost if she commits herself to love a man:

> Allas! syn I am free,
> Sholde I now love, and put in jupartie
> My sikernesse, and thrallen libertee?   (2.771–3)

[Alas, since I am free, should I now fall in love and jeopardize my security and enslave my liberty?]

The love-affair that Chaucer explores with such sensitivity and in such detail in *Troilus and Criseyde* takes its course in a public world that from the very outset has a profound influence on the relationship of the couple, and eventually tears them apart. This private/public symbiosis is captured in Criseyde's constant references to her *honour*, which for her is not some abstract element in a courtly ideal but the guarantee of her status in society on which her security depends. She knows that she is finished if she loses her reputation. Criseyde's love for Troilus takes root, flourishes and dies in the context of the complex social and political organization of the city of Troy.

CHAPTER 4

History and Romance

Definitions

The title of this chapter needs some explanation, since for us history and romance are antithetical concepts. History relies on facts, romance on imagination. And yet we know, and it troubles us, that facts are slippery customers and not all they seem, and that a good deal of imagination is required in their interpretation. History, as the Middle Ages agreed, is not a collection of facts but a narrative interpretation of facts, and through this narrative we learn of the past and gain understanding of the present, thus exploring our society past and present and defining ourselves within a social context. What we classify as romance was to the Middle Ages another way of tackling that same task of interpreting the past. In Middle English the same terms were used to classify both: *story, geste, romance*, and none of them fits neatly into our own definitions of genre (Strohm 1971).

There is indeed no way of defining medieval romance as a genre, though many have tried to do so. The term *romance* itself in Middle English means primarily something in a romance language, and thus a work of a kind particularly associated with French, and therefore often a work about a chivalric hero. But bibliographies and studies of Middle English romances include a good number of works that are actually histories, such John Clerk's *Destruction of Troy*, a poem of over 14,000 lines in which the author begins by asserting the veracity of what he is about to recount and dismisses the 'fablis and falshed' of the Greek account of Homer and others. Our own historical knowledge tells us that these accounts of Troy, of Alexander the Great and of King Arthur are largely fictional, and so we fall back on the old, bad division between truth and falsehood in order to classify these works as romances rather than histories. There can be no doubt that to medieval readers they were historical narratives of an imaginative kind, like the stories of Arthur of which Robert Manning says in his *Chronicle*:

> Not alle is sothe, ne alle lie,
> Ne alle wisdom, ne alle folie. (10399–400)

There is not a generic divide but a spectrum. At one end are the accounts that even today are used as prime sources of historical knowledge, some of the chronicles and monastic histories. At the other end are the tales of Celtic faerie and love which contemporary readers would have appreciated as tales of the imagination, as we do ourselves. In this chapter these opposite ends of the spectrum are represented by *The Peterborough Chronicle* and *Sir Orfeo*. And yet. Here is the famous scene where Orfeo in the desert witnesses the faerie hunt as it rides past him with hounds and horns:

> He miʒt se him bisides,
> Oft in hot undertides,   *undertides* mornings
> Þe king o fairy wiþ his rout   *rout* company
> Com to hunt him al about
> Wiþ dim cri and bloweing,
> And houndes also wiþ him berking;
> Ac no best þai no nome,   *nome* captured
> No never he nist whider þai bicome. (281–8)

[*No . . . bicome* Nor did he ever know where they went]

And here is the same scene from *The Peterborough Chronicle*, where the chronicler has just described the arrival of the wicked new abbot to Peterborough:

Þa son þæræfter þa sægon and herdon fela men feole huntes hunten. Ða huntes wæron swarte and micele and ladlice, and here hundes ealle swarte and bradegede and ladlice, and hi ridone on swarte hors and on swarte bucces. Þis wæs segon on þe selve derfald in þa tune on Burch and on ealle þa wudes ða wæron fram þa selva tune to Stanforde; and þa muneces herdon ða horn blawen þet hi blewen on nihtes. Soðfeste men heom kepten on nihtes; sæidon, þes þe heom þuhte, þet þær mihte wel ben abuton twenti oðer þritti hornblaweres. (year 1127, ll. 63–71)

[Soon afterwards many people saw and heard many huntsmen hunting. The huntsmen were black and huge and horrible, and their dogs all black and broad-eyed and horrible, and they rode on black horses and on black goats. This was seen in the town of Peterborough in the deer-park itself and in all the woods between that town and Stamford; the monks heard the horns blow that they blew at night. Honest men observed them at night; they said that, as they thought, there might well be about twenty or thirty horn-blowers.]

The difference between these two accounts of the faerie hunt has nothing to do with 'fact', but rather with the context in which the story is offered. The chronicler actually presents the extraordinary phenomenon as a way of emphasizing the true awfulness of the new abbot, introducing the episode with 'þet we soð seggen' (1127, l. 60) – 'what we say is true'. *Sir Orfeo*, as we shall see, defines itself in terms of a romance of a particular kind, the Breton Lay, and Orfeo's vision is part of the world of wonder and mystery that the poet creates. Yet even a tale of wonder such as *Sir Orfeo* has a contribution to make to contemporaries' understanding of their society – again, as we shall see.

Monastic History

The Peterborough Chronicle marks the end of a remarkable tradition of vernacular historical writing that began in the late ninth century during the reign of King Alfred. The 'First Compilation' of the *Anglo-Saxon Chronicle* was assembled from a great variety of sources, beginning with brief annals about the Roman occupation. It concentrated upon the history of the West-Saxon kingdom, from King Cerdic at the end of the fifth century up to Alfred. Naturally the early entries are usually very brief; the complete annal for the year 611 recording the accession of Cynegils is typical enough:

Her Kynegils feng to rice on Weast Seaxum and heold xxxi wintra.

[In this year Cynegils succeeded to the kingdom of Wessex and reigned for 31 years.]

It consists of two facts, the accession and the length of his reign, and is expressed in the formulaic language (e.g. *feng to rice*, 'came to the throne') regularly used in the *Anglo-Saxon Chronicle*. On other occasions the compilers were in possession of fuller material, and here we sometimes see a different style of writing. The most celebrated of the early entries is the tragic story of Cynewulf and Cyneheard entered under the year 755. The source of this account of loyalty to one's lord until death was probably a heroic lay. The story is carefully patterned, bringing out the parallelism of the two battles it describes; the material is presented in such a way that nothing is superfluous, and so that cause and effect emerge from the narrative with no need of commentary from the writer.

Different versions of the *Anglo-Saxon Chronicle* were maintained throughout the tenth century, extending the historical record until shortly after the Norman Conquest. In 1116 much of Peterborough Abbey was destroyed in a fire which consumed the books in the library. Early in the 1120s the monks borrowed a text of the *Anglo-Saxon Chronicle* and a scribe wrote out a new copy, interpolating a number of details relating to the history of the Abbey. The scribe then continued his copying at intervals, adding annals from 1122 to 1131 to keep the record up to date. It was then set aside for a time, and about 20 years later, probably in 1155, another scribe wrote the final continuation, recording the events of the intervening period, ending with the reign of King Stephen (1135–54). *The Peterborough Chronicle* ends with these words on the newly appointed abbot William of Waltevile: 'Nu is abbot and fair haved begunnon; Crist him unne þus enden' (1154, l. 19) – 'He is now abbot and has made a good start; may Christ grant that he end just as well.'

There is stylistic variety in *The Peterborough Chronicle* as there is throughout the *Anglo-Saxon Chronicle*. Some entries are brief and factual, as is the short annal for 1138 sandwiched between the two long entries for the reign of Stephen. This 1138 entry reports the attempted invasion of David of Scotland and his defeat by William of Aumale at the battle of the Standard. It begins:

On þis gær com David king of Scotland mid ormete færd to þis land; wolde winnan þis land.

[In this year King David of Scotland came to this country with a huge army; he intended to conquer this country.]

The sentence structure of the annal is of the simplest, consisting essentially of a series of main clauses. The vocabulary is also simple and typical of the chronicle style. No attempt is made at variation of common nouns such as *land . . . land*. This is the plain annalistic style used for the recitation of facts. There is no authorial intervention, no attempt to assess the considerable historical significance of the defeat of the Scots.

Side by side with this is writing of quite a different character. A series of events that affected Peterborough Abbey deeply and directly began with the appointment of the new abbot in 1127, whose arrival was accompanied by the dire portent of the faerie hunt quoted above. The Frenchman Henry, abbot of Saint-Jean d'Angély, was imposed on Peterborough Abbey by the king, and was bitterly resented by the monks for his use of the abbey's resources for his own enrichment, 'eallriht swa drane doð on hive' (1127, l. 56) – 'just as a drone in a hive does'. The quarrels grew worse, until in 1131 the monks deposed him and chose a new abbot from amongst their own number. The chronicler comments:

Hi scolden nedes. On fif and twenti wintre ne biden hi næfre an god dæi. Her him trucode ealle his mycele cræftes: nu him behofed þet he crape in his mycele codde in ælc hyrne, gif þær wære hure an unwreste wrenc þet he mihte get beswicen anes Crist and eall cristene folc. (1131, ll. 25–9)

[They had to do it. They didn't have one good day in twenty-five years. Now all his great tricks failed him; now he had to crawl into every corner of his great bag to see if there might be at least one dirty trick so that he could once more betray Christ and all Christian people.]

Here the constructions are rather more complex that in the 1138 annal. There is rhythmic variety in the short and punchy clause of the first sentence contrasting with the longer sentence of explanation that follows. There is also a powerful metaphor expressing the writer's indignation: the simple word *codde* has a range of meanings and associations including 'bag', 'wallet', '(pea)pod', 'belly', 'scrotum' (from which comes the later expression *codpiece*). Abbot Henry is the charlatan with his bag of tricks, and also the worm crawling into the pod intent on destroying the crop. This is a style that works best in the vernacular, and it is interesting to note that Hugh Candidus, a contemporary Peterborough monk who tells this same story in Latin, does not include this colourful passage. It is not the expected dry chronicle style, but a passionate and committed expression of contempt for a hated ex-superior.

The famous description in *The Peterborough Chronicle* of the dreadful sufferings during the civil war of King Stephen's reign has gained the respect of historians for its accuracy and of critics for its artistry (King 1994). It is certainly not a chronicle account set out as a series of annals, but is presented as a pair of narratives written after the event. The two substantial entries for the reign are labelled 1137 and 1140. The latter gives an account of the political events during the Anarchy, the years 1135–54. King Stephen is opposed by the empress Matilda and Robert, earl of Gloucester, daughter and illegitimate son of the previous king, Henry I. Supporting the rebels are a number of Stephen's enemies, including his own brother the bishop of Winchester, and Randolph, earl of Chester. The writer succeeds very well in imposing a thematic pattern upon the fast-moving events that unfolded in the unstructured way that events appear to happen, with protagonists attacking and besieging one another in different parts of the country. Robert imprisons the king, but is then himself imprisoned, until terms are agreed to release them both. The future Henry II lands in England to join the struggles, and eventually settles with Stephen. To impose a structure involves the writer in some juggling with chronology, and consequently it would be impossible to divide the 'annal' into individual year-entries. The author captures the breathless and often futile succession of events as one bit of double dealing follows hard on the heels of another. There are some fine cameo scenes, such as that where the besieged empress escapes from her tower at dead of night by means of a rope.

Since we take it to be the business of the historian to analyse the political causes of events, we should expect that the description of the consequences of the struggles between the king and his enemies would follow rather than precede the account of the wars. The fact that this description comes first, in the entry for 1137, shows that the chronicler's motivation is not that of a modern historian. His purpose, not inappropriate to a monk, is to demonstrate the hand of God in the affairs of the world. This annal is in three sections or movements. At the beginning of the first movement, Stephen is said to have acted *sotlice*, 'foolishly', and he is surprisingly characterized by the seemingly positive adjectives 'milde . . . and softe and god' (1137, l. 10). In fact it is a sign of weakness in a king facing ruthless opposition to be seen as possessing such qualities of generosity together with a lack of political judgement. His enemies have built castles to establish power-bases for themselves, and Stephen's response is to imprison a group of three of the old king's supporters until they give up their castles. The effect is merely to encourage all his powerful enemies to build castles of their own. The writer, having briefly explained how this situation came about, says nothing more about political matters but concentrates entirely upon the sufferings inflicted on the people of the country as the lords press-ganged them into building their castles, looted the surrounding villages, and devastated the estates around enemy castles as a tactic to prevent their rivals from living off the lands. The castles are peopled with 'deovles and yvele men' (17). They seized those who have some wealth and 'tortured them with indescribable torture (*pining*)' (20), the same word that is later used of Christ's tortures. The savage torments inflicted on them are vividly described in painful detail, and the writer comments that 'never were martyrs so tortured as they were' (20–1). Using this religious vocabulary of *deovles*, *pining* and *martyrs*, the monkish author sets out a polarity of good and evil. Indeed, he goes on to say that *hethen men* (probably thinking specifically of the earlier Viking invaders) never caused so much suffering in the country as these evil men did (45–6). This leads him into an account of the pillaging and burning of churches and the robbing of monks and clergy, which understandably seems to him outrageous. The church does what it can by excommunicating the evildoers, 'but it meant nothing to them for they were all damned and perjured and lost' (52–3). The description of the Anarchy concludes with these memorable words:

Hi sæden openlice ðat Crist slep, and his halechen. Swilc and mare þanne we cunnen sæin we þoleden xix wintre for ure sinnes. (1137, ll. 56–7)

[It was openly said that Christ and his saints were asleep. Such, and more than we can relate, did we suffer over nineteen years for our sins.]

This is a bleak picture indeed. There are two statements here: one is from the viewpoint of the writer, 'we þoleden . . . for ure sinnes'. The other is the understandable conclusion of those who are suffering 'ðat Crist slep', and it is the writer's purpose to show that they are wrong in this view, which he does over the two other movements of the entry.

The second movement is in direct contrast to the first: order vs. disorder, construction vs. destruction, good vs. evil. It leaves the national scene for the local community of Peterborough. Here we read how during the same years the good and practical Abbot Martin was building up the fortunes of the abbey after the great fire of 1116, acquiring lands and managing the estates to produce the income to feed the monks and construct the new church. He travelled to Rome to negotiate with the pope for legal documents to secure the abbey's property for the future. We must dismiss any uncharitable suspicion that the abbot, certainly a 'manly man', was in any other respect cousin to Chaucer's worldly Monk. Martin performs vital service to his abbey for which he is described as 'god munec and god man' (74). While the country is in turmoil, the abbot is quietly rebuilding, planting a vineyard, improving the conditions of the town, refurbishing to the honour of God.

So Christ is not asleep but still working and suffering in the world, and in direct proof of this the final movement of the entry tells the story of St William. It is the earliest example of what is to become throughout the Middle Ages a standard anti-semitic calumny, the accusation of the ritual murder of a child by Jews. This happened 'on Stephnes kinges time' (76–7), the first reference to Stephen since the very beginning of the whole entry, inviting us once more to recall the account of the appalling events of the Anarchy. The chronicler reports that the young Norwich boy William was sacrificed by Jews on Good Friday as an insult to Christians. In the chronicler's description, it was a precise re-enactment of Christ's sacrifice. As a result of this evil act another saint was added to the martyrology, and little St William 'through our Lord performed many wonderful miracles' (83–4).

The entry for 1137 is therefore most artfully structured, as a sophisticated piece of writing in which the chronicler uses the events of Stephen's reign as a way of casting a moral perspective on the affairs of the world. The viewpoint of a monk deeply involved in the activities he describes is everywhere evident. His sympathy for the wretched people (*wrecce men*) of the country oppressed by high-born Normans is underlined by his use of Norman-French words to describe the rulers' *tresor*, their *castles* each with its *prisun*, and their demands for protection money which they call *tenserie*. So far from hiding behind a curtain of objectivity, he exclaims passionately: 'I ne can ne I ne mai tellen alle þe wunder ne alle þe pines ðat hi diden wrecce men on þis land' (35–6) – 'I have neither knowledge nor skill to tell of all the atrocities or all the tortures that they inflicted on poor men in this land.' As is all historical interpretation, this is partisan, but it is honestly and openly so, and the reader cannot mistake it for an objective recital of facts.

The History of St Erkenwald

Chaucer's Prioress provides a later version of the 'blood libel' of the child murdered by Jews. The Prioress's Tale is set vaguely in 'Asye' and is told as a miracle of the Virgin, who places a *greyn* on the dead boy's tongue, so giving him the power to sing and thus direct his grieving mother to his body. *St Erkenwald* is also a *miraculum*, that is, a story centred on a saintly miracle, and it also involves a body granted the power of speech. A significant difference between *St Erkenwald* and the Prioress's Tale is that the former is given the precise local and historical setting of St Paul's Cathedral in London during the time of bishop Erkenwald (AD 675–93).

Most of the known facts about Erkenwald come from the other prime authority for Anglo-Saxon history, Bede's *Ecclesiastical History of the English People* (*Historia Ecclesiastica Gentis Anglorum*), written in 731 in Latin, translated into Old English during the reign of Alfred, at much the same time as the 'First Compilation' of the *Anglo-Saxon Chronicle* was written. Bede, who begins with the coming of the Romans, is principally concerned with the conversion of the English by St Augustine at the end of the sixth century and the succession of Anglo-Saxon saints and saintly kings. He is an obvious source for a poet who wished to write about St Erkenwald, but the details offered by Bede are meagre. Erkenwald, he says, built a monastery for himself at Chertsey and another for his saintly sister at Barking in Essex, and Bede reports a number of miracles associated with both brother and sister. The horse-litter on which Erkenwald was carried was preserved until Bede's own day and was effective in curing the sick. Later histories report that Erkenwald rebuilt St Paul's and was buried there.

As is the way with saints, further legends grew up around Erkenwald, one of which may have been the legend that the poet relates, though there is no other record of it in Erkenwald's portfolio. *St Erkenwald* opens with a detailed historical introduction, based partly on Bede and partly on Geoffrey of Monmouth's *History of the Kings of Britain*, perhaps from memory since minor details are not quite accurate. Thus the poet says that St Augustine landed at Sandwich, an important port in the later Middle Ages, though Bede had located the landing at the Isle of Thanet some little way to the north. The lively account of how Augustine converted the Londoners, driving out the heathen idols and rededicating pagan temples to Christ, effectively introduces Erkenwald as Augustine's successor and bishop of his province, now rebuilding St Paul's as a way of confirming the new faith of the Londoners.

The introduction prepares readers for the poet's approach, which is to present the *miraculum* of St Erkenwald in its full historical context. If readers do not believe the story, or at least suspend their disbelief, then the poet fails in his aim of demonstrating God's scheme of salvation through a saintly miracle. The rich detail of the account is delightful, but its purpose is to persuade us that this miracle actually occurred, even though, like all miracles, it is outside the natural order.

And so the poet relates that workmen constructing the footings of St Paul's and digging deep into the ruins of the former pagan temple discovered an elaborate marble tomb with strange gold letters on its lid. The mayor and the city officials ordered the tomb to be opened, and in it was revealed a body lying as if asleep, dressed in a robe edged with miniver, wearing a lawyer's coif and with a crown and sceptre. Bishop Erkenwald was on a visit to his abbey in Essex, but returned to London on hearing the news. Rather than investigating the tomb immediately, he spent the night in prayer, and the next morning robed himself to sing a solemn mass before the excited people. Only then did he approach the tomb. The dean gave him an account of the discovery and told him of the inability of anyone to identify the body of what appeared to be a king, and the bishop reminded him that only God can explain the significance of miracles.

Turning to the tomb, he asked the body who he was and whether he was in heaven or hell. The body replied in a mournful voice that he had been a lawyer in the pagan time of the ancient British king Belin. Because he never swerved for fear or favour from his devotion to justice, he was buried in royal estate as a king of justices. His body and clothes had miraculously remained uncorrupted through a dispensation of God, who values the just above all others. Erkenwald then asked him about the state of his soul, which he assumed had won an eternal reward. At that the judge groaned, saying that, as a pagan who never knew God's covenant, he was not among those bought by the blood of Christ, and so was excluded from the glorious feast of heaven:

> My soule may sitte þer in sorow and sike ful colde,
> Dymly in þat derke dethe þer dawes never morowen,
> Hungrie inwith helle-hole, and herken after meeles.   (305–7)

> [My soul may sit there in sorrow and sigh miserably, abjectly in that dark death where morning never dawns, hungry in the pit of hell, and long for food.]

Erkenwald, greatly troubled, wished that the judge could retain life for as long as it took to get water and say 'I baptise thee in the name of the Father and his noble Son and the gracious Holy Ghost', and weeping as he uttered those words of baptism, a single tear dropped on the judge's face. With that, the judge sighed for joy, for 'Ryȝt now to soper my soule is sette at þe table' (332). As soon as he stopped speaking his body turned to dust. The Londoners praised God and all the bells of the city miraculously rang in unison.

This narrative involves a precise concept of the past in one location at two periods of time, BC and AD. It depends upon historical records, on what the poet calls 'crafty cronecles' (44), and is itself a historical record. Because our attitudes to historical evidence have changed, and because, unlike the Middle Ages, we are not used to reading our history in verse, it is easy for us to miss the rather obvious fact (obvious at least to the contemporary reader) that *St Erkenwald* is a historical account.

The dean and his learned clerics search through their chronicles for some account of the judge, but in this case the historical record fails them:

> And we have oure librarie laitid þes long seven dayes,
> Bot one cronicle of þis kyng con we never fynde.   (155–6)

[And we have searched in our library for these seven long days, but we cannot find a single chronicle of this king.]

History is revealed through the miracle of the judge's power of speech; he is living history. Through his words the distant pagan past comes to life: the 'felonse and fals and frowarde' (231) inhabitants of New Troy, as London was then called; their lamentation when their revered judge died (246); their honouring of him with a richly elaborate burial. The judge is utterly precise about when he lived (205), even if his style of chronology 'is too much for anyone to make a number of' (206).

Even more vividly does Anglo-Saxon London spring to life through the poet's description. The bustling city is full of people of all social levels; the builders at work:

> Mony a mery mason was made þer to wyrke,
> Harde stones for to hewe with eggit toles;   *eggit* sharp-edged
> (39–40)

the tonsured cathedral clergy trying in vain to interpret the inscription on the tomb (55–6); the sexton, mayor and burgesses excitedly puzzling over the wonder (65–6); the nobility coming to hear high mass (134–5). We are given a lively impression of the jostle and confusion of 'þe grete prece' (141), the London crowd, 'with troubull in þe pepul' (109), and in sharp contrast the commanding figure of their bishop, calmly convinced that God will provide answers where human knowledge and reason fail. This demonstration of God's omniscience will act to confirm the unstable faith of those newly Christian Londoners, 'in fastynge of ʒour faith and of fyne bileve . . . Þat ʒe may leve upon long þat he is lord myʒty' (173–5) – 'in confirming of your faith and unsullied belief, so that you may believe in the end that he is the almighty lord'.

The effect, then, of this weight of circumstantial detail is to bring history into focus and thus to reassure the reader that this is an account of a historical event and not a pious fiction. Furthermore, the detail appropriately emphasizes the physical context of the miracle, for without a body there would be no miracle. The rich description of the judge's body makes it clear that this is not some mummified corpse but a rosy-cheeked figure lying as if asleep:

> And als freshe hym þe face, and the flesh nakyd
> Bi his eres and bi his hondes þat openly shewid,
> With ronke rode as þe rose and two rede lippes
> As he in sounde sodanly were slippid opon slepe.   (89–92)

[And his face was as fresh, and the naked flesh openly revealed by his ears and hands, with complexion as ruddy as a rose, and two red lips, as if he had in good health suddenly fallen asleep.]

Since the dead cannot be baptised, it is important to recognize that the judge is in some miraculous way still alive 'by virtue of some spirit-life' (192). Most physical of all is the baptism itself, which can only be fulfilled by a precise verbal formula and the contact of water with the body. Despite the unusual circumstances in this case, the description shows that all the proper conditions have been met. The baptismal formula is almost accidentally pronounced and then:

> With þat worde þat he warpyd, þe wete of his eghen
> And teres trillyd adoun and on þe toumbe lighten,
> And one felle on his face, and þe freke syked.   (321–3)

[As he uttered that phrase, the moisture of his eye and his tears flowed down and dropped on the tomb, and one tear fell on the man's face, and he sighed.]

St Erkenwald occupies two time-slots in the past: the reign of Belin and the episcopate of Erkenwald. There is a third period that is important: the poet's present. Erkenwald's aim is to confirm the faith of his people; the poet's is to take sides in one of the major theological debates of the age about the salvation of the righteous non-believer. Some held the view that salvation could be achieved only through faith; others argued that there was sufficient merit in good works, at any rate for those denied the opportunity of faith. For the latter party there could be no question but that this judge merited salvation, since he lived before the time of Christ and fulfilled the laws of right and justice so far as was in him. Even Erkenwald assumes he is saved. But he is not. For the poet, the sacrament of baptism is necessary for salvation.

We have seen that the miracle of *St Erkenwald* is not one elsewhere associated with this saint. There are various versions that relate it of the Roman emperor Trajan, who died a pagan in AD 117. Through the intercession of Pope Gregory, his soul was transported to heaven in recognition of his compassion and devotion to justice. The closest analogue to *St Erkenwald* is a version of about 1330 by Jocopo della Lana commenting on Dante's interpretation of the story in *The Divine Comedy* (Whatley 1986). Langland tells the same story very differently and to the opposite effect in *Piers Plowman*, for here Trajan is saved 'Nought thorugh preiere of a pope but for his pure truthe' (B.11.155) (Burrow, 1993). Langland is, then, of the party that accepted salvation through good works alone, for Trajan was redeemed even though he had the opportunity to know Christ. Some similarities of phrasing suggest the possibility that *St Erkenwald* is an answer to Langland's treatment, or vice versa.

Is *St Erkenwald* a pious fraud? Did the poet read Langland's account and, knowing another version of the Trajan story more suited to his purpose, graft it onto the history of Erkenwald? Possibly so, since the doctrinal end would justify the means. It seems to me as likely, though, that the story had already become attached to the saint, so that the poet had every justification for shaping it into a fully developed historical narrative. In any event, it was written in such a way as to impress the reader as an authentic account of an event in London's past.

Englishing Arthur

For the history of Britain from the earliest settlement until the domination of the Anglo-Saxons, the Middle Ages relied on Geoffrey of Monmouth's *History of the Kings of Britain*. Geoffrey's Latin history was completed in 1136, and is thus contemporary with *The Peterborough Chronicle*. It became immensely popular, so much so that over 200 copies still survive. It was widely translated and adapted, and its influence penetrated deeply into historical and non-historical works of the Middle Ages. It gave the Europeans, and in particular the British, a noble Trojan ancestry and a glorious past, and although Geoffrey's purpose was to serve the interests of his Norman patrons, his history could also be interpreted as an encouragement of the political aspirations of the Welsh and, by a blatant misappropriation of the legend, the English as well.

Geoffrey's *History* begins with the departure of Aeneas from the ruined city of Troy and the fortunes of his great-grandson Brutus, who settled in Britain, founding his capital New Troy on the banks of the Thames. Among his many successors, including Lear, Belin and Cymbeline, is Arthur, to whom Geoffrey devotes over a fifth of his *History*. Arthur drives out the Saxon invaders, marries Guenevere, achieves great victories abroad, leads his army against the Roman emperor but is summoned home to deal with Mordred's treachery, and is mortally wounded at the battle of Camblam. The history of the British kings after Arthur is a depressing account of feeble leadership, duplicity, and eventual defeat by a cunning and unscrupulous enemy, the Saxons.

Geoffrey acknowledges his use of Bede and the sixth-century historian Gildas, neither of whom makes any mention of Arthur, and he also followed the ninth-century *Historia Brittonum* once attributed to 'Nennius', who refers to Arthur briefly. However, Geoffrey claims to be translating 'a certain very ancient book written in the British language', that is, Welsh or Breton. More probably, living as he did on the Welsh border, he gathered up a variety of Celtic tales and added a large dash of his own imagination to construct an account that held the Middle Ages in its grip for 400 years. Doubts about the authenticity of his work surfaced early and were repeated by more sober historians, but the wish to believe in the Trojan Britons swept all doubt aside, and it was not until the sixteenth century that the Trojan myth was generally discounted.

An early translator of Geoffrey's *History* was the Norman cleric Wace, who completed his version in French couplets in 1155 (see p. 11). Wace expands the work considerably, romanticizing it by putting more emphasis on the court and on contemporary chivalric interests, for example introducing the story of Arthur's creation of the Round Table. Wace's *Roman de Brut* is the direct source of Laȝamon's *Brut*, probably written around 1200, surviving in two thirteenth-century manuscripts, both now in the British Library. In his prologue Laȝamon authenticates his history by describing his travels in search of sources, of which he lists three: the English book that St Bede made, another in Latin that St Alban made (whatever that may be), and Wace. His *Brut* is a much-expanded version of Wace. It is an extraordinary work, a highly ambitious recasting of its source. Nothing that survives from the period is in any way like it, and although we may have lost other works that would set it in some context, it must be doubtful that there was ever anything truly to compare with it. Its verse-form is an eclectic melding of alliterative and rhymed verse, which owes something to late developments of Anglo-Saxon verse. The metre is so flexible that its features are difficult to analyse in a formal way, but the fundamental unit is the half-line, usually of two stresses, with or without alliteration, with or without rhyme. Over long passages the metre is strangely hypnotic; very much a long-poem style, so that quotation of short passages cannot do it justice.

The vocabulary of the poem is also remarkable. By Laȝamon's time words of Norman French origin were embedded in the English language, but they are scarcely present in Laȝamon's vocabulary, despite the fact that he was translating a French source. This must mean that words of Norman origin could still be identified as such, and that Laȝamon deliberately excluded them in favour of words and expressions of Anglo-Saxon origin. Some of the most striking of these were heroic words in Old English, associated with verse rather than prose, such as: (for 'knight, man') *beorne, gume, kempe, leode, haleþe, rink, segge, scalc*; (for 'people', 'court') *hired, duȝeþe*; *blonke* for 'horse'; and *aþele* for 'noble'. Laȝamon makes effective use of the poetic compound-noun, also a notable feature of the Old English verse tradition, as *here-feng*, 'battle-capture', i.e. 'booty', *here-gumen*, 'men of battle', *here-scrud*, 'battle-garment', i.e. 'armour', *here-toȝe*, 'leader', *leod-kinge*, 'king of the people', *leod-cwide*, 'nation-language', i.e. 'English', *leod-scome*, 'national shame', *leod-scop*, 'poet of the people', *leod-swike*, 'traitor to his country'. This vocabulary is preserved in one manuscript, Cotton Caligula A.IX, but must have been recognized as a peculiar and archaic feature of Laȝamon's style, since it is revised wholesale in MS Cotton Otho C.XIII, where much of the distinctive vocabulary is removed and replaced by more commonplace words, sometimes of French derivation. Thus *rink, segge* and *scalc* are replaced by *man* or *cniht*, *grith* by *pais* 'peace', *leod-swike* by *wikede*, and so on (Cannon 1993; Stanley 1969).

What is Laȝamon doing in his choice of verse-form and vocabulary? He is writing heroic epic, an aspect of his work that is reinforced by other stylistic features. Just as *Beowulf* (and, for that matter, Homeric epic) does, he makes great use of the formula, a half-line consisting of a repeated expression or syntactic structure:

> Ærst sweor Arður, aðelest kingen   (11410)
> Al for Arður æiȝe, aðelest kingen   (11418)
> Hail seo þu, Arður, aðelest kinge   (11425)

[*Ærst sweor* First swore; *aðelest kingen* noblest of kings; *æiȝe* respect for; *Hail seo þu* Greetings to you]

These expressions are formal signatures of high style, in a kind of poetry where what matters about a hero is his heroic nature shared with other heroes throughout the ages, and where every villain is most hateful of all men, 'laþest alre monne'.

Another striking feature of Laȝamon's style is his use of poetic similes, some of which are particularly elaborate and extend over as many as 16 lines. These extended similes are prominent in the section of the poem dealing with Arthur's battles against the Saxons. Often they liken the combatants to animals, birds or fish. So in one passage the Saxons wander like the crane in the moor-fen; the crane is pursued by hawks, attacked in the reeds by dogs, safe neither on land nor in water. In the end:

> Havekes hine smiteð, hundes hine biteð;
> Þenne bið þe kinewurðe foȝel fæie on his siðe.   (10066–7)

[Hawks strike him, hounds bite him; then the kingly bird is on the road to death.]

The inspiration must have been Latin heroic poetry, the classical epic of authors such as Virgil and Statius, as well as twelfth-century versions of epic, such as Walter of Châtillon's *Alexandreis* and other Latin poems praising rulers and describing their victories (Salter 1988, 48–70).

Drawing on a variety of models in English, Latin and French, Laȝamon ambitiously constructed a national epic with Arthur as its central hero. For Wace, Arthur was an exemplar of the chivalric values that preoccupied contemporary courts; for Laȝamon he is a war-leader from a heroic past. Laȝamon daringly fashions British Arthur into a national hero; he was the first but by no means the last to do so, since English kings from Edward I onwards used the appeal of Arthur to ratify their own political ambitions. A small example will show how Laȝamon goes about this transformation. The arming of the hero is a set-piece in epic (see, for instance, *Beowulf* 1441–72), and Laȝamon expands Wace to give prominence to the motif. Wace describes Arthur's sword Chaliburne (Welsh 'greedy?') made in the Isle of Avalon, the gleaming helmet of gold with the dragon painted above that had belonged to Uther, his shield Pridwen (Welsh 'blessed form'), and his lance Ron (Welsh 'spear'). Laȝamon includes these pieces of armour, which have names of Welsh origin, but begins:

> Þa dude he on his burne ibroide of stele
> Þe makede on alvisc smið mid aðelen his crafte:
> He wes ihaten Wygar, þe Witeȝe wurhte.   (10543–5)

> [Then he put on his mail-coat woven of steel which an elvish smith made with his noble skills: it was named Wigar (OE 'battle-hard'?), which Witeȝe had made.]

The elvish smith Witeȝe who fashions the corslet takes us to Germanic legend, for he is perhaps to be identified with Widia, son of the smith Weland who forged Beowulf's corslet. The helmet is given the thoroughly English name 'Goosewhite'. This is not a solecism, confusing Arthur with his Saxon enemies, but an artful re-visioning of the hero, dissolving the historical division between British and English.

In Laȝamon, as in Wace, Arthur is ferried to the Isle of Avalon. In Wace, the Britons still await his return to this day, whereas at the same point in Laȝamon's account Merlin prophesies that Arthur will return 'Anglen to fulste' (14297) – 'to help the English'. It is the culmination of his story of Arthur. If we refer it to a concept of nationalism as defined by the racial origins of its people, Arthur is a most unsuitable hero for the descendants of his Saxon enemies. For Laȝamon, though, the nation is defined by its territory (Cannon 2004), and it is noteworthy that he frequently uses the same term, *leode*, to mean both 'land' and 'people, nation'. In this first English account of Arthur, Laȝamon paves the way for the celebration in the centuries to follow of Arthur as a national hero.

The Fairy World

This 'historical' tradition of Arthur is used again as a framework for *Sir Gawain and the Green Knight*. The account of Brutus' settlement of Britain, familiar from histories of England, introduces the story, and at the end of the poem is a reference to the 'Brutus bokez' as one of the poet's authenticating sources. For historians such as Laȝamon, and even more for Robert of Gloucester and Robert Manning, Trojan ancestry underpins expressions of pride in the nation that is now England, and therefore the focus is on Brutus as founding father (Turville-Petre 1996, 71–107). The prologue to *Gawain* shifts the focus to the descendants of Aeneas as settlers throughout Europe who have escaped from the destruction of their city, Troy, and who set about constructing (9), naming (10), settling (12), establishing (14). In Europe and finally in Britain the Trojans become *patrounes* (6), protectors and overlords. In short, they give birth to European civilization. In this way the *Gawain*-poet defines Arthur's court in terms of a European identity inherited from the ancient Trojans, sharing an international court culture. To convey the quality of the gracious behaviour that greets Gawain in the Cheshire castle beyond the 'wyldrenesse of Wyrale', the poet uses the surprising anachronism *Frenkysch fare* (1116), 'French manners'. Even in the north-west midlands, knightly society is characterized by European qualities of chivalry and politeness.

At the same time the poet refers to other sources that point away from the 'historical' tradition and to the Arthur of the chivalric romances. At the end of the poem another source is characterized as 'þe best boke of romaunce' (2521), while the prologue defines the story to follow as 'þis laye' and 'an outtrage awenture' (29–30). We shall look into the associations of the term *lay* in connection with *Sir Orfeo*; the designation *aventure* is a classic term for a chivalric romance in which a knight risks all to pursue a noble quest (Barron 1983). This is not the world of the warrior Arthur leading his troops into battle against the Saxons, but the realm of French romance, where Arthur presides over a court whose qualities of bravery, honour, fellowship, generosity, purity and courtesy will be tested by individual adventures.

This realm was essentially created in the late twelfth century in a series of romances by Chrétien de Troyes, who drew some motifs and stories from the 'historical' Arthurian tradition of Wace and others from Celtic tales. The romances tell of individual knights, Erec, Cligés and Yvain, of the adulterous love between Lancelot and Guenevere, and of Perceval's quest for the mysterious Holy Grail. The emphasis is upon *courtoisie*, an elaborate code of conduct in which the knight, often motivated by his ennobling love for a lady, expresses his self-discipline as well as his bravery, his politeness as well as his ability to keep his pledged word. Chrétien's chivalric romance was immensely popular, not only in France, where it had profound influence on later writers, but also among the nobility of England, who listed such books in their wills and inventories (Putter 1995, 2).

Another branch of French romance owes its inception and popularity to the Anglo-Norman settlers. In this 'insular' romance, the concern is predominantly with family origins, and typically the young hero, driven from his inheritance, undergoes a series of adventures in exile and returns to claim what is rightfully his, both wife and land. Justice triumphs over wrong and the hero founds a lineage which the Anglo-Norman families could claim as their own (Crane 1986, 13–52). These romances were sometimes translated into English, as *Guy of Warwick*, *Bevis of Hampton* (Southampton) and others. There are several of these English versions in the Auchinleck manuscript of the 1330s. Their nationalistic concerns for territorial rights and family settlement are quite distinct from the courtly ethos of Chrétien and the *Gawain*-poet.

The exploration of chivalric virtue as tested through the pressures and ambiguities of the quest is characteristic of Chrétien and his successors. Gawain figures in Chrétien's romances as a brave and courteous knight. The specific plot elements of *Sir Gawain and the Green Knight* are most closely paralleled not in Chrétien but in a number of romances by his followers (Brewer 1992; Brewer 1997). The most distinctive element, the Beheading Game, has a close analogue in an anonymous continuation of Chrétien's unfinished *Perceval*, known as *Le Livre de Caradoc*. In this, Caradoc accepts the challenge of a huge knight who rides into Arthur's court. Having agreed to submit to a return blow from the challenger, Caradoc decapitates him with his sword, but the knight replaces his head on his shoulders and rides out. A year later the knight returns to claim his blow, but after threatening Caradoc and accusing him of cowardice, hits him with the flat of the sword, revealing that Caradoc is his son. Several other

thirteenth-century romances tell the same basic story, in the case of
La Mule sans Frein, 'The Mule without a Bridle', of Gawain himself.
The motif is ultimately derived from Celtic tales, and first appears in
the Middle Irish *Fled Bricrend*, 'Bricriu's Feast'. In this Cuchulainn,
competing for the hero's prize, agrees to cut off the head of a giant
Terror, who spares him on account of his bravery in turning up the
next day to receive his blow. This is an unusually well-documented
example of the classic pattern of dissemination of folk-tale material,
from Celtic story to French romance, and thence to English romance.
In turning to *Sir Orfeo*, we can further investigate the connection
between Celtic and French.

The prologue attached to *Sir Orfeo* defines the poem as a 'Breton
Lay':

> In Breteyne þis layes were wrou3t,
> First yfounde and forþ ybrou3t,
> Of aventours þat fel bi dayes,   *bi dayes* in past times
> Wherof Bretouns made her layes.
> When kinges mi3t our yhere   *our yhere* hear anywhere
> Of ani mervailes þat þer were
> Þai token an harp in gle and game
> And maked a lay and 3af it name.   *3af* gave.
>   (13–20)

This characterization of lays as lyrics performed by Breton minstrels,
consisting of both music and narrative, is repeated elsewhere. Chaucer's
Franklin announces he will recount a Breton Lay as his contribution
to the Canterbury Tales, and in his prologue recalls that:

> Thise olde gentil Britouns in hir dayes
> Of diverse aventures maden layes,
> Rymeyed in hir firste Briton tonge,
> Whiche layes with hir instrumentz they songe
> Or elles redden hem for hir plesaunce.   (*CT* V.709–13)

Eight English versions of the Breton Lay survive from the early fourteenth century to the early fifteenth. Two of them, including the
earliest text of *Sir Orfeo*, are in the Auchinleck manuscript. In France
the form was popular in the late twelfth century, particularly associated with the court poet Marie de France, who wrote a series of

French *lais* in which she several times acknowledges her debt to Breton minstrels, performing their lays 'on harp and rote'. At the beginning of *Equitan* she writes of them:

> The Bretons, who lived in Brittany, were fine and noble people. In days gone by these valiant, courtly and noble men composed lays for posterity and thus preserved them from oblivion. These lays were based on adventures they had heard and which had befallen many a person. (trans. Burgess and Busby 1986, 56)

The Bretons were Celtic speakers descended from the inhabitants of Britain who had emigrated after the invasion of the Angles and Saxons during the fifth century. They kept their language and their fund of Celtic stories, which they shared with their cousins who had retreated to Cornwall, Wales, Scotland and Ireland, and they performed their lays to the courts of France and further afield.

The fairy world of the extant Breton lays is a sensitive recreation of Celtic folk-tales and beliefs. The *lais* of Marie de France are characterized by simplicity of plot, the refined treatment of love and a delicate *aventure* involving the fairy world. The prologue to *Sir Orfeo* characterizes the subject matter thus:

> Sum beþe of wer and sum of wo,   *beþe of wer* are about war
> And sum of joie and mirþe also,
> And sum of trecherie and of gile,
> Of old aventours þat fel while,   *fel while* happened once
> And sum of bourdes and ribaudy,
>   [*bourdes and ribaudy* frivolity and lewdness]
> And mani þer beþ of fairy.   (5–10)

There is no French version of the Orfeo story now in existence, but there are references in French works to a Breton musical 'lai d'Orphey', so we may take it that some version of the story was known in French, and it is most probable that the English *Sir Orfeo* is an adaptation of a French *lai*, which in turn was modelled on a celticized version of the classical story of Orpheus and Euridice. In Ovid's account, Euridice is fatally stung by a snake and the poet Orpheus goes into the underworld to win his bride back. He plays his harp so beautifully that he is allowed to take her away, provided that he does not look back at her on the journey out of Hades. He looks back, and loses her. What we seem to have here is a classical story that has been picked up by the Bretons in the early Middle Ages and reinterpreted by them as a Celtic myth. There are many reports, indeed up to recent times, of the fairy abduction of a human to the Other World, perhaps at the point of death and sometimes leaving a changeling in exchange (Allen 1964). There are also descriptions of the Celtic Other World, the parallel universe of the fairies, which humans enter at their peril through a barrier of rocks or water (Patch 1950). These are the Celtic elements of *Sir Orfeo*, but it is clear that the English poem has been adapted to shape a version of the story for the fourteenth century.

The fairies of *Sir Orfeo* disrupt the world of humans just when it seems most secure. Queen Herodis steps out into the castle garden with her maidens one May morning, into 'our orchard' as she calls it. This is the traditional courtly setting, seen again when Criseyde walks in the garden with her nieces and Antigone sings to them of love. In the warm sun Herodis falls asleep under a fruit tree, but the calm beauty of the scene is shattered by her terrible cries as she awakes, scratching her face until it bleeds and tearing her fine clothes. Driven out of her mind (82), she is carried by her knights and damsels to bed, where they hold her down despite her cries that she must get away. In one sense she has already gone. When Orfeo hurries to her chamber he finds her utterly changed (97–112), so that even her eyes 'Lokeþ so man doþ on his fo' (Pearsall 1996, 53). She tells him that while she was asleep a king had appeared with one hundred knights and one hundred damsels all on snow-white steeds, and had forced her to ride with him to his palace, telling her that the next day she must go with him for ever. In a futile gesture of love, Orfeo assembles a thousand armed knights to protect her, but Herodis is magically snatched away. Devastated by his loss, Orfeo tells his barons that he will for ever retire to the wilderness alone, taking only his harp. He appoints a steward in his place, and instructs his people that they should assemble a *parlement* (216) to appoint a new king to replace him when they hear that he has died.

The wilderness where Orfeo lives in wretchedness for 10 years is a landscape untouched by civilization, as the poet emphasizes by a series of contrasts between Orfeo's courtly past and his desolate present existence, beginning:

He þat hadde ywerd þe fowe and griis,
And on bed þe purper biis,
Now on hard heþe he liþ,
Wiþ leves and gresse he him wriþ.   (241–4)

[He who had worn the fine furs, and had the silk of royal purple on his bed, now lies on the hard heath, wrapping himself in leaves and grass.]

This is a liminal place, on the threshold between the human and fairy worlds (Pearsall 1996, 57). Orfeo plays his harp to the animals who gather to listen, sometimes seeing the fairy king out hunting. One day he sees ladies hawking, and Orfeo, remembering how he had once enjoyed that sport, follows them and recognizes Herodis among them. They disappear through a rock, and Orfeo boldly goes in after them.

The castle before him, glittering like crystal, is splendid on the surface but terrible within, for as Orfeo enters he sees a gruesome sight: people who had been supposed dead but in fact had been snatched away – headless, strangled, drowned, women in childbirth or gone mad, in the attitudes they had when they disappeared:

Sum stode wiþouten hade,	*hade* head
And sum non armes nade,	*nade* had
And sum þurth þe bodi hadde wounde,	*þurth* through
And sum lay wode ybounde,	*wode ybounde* restrained as mad people
And sum armed on hors sete,	
And sum astrangled as þai ete,	*astrangled* choked
And sum were in water adreynt,	*adreynt* drowned
And sum wiþ fire al forschreynt.	*forschreynt* scorched to death
	(391–8)

Among these is Herodis asleep under her orchard tree. Orfeo plays his harp so beautifully to the king and queen that the king promises him anything he wants as a reward. He boldly asks for Herodis, and takes his wife back to his own world.

Central to *Sir Orfeo* is the virtue of personal loyalty, first demonstrated by Orfeo's utter commitment to Herodis, which leads him to abandon his wealth and his kingdom, vowing:

Whider þou gost ichil wiþ þe,
And whider y go þou schalt wiþ me.   (129–30)

[Wherever you go, I'll go with you, and wherever I go, you'll come with me.]

When Herodis is snatched away from him, Orfeo refuses to take a new queen and retreats from the world to become a wild man:

> Never eft y nil no woman se.
> Into wildernes ichil te
> And live þer evermore
> Wiþ wilde bestes in holtes hore. (211–14)

[I'll never see another woman. I'll go into the wilderness and live there for ever with wild beasts in hoary woods.]

To reach the fairy world he must risk all for his love. In striking a bargain with the fairy king, he reminds him of the importance of maintaining his pledged word: 'nedes þou most þi word hold' (468). Even in the fairy court, loyalty is the foundation on which society rests.

The poem could end at the point at which Orfeo wins Herodis back, but the poet wants to emphasize the political as well as personal significance of loyalty, and so relates how Orfeo's steward proves *trewe* in waiting for his master's return against all odds for 10 years:

> King Orfeo knewe wele bi þan
> His steward was a trewe man. (553–4)

As a result, Orfeo's queen and crown are both restored to him, with his loyal people proclaiming 'ȝe beþ our lord, sir, and our king!' (582). The steward is in turn rewarded, because Orfeo 'founde þe þus trewe' (569), by succeeding to the throne after the king's death. At every point of the plot, the disaster and loss that threaten are averted by the power of loyalty.

The emphasis upon the social consequences of loyalty links *Sir Orfeo* with other texts assembled in the Auchinleck manuscript that show a particular concern with contemporary life, the ideals that underpin society and an analysis of its current ills, perhaps responding to the factional battles that led to Edward II's deposition and murder (Turville-Petre 1996, 108–41). Another of the Auchinleck romances is a translation of an Anglo-Norman 'insular' romance, *Amis and Amiloun*, which is entirely devoted to a celebration of *treuthe*. The two sworn friends are prepared to sacrifice everything for their loyalty to one another; their troth-plighting is a bond to be kept whatever the consequences. In rescuing his friend, Amiloun sacrifices his health and is cast out by his wife and kin to beg with his loyal squire. Amis goes to the lengths of slaughtering his own children in order to restore his friend to health with their blood. It is a rather absurd story, but one focused on the importance of loyalty to a society that was in the process of disturbingly radical change.

Prompted by the poem's presentation of Orfeo as a medieval king ruling in conjunction with a *parlement* of his barons, the Auchinleck scribe makes three small but curious alterations to the text of *Sir Orfeo*, not present in the two other versions of the poem, in order to reinforce the local and historical contexts. Orfeo is introduced as 'a king / In Inglond' (39–40); his homeland of Thrace is identified with Winchester, 'For Winchester was cleped þo ["then called"] / Traciens, wiþouten no' (49–50); and it is to Winchester, 'his owhen cité' (479), that he returns with his restored wife at the end of the poem. These additions are out of keeping with the tone of a Breton Lay, with its atmosphere of fairy-tale and myth. Orfeo's Thrace is a land of romance, so distant both in time and space as to be outside time and space, in a realm where fairies might well be expected. To make Orfeo king of England, with his throne in the ancient city of the Anglo-Saxon kings, cuts across the grain of the fantasy. But with these alterations, the Auchinleck scribe provides what is in effect a new interpretation of *Sir Orfeo*, turning it into a historical poem about England, about a model society of a past time in which loyalty triumphed over all adversity.

The fairies have many human features, are handsome, well equipped, with hounds and with banners displayed, but they have mysteriously limited contact with our world. This is well captured in the contrast between the splendid hunting-army of the fairy king that catches no prey (287) and the hunting-party of the abducted ladies who set their falcons onto the water fowl and 'ich faucon his pray slouʒ' (313). The Green Knight is a more ambiguous figure than the fairies of *Sir Orfeo*. In his role as challenger, he is a descendant of the shape-shifting giant of Celtic fairy-tales, although the poet hesitates to define him precisely. He is giant-like in stature, certainly; at any rate he is the largest of men:

Half etayn in erde I hope þat he were,
Bot mon most I algate mynn hym to bene. (140–1)

[I suppose he was really half-giant, but in any event I declare him to be the largest of men.]

Arthur's knights, abruptly interrupted in their New Year's feast, are equally perplexed by this elegant figure who wears courtly clothes, and yet is completely green, 'overal enker grene' (150), but they conclude that he must be a fairy phantom: 'Forþi for fantoum and fayryȝe þe folk þere hit demed' (240).

Unless the Green Knight has supernatural powers, his challenge to a beheading game presents Gawain with manageable difficulties. Arthur reassures him, too optimistically as it turns out:

If þou redez hym ryȝt, redly I trowe
Þat þou schal byden þe bur þat he schal bede after. (373–4)

[If you manage him correctly, I believe you'll easily cope with the blow that he'll deal you then.]

For in the last analysis the Green Knight is undoubtedly supernatural. Picking up his bloody head from where it has rolled across the floor, he appears hale and hearty in his headlessness, 'as non unhap had hym ayled, þaȝ hedlez he were' (438). He reminds Gawain sternly of his agreement to meet at the Green Chapel, and rides out swiftly, 'his hed in his hande' (458). Even so, unlike the fairies of *Sir Orfeo*, the Green Knight is 'really' a man, Sir Bertilak de Hautdesert, exemplar of gracious manners, genially entertaining Gawain in his castle, concerned about his guest's health and comfort. There is no reassuring barrier between the supernatural and the human, so that when Gawain is offered a magic girdle that will save his life, neither the hero nor the reader places much trust in its powers. In the end Gawain faces the Green Knight alone, unaided by magic, and there he learns the identity of his host-challenger: 'How norne ȝe yowre ryȝt nome?' (2443) – 'what is your real name?' – he asks him. Sir Bertilak explains to him that he has been enchanted by Morgan la Faye, who has learnt her magic arts from Merlin.

Morgan has sent the Green Knight to test the qualities of Arthur's famous court, and the test is the more severe in that the Green

Knight/Bertilak shares the same courtly values as Arthur's knights. This complex of virtues is summed up in the word *trawþe*, which includes the sense 'loyalty', as in *Sir Orfeo* (Green 1999, 8–31). At its broadest *trawþe* means 'a commitment to the ideal one has set for oneself', and it has both personal and communal significance, emblematized by the Pentangle that Gawain wears to signify a variety of personal, courtly and religious qualities all 'in bytoknyng of trawþe' (626) (Burrow 1965, 41–51). It is this concept that the poet explores, and we follow how Gawain's *trawþe* is expressed in his fidelity to his pledged word when he commits himself to keeping his side of the beheading agreement (*trawþe* 394, 403, and cf. *trwe* 392, 638); how it is tested when he pledges himself to follow the rules of the Christmas game of exchange proposed by his host in the Cheshire castle (*trawþe* 1108; cf. *trwe* 1091); how it is displayed when he swears to submit to the death-dealing blow of the Knight at the Green Chapel (*trawþe* 2287; cf. *trwe* 2241, 2354). The Green Knight praises Gawain for his *grete trawþe* in pursuing his *awenture* to its successful conclusion (2470), but Gawain himself is miserably oppressed by his sense of failure, by what he identifies as his *untrawþe* (2383, 2509) in the exchange agreement with his host. Gawain, held up by the Green Knight and Arthur's court as the great exemplar of chivalric *trawþe*, is in his own eyes shamefully unable to live up to the ideals of his Pentangle. Success and failure, virtue and vice, are in practice more difficult to distinguish than the young Gawain had imagined, a conundrum adumbrated in the opening lines of the poem by the Aeneas of Troy who 'þe trammes of tresoun þer wroȝt' – 'carried out the treasonable plots' – yet who is even so 'þe trewest on erthe' (3–4).

CHAPTER 5

Piety

From Pecham to Arundel

In 1281 Archbishop John Pecham issued instructions that the laity should regularly be taught the basic points of doctrine in simple terms in the vernacular (*vulgariter*). The archbishop was concerned to carry forward the decree of the Fourth Lateran Council of 1215, which had made annual confession to the parish priest compulsory and which called for a well-educated clergy who could in turn teach their parishioners the elements of faith. Pecham's Constitutions gave an impetus to the writing of works of pastoral guidance in English designed for the clergy to use in teaching the laity (Gillespie 1989, 318). Works such as *Cursor Mundi* and the *Northern Homily Cycle* of c. 1300, Robert Manning's *Handlyng Synne* of about 1317, *Speculum Vitae* (before 1354) and the *Prick of Conscience* of about the same date are lengthy compositions in verse designed to provide religious instruction for lay people, but in depth and subtlety going far beyond Pecham's instructions. All these works begin by stressing that their intention is to address the *lewed* rather than the *lered*, the laity rather than the clergy, those who don't know Latin rather than those who do. The preface to the *Northern Homily Cycle* makes clear that priests are to communicate the text to their parishioners, in the relationship envisaged by Pecham's Constitutions (Turville-Petre 1996, 31–3), and many of the manuscripts of these works were indeed owned by priests and religious houses, though later evidence shows that the literate laity were beginning to possess their own copies (Gillespie 1989, 318). The scope and ambition, as well as the popularity, of these works are alike impressive. The *Speculum*

Vitae, over 16,000 lines preserved in more than 40 manuscripts, discourses with considerable sophistication on such matters as the meaning of the Lord's Prayer, the Ten Commandments, the seven sacraments, the four cardinal virtues and the seven deadly sins. *Handlyng Synne* at some 13,000 lines is an aid to confession, which illustrates the consequences of sin in a series of tales. It is sometimes seen as the precursor of another story-collection, the *Canterbury Tales*. Comparison with Gower's *Confessio Amantis* is rather more apt, since Gower adopts the form of the confessional manual, with a priest of Venus examining the lover for his sins against love, taking each of the seven deadly sins in turn (see chapter 6). Most popular of all these works of pastoral guidance was the *Prick of Conscience*, to judge from some 120 surviving manuscripts in three versions. For its study of the world, hell and earth, the poem draws on a range of learned Latin authors, from Augustine to Bartholomaeus Anglicus, whose comprehensive encyclopedia was later translated by John Trevisa.

Other texts took spiritual instruction in another direction. Richard Rolle of Hampole in Yorkshire, who died in the plague year of 1349, was supported as a hermit by the local gentry (Hanna 2004). He composed several Latin works describing his mystical thoughts and experiences, and in English wrote devotional lyrics, meditations on the Passion and epistles of guidance for his disciples (Woolf 1968, 58–79). Rolle wrote two works for the anchoress Margaret Kirkeby: the *Form of Living* as a treatise on the contemplative life, and the *English Psalter*, which gives the Latin text of each verse of the Psalms together with a literal translation into English, followed by a commentary. Here, for example, is part of Psalm 56.7 (AV 57.6):

> *Foderunt ante faciem meam foveam, et inciderunt in eam.* 'Þai grove a pitte byfore my face, and þai felle þareinne.' Þat es: þai graythed studyousely þat I knew flescheli lust to take me with, þat es a depe pitte til al þat folowys it; and 'þai felle þarein', þat es: þai noyed til þamself noght tille me, for I understode þat alle þe joy of þis werld es bot als a floure of þe feld. (*English Psalter*, Psalm 56, ll. 61–8)

> ['They dug a pit before my face and they fell into it.' That means: they worked assiduously to capture me by acquainting me with carnal lust, which is a deep pit to all who follow it; and 'they fell into it', that means: they caused trouble to themselves and not to me, since I understood that all the joy of this world is but a flower of the field.]

Rolle, writing in the first instance for those who had committed themselves to the religious life, takes the remit of the vernacular pastoral
guide yet another stage, beyond the avoidance of sin and the fundamental worship of God to a higher state of rejoicing in the presence of
God (Watson 1999, 548). We shall see the further development of
this in the *Cloud of Unknowing*. Rolle describes the value of the psalms
in the development of personal piety:

> Sothely þis shinand boke es a chosen sange bifor God, als laumpe
> lyghtenand oure lyf, hele of a seke hert, huny til a bitter saule, dignité of
> gastly persones, tunge of privé vertus. (*English Psalter*, Prol., ll. 15–18)

> [Truly this shining book is a select song before God, like a lamp that
> lights our life, cure for a sick heart, honey to a bitter soul, treasure of
> spiritual people, voice of secret virtues.]

Unlike the parish priest, Rolle is concerned not with the examination
of social sins but with the development of the inner spirituality of the
individual. Here as elsewhere, Rolle is directly instructing his disciples
without the intermediary of a priest, enabling the contemplative to
make personal contact with God. For those able to read Rolle for
themselves, what need, they might ask, is there for the guidance of
the church?

In line with the developing social role for writings in English in
general, religious writings came to address a more diverse readership
on a wider range of topics. In *Piers Plowman* Langland confronts many
of the most bitterly contested religious issues of the day, including
dangerous topics concerning the corruption of the clergy, the
disendowment of the church and the value of pardons. Through his
story of the emperor Trajan, for example, Langland takes a liberal line
on the thorny issue of whether salvation is attainable through good
works alone, and the same question figures in *Pearl*, and is the subject
of *St Erkenwald*, which reaches a much more conservative conclusion,
as we have seen.

This increasingly deep involvement in sensitive theological matters
led to two particular anxieties. Firstly there were concerns that English, with its limited vocabulary and 'lack of grammar', was not a
suitable vehicle for complex thought, and that translations of Latin
works would inevitably falsify and simplify the originals. Secondly

there was constant discussion about the dangers of making material available to the unlearned that was liable to misinterpretation. Dame Study in *Piers Plowman* expresses the hostility to be expected from such a figure when she reproves her husband Wit for discoursing learnedly with the ignorant Will:

> 'Wel arto wyse', quod she to Wyt, 'suche wysdomes to shewe
> To eny foel or to flaterere or to frentike peple!'
> And sayde, '*Nolite mittere*, ʒe men, margerie perles
> Among hogges þat han hawes at wille.
> They do bote drevele theron, draf were hem levere
> Then al þe preciouse perye þat eny prince weldeth.'   (C.11.5–10)

> ['You're pretty smart', she said to Wit, 'to reveal such wisdoms to any fool or flatterer or to deranged people!' And she said 'Do not cast pearls, sirs, among hogs who have all the haws they want. They merely dribble on them and would rather have swill than all the precious jewellery that any prince possesses.']

When John Wycliffe and his followers expressed their theological views in English, the leaders of the church were especially hostile to their assumption that everyone, learned and unlearned alike, should be able to discover the Wycliffites' unorthodox beliefs concerning the authority of the church (Hudson 1985, 141–63; Hudson 1988). The Wycliffites made it their business to circulate their challenging arguments among the *lewed*, and writing in English became a symbol of their anti-clericalism. Their views on the primacy of scripture inspired two complete translations of the Bible into English in the late fourteenth century. We shall see that Bible translation had always been practised, but in the new climate of suspicion it provoked particular hostility from scholars who argued that the laity were in no position to understand the complexities of biblical interpretation, and would inevitably fall into heresy without the guidance of the learning of the church. In an early fifteenth-century debate on biblical translation, Thomas Palmer counselled the laity to concentrate instead on 'things to avoid, that is, the seven deadly sins; things to fear, that is, the pains of hell; things to believe, found in the Creed; things to do, the ten commandments; things to hope for, everlasting reward' (Watson 1995, 842). Richard Ullerston agreed that if translations were made available to everyone, 'all the sacraments of the church will be vilified and clerics will be regarded by the laity as useless' (Watson 1995, 843, n. 60). 'Every lewde man is becomen a clerke and talkys in his termys', complains another writer (Hudson 1985, 156–7). On the other side it was argued that Christ himself taught the laity, the people of God, in the vernacular, and that Englishmen from Bede to Rolle had trans-lated the scriptures. Before the matter had become quite so contro-versial, John Trevisa played out some of these arguments in his *Dialogue between a Lord and a Clerk* of the 1380s, in which the Clerk objects that books that draw heavily on the Bible 'sholde noȝt be translated ynto Englysch' in view of the danger of error, and the Lord in reply points to the long and distinguished tradition of translation (*BOME* 12.108–36).

It was, however, the instinct to repress that won the day. In 1409 Archbishop Thomas Arundel published his Constitutions banning bib-lical translation. The Constitutions invoked the instructions of Arch-bishop Pecham, limiting the topics that could be covered in sermons to the basic articles of faith as laid down by Pecham and, most sweep-ingly, banning all translation of scripture, even the translation of brief extracts of the Bible, and prohibiting the ownership of any translation made in or after the time of Wycliffe, without express permission (Hudson 1985, 146–7; Watson 1995, 825–30). Even though Arundel tactically associated himself with his predecessor, the effect was quite different. Whereas Pecham had decreed the minimum that Christians should know, Arundel's Constitutions defined this as the maximum to which the laity should have access (Watson 1995, 828). The new climate of fear and repression may have inhibited the composition of new religious works in English and have led to the destruction of many suspect vernacular texts; even so, the preservation of some 250 manuscripts containing the Wycliffite Bible in whole or in part shows that it became immensely popular and widely copied, owned by both orthodox and Lollards alike.

Christ the Lover and God the Unknowable

Ancrene Wisse, 'The Guide for Anchoresses', is one of a number of associated prose works in English from the earlier thirteenth century addressed to female recluses, thus preceding Rolle's *Form of Living* by more than a century. Other writings in the group include the lives of three virgin martyrs, Margaret, Katherine and Juliana, a translation of a Latin treatise on the nature of the soul called *Sawles Warde*, and *Hali Meiðhad* in praise of virginity (both eds. Millett and Wogan-Browne 1990). *Ancrene Wisse* was initially written at the request of three young sisters who had chosen to live as recluses in 'Godes prisune' (2.877), and was later revised for an expanded group of 20 or more anchoresses. They have shut themselves off from the world and will never leave their cells in the anchor-house; it is, so the writer says, their grave. As he describes it, each cell has three windows, a church window looking on to the altar so that the anchoress can take part in the mass, a house window through which she can communicate with the maids who care for her, and a tiny parlour window, to be kept heavily curtained, through which she can speak as necessary to visitors (2.21–3; 2.340–3). The anchoresses have effectively committed themselves to a life-sentence of solitary confinement.

To make an existence such as this endurable, the author (their spiritual advisor) needs to reassure the young women of the great value of their self-sacrifice, and to remind them why they have chosen this life. He asks them to reflect on what they were searching for when they forsook the world; their purpose was:

> biwepen þine ahne ant oþres sunnen ant forleosen alle þe blissen of þis lif forte cluppen blisfulliche þi blisfule leofmon i þe eche lif of heovene. (2.881–3)

> [to weep for your own sins and those of others, and to lose all the joys of this life so as to embrace joyfully your joyful beloved in the eternal life of heaven.]

This reflection provides the basis for the structure of what the author calls the 'inner rule' in six parts, which guides his readers to a recognition of sin, its effects and how it must be dealt with, so leaving the heart pure and in a state to receive the love of Christ. Their imprisonment as recluses indeed makes them companions of Christ, who himself was first a recluse in Mary's womb, then enclosed in a cradle, fixed with nails onto a cross and finally shut into a stone tomb: 'Marie wombe ant þis þruh weren his ancre-huses' (6.424–5) – 'Mary's womb and this tomb were his anchor-houses'.

Literary critics analyse the fine writing, the rhetorical devices, the restrained use of alliteration and above all the arresting imagery; for the author these are the means to the end of engaging the attention of the anchoresses, focusing their minds on a series of pictures, analogies and reflections to direct their thoughts and to comfort them in their self-imposed isolation. So the anchor-house, though described as a prison and a grave, is also a refuge: an enclosure to protect them from the lion of hell that roams the streets (3.618–19), a tower against the Devil's blast (4.697–701), a strong castle surrounded by a moat of deep humility and tears (4.947–50), God's orchard protected by thorns (6.436–8), and an anchor (a pun) to secure their ship in the storm (3.329–33).

The brief 'outer rule' (parts 1 and 8) gives advice on practical matters, and thereby offers us a remarkable insight into the day-to-day routine of these women. Far from being the empty life we might imagine, it is in fact busy and tightly organized. There are the devotions that have to be recited at the appointed times throughout the day, starting with matins at daybreak in summer or during the night in the winter (1.87–8). Reading is strongly commended as a remedy against the sin of sloth: 'Often, dear sisters, you should pray less in order to read more' (4.1553–4). Practical activities include sewing vestments for the clergy and making clothes for the poor (8.169–70), as well as supervising their women attendants: most anchoresses, he says, will need two servants. Although enclosed, they may get a stream of visitors to their curtained window, perhaps pious women seeking their prayers and guidance, cackling crones hoping to share gossip, men asking impertinently where they sleep (just say you're well provided for), or the bishop troublingly insisting on having a sight of them (2.235–49).

Two frequent visitors to the anchor-house are the Devil and Christ. The Devil is imagined in various guises: he may, for instance, slink up as the dog of hell to stir lustful thoughts. Don't yawn and say sleepily 'Ame dogge, ga herut!' (4.1599–600) – 'Good dog, out with you!' – but pick up the staff of the cross and violently beat him with it, call repeatedly on Jesus' name and beg for his help through his death on the cross, flee into his wounds and creep inside them with your thoughts. These are characteristically physical terms in which to describe the anchoresses' struggle with lust. Throughout the *Ancrene Wisse* and its associated texts, thoughts, fears, temptations and longings take vivid physical shape. A memorable example is the terrifying scene in the life of St Margaret that describes the Devil in the form of a dragon assailing the virgin in the dungeon:

> His lockes ant his longe berd blikeden al of golde, ant his grisliche teð semden of swart irn. His twa ehnen steareden steappre þen þe steoren ant ten ʒimstanes, brade ase bascins in his ihurnde heaved on eiðer half on his heh hokede nease. Of his speatewile muð sperclede fur ut, ant of his nease-þurles þreste smorðrinde smoke, smeche forcuðest, and lahte ut his tunge se long þet he swong hire abuten his swire. (*Seinte Margarete*, eds. Millett and Wogan-Browne 1990, 58.12–17)

> [His hair and his long beard shone all of gold, and his terrifying teeth seemed to be of black iron. His two eyes shone brighter than the stars and the jewels, broad as basins in his horned head on either side of his high, hooked nose. From his horrible mouth fire sparkled out, and from his nostrils poured suffocating smoke, most horrible of fumes, and he stretched his tongue out so far that he swung it about his neck.]

Like all great lords, the Devil holds court, and his courtiers are those who act out each of the seven deadly sins. One of his entertainers, for example, is a smutty child sitting by the great fire in the Devil's hall:

> Þe ʒiscere is his eskibah, feareð abuten esken ant bisiliche stureð him to rukelin togederes muchele ant monie ruken, blaweð þrin ant blent himseolf, peaðereð ant makeð þrin figures of augrim as þes rikeneres doð þe habbeð muche to rikenin. Þis is al þe canges blisse, ant te feond bihalt tis gomen ant laheð þet he bersteð. (4.515–19)

> [The miser is his ash-fool, occupies himself with ashes and busily arouses himself to heap together many huge heaps; he blows on them and blinds himself, pokes them and draws in them arithmetical figures as these accountants do who have much to count. This is the whole of the fool's joy, and the fiend looks at this game and laughs until he bursts.]

By this the anchoresses are to understand the absurdity of valuing worldly possessions. They must realize:

> þet gold ba ant seolver ant euch eorðlich ahte nis bute eorðe ant esken þe ablendeð euch mon þe ham in blaweð, þet is, þe bolheð him þurh ham in heorte prude. (4.520–2)

[that both gold and silver and every earthly possession are but earth and ashes that blind everyone who blows on them, that is, who puffs himself up in pride of heart as a consequence of them.]

Christ also takes physical shape, represented throughout *Ancrene Wisse* as a lover. Here the author draws upon twelfth-century movements in devotional practice, as promoted in particular by St Bernard of Clairvaux (d. 1153), to whom the author of *Ancrene Wisse* frequently refers (Shepherd 1959, xxviii–lvi). Bernard envisaged a very personal relationship between God and man, most prominently in his sermons on the Song of Songs, in which God is the bridegroom and the soul is the bride. In *Ancrene Wisse* the Song of Songs is the 'luve boc' (6.404) in which Christ is the lover. There is in this construction an increased emphasis on the humanity of Christ and a heightened intensity in imagining his bitter sufferings at the crucifixion, which finds expression in the art of the period, as in plate 7, where Christ's emaciated body is twisted in agony. The anchoresses, by redirecting their feelings of carnal love, will experience that passionate love of Christ that alone gives point to all their mortifications and deprivations:

Seinte Pawel witneð þet alle uttre heardschipes – alle flesches pinsunges ant licomliche swinkes – al is ase nawt aʒeines luve, þe schireð ant brihteð þe heorte. (7.1–3)

[St Paul attests that all external hardships – all bodily mortifications and physical labours – all are as nothing in comparison with love, which makes the heart pure and bright.]

Therefore they need to meditate constantly upon Christ's physical torments, dwelling on the details of 'hokeres, buffez, spatlunge, blindfeallunge, þornene crununge' (4.141–2) – 'insults, blows, spitting, blindfolding, crowning with thorns' – and remember

his swete bodi ibunden naket to þe hearde piler ant ibeate swa þet tet deorewurðe blod ron on euche halve. (4.143–5)

[his sweet body bound naked to the hard pillar and beaten so that the precious blood ran down on every side.]

7 Crucifixion, de Lisle Psalter, BL MS Arundel 83, pt 2, f. 132.
The psalter was made in about 1335, for Robert de Lisle's daughter Audere.
Christ's body is contorted in his death-agony, with the sorrowing Mary on
his left and John on his right. Below a dead man rises from his grave.
Sandler (1986, no. 38). Photograph © British Library, London.

It is the great reward of the life that they have chosen that it puts them on the cross with Christ: 'all their joy is to be hung painfully and shamefully with Jesus on his cross' (6.88–9).

Love is the subject of part 7, which is the conclusion of the 'inner rule' and the climax of *Ancrene Wisse*. Here a remarkable allegory combines the image of Christ as lover with Christ as knight, drawing on a scene from the chivalric romances in which the knight rescues a lady from her enemies or jousts in her honour in order to gain her love (Woolf 1986, 99–117). The story begins:

> A leafdi wes mid hire fan biset al abuten, hire lond al destruet, ant heo al poure inwið an eorðene castel. A mihti kinges luve wes þah biturnd upon hire swa unimete swiðe þet he for wohlech sende hire his sonden, an efter oðer, ofte somet monie, sende hire beawbelez baðe feole ant feire, sucurs of liveneð, help of his hehe hird to halden hire castel. (7.68–73)

> [A lady was besieged all around by her enemies, her land entirely destroyed, and she quite destitute inside a castle of earth. A mighty king's love was however directed towards her so immeasurably greatly that in order to woo her he sent her his messengers, one after another, often many together, sent her many beautiful jewels, assistance in provisions, help from his noble army to preserve her castle.]

But the lady responds to these missives with the haughty disdain characteristic of the courtly mistress, and so eventually the lover-knight must come in person, to show his face and to speak words so sweet they might raise the dead to life. He tells her of his kingdom and offers to make her queen of all his realm. Still she refuses him, but so deep is his love for her that he takes on the battle to rescue her from her enemies, knowing that he himself will lose his life:

> Nere þeos ilke leafdi of uveles cunnes cunde ʒef ha over alle þing ne luvede him herefter? (7.93–4)

> [Wouldn't that lady be come of evil stock if after that she didn't love him above all things?]

Unlike this haughty lady, the anchoress should offer herself to Christ, who asks her to turn away from other lovers:

Ne schaw þu na mon þi wlite, ne ne leote bliðeliche here þi speche, ah turn ham ba to Jesu Crist, to þi deorewurðe spus. (2.752–3)

[Show no man your face, nor let him gladly hear your voice, but turn both to Jesus Christ, to your precious husband.]

In *Ancrene Wisse*, as in the other prose writings for female recluses, the motif of Christ the lover with his love-letters, kisses and physical sacrifice is taken as far as it can go in order to stimulate in the readers an emotional response of passionate intensity.

A very different approach is taken by the author of several works of spiritual guidance written 150 years later. *The Cloud of Unknowing* is addressed to a spiritual friend aged 24 who intends to become a contemplative. The author, who also wrote the *Book of Privy Counselling* and other treatises of spiritual guidance, indicates that he lived as a recluse, and he seems to have had a connection with the Carthusians, a contemplative order vowed to silence and prayer, who distributed his works. This one-to-one address to his 'spiritual friend' is urgent, personal and colloquial. Though the writer intends to reach a wider (but select) audience, he chooses this intimate form of address so that he can concentrate on points of particular application. As he explains at the opening of the *Book of Privy Counselling*: 'I speke at þis tyme in specyal to þiself, and not to alle þoo þat þis writyng scholen here ["will hear"] in general' (75.2–3).

The aim of the contemplative is to reach a mystical union with God. Since God is unknowable, this union must be achieved through a long process of unknowing, that is to say, of setting aside the experiences of both the senses and the intellect. These ideas have a long history and can be traced back to the *via negativa* of the *Mystical Theology* ascribed to Dionysius the Areopagite (c. 500) (Hodgson 1982, xli–lvii). The novice contemplative must enter 'a derknes, and as it were a cloude of unknowyng' (9.29–30), leaving behind those faculties which strive to know and comprehend:

And þerfore schap þee to bide in þis derknes as longe as þou maist, evermore criing after him þat þou lovest, for ʒif ever schalt þou fele him or see him as it may be here, it behoveþ alweis be in þis cloude and in þis derknes. (9.34–7)

[And therefore be prepared to wait in this darkness as long as you can, always calling on him whom you love, for if you are ever going to feel him or see him here, so far as it is possible, it must always be in this cloud and in this darkness.]

The disciple is instructed to put another cloud beneath him, a cloud of forgetting between himself and all created beings, whether they are physical or spiritual, whether they are good or bad (13.26–37). Having interposed this cloud of forgetting between himself and created nature, the contemplative may strive to 'smyte apon þat þicke cloude of unknowyng wiþ a scharp darte of longing love' (14.29–30).

The natural inclination for the novice to dwell on his own unworthiness, to lament his sinfulness, is to be resisted. Here is a sharp and significant contrast with *Ancrene Wisse*, as the author of the *Cloud* sternly warns his friend of the need to drive out meditation, whether it is on the wickedness of sin or the kindness of God. Dissection of the seven sins is a hindrance to contemplation: think of sin simply as 'a lump' (40.30). Certainly meditations on the Passion are good and holy spiritual exercises: the author acknowledges their value for the life of the spirit, as Rolle did also; yet those who strive to reach a state of mystic union with God, such as Rolle himself and the reader of the *Cloud*, need to abandon such meditations 'and put hem and holde hem fer doun under the cloude of forʒetyng' (15.21–2). It is certainly difficult to dismiss such thoughts, which persist in intruding, but the writer suggests a couple of tricks. One is to 'fonde ["try"] to loke, as it were, over þeire schuldres, seching ["seeking"] anoþer þing, þe whiche þing is God, enclosid in a cloude of unknowyng' (37.2–4). Another trick, if you feel you really can't resist such thoughts, is 'koure þou doun under hem as a cheitif and a coward overcomen in batayle, and þink þat it is bot a foly to þee to stryve any lenger wiþ hem; and þerfore þou ʒeeldest þee to God in þe handes of þin enmys' (37.10–13) – 'cower down under them as a captive and a coward defeated in battle, and consider that it is just folly for you to struggle any longer against them; thus you surrender yourself to God in the hands of your enemies'.

Through the very physical imagery of passages such as this, the author draws a sharp distinction between what is *bodely* and what *goostly* (spiritual) (Burrow 1984, 132–47). Inevitably 'speche is a bodely werk wrouʒt wiþ þe tonge' (63.32–3), and so it is important that the novice should not take literally words such as 'UP or DOUN, IN or OUTE, BEHINDE or BEFORE' (63.29–30). Failure to observe this distinction between the body and the spirit can lead the enthusiast into ludicrous and dangerous delusion, as he simple-mindedly misunderstands instructions to draw his perceptions 'within' himself or climb 'above' himself. This foolish contemplative may signal his failure to demarcate the bodily from the spiritual by odd and unseemly gestures:

> Som kan nouþer sit stille, stonde stylle, ne ligge stille, bot ʒif þei be
> ouþer waggyng wiþ þeire fete or elles sumwhat doyng wiþ þeire handes.
> Som rowyn wiþ þeire armes in tyme of here spekyng, as hem nedid for
> to swymme over a grete water. Som ben evermore smyling and leiʒing
> at iche oþer worde þat þei speke, as þei weren gigelotes and nice japyng
> jogelers lackyng kontenaunce. (55.6–12)

> [Some can neither sit still, stand still nor lie still without wagging their
> feet or doing something with their hands. Some row with their arms as
> they speak, as if they had to swim across a great lake. Some are always
> smiling and laughing with every other word that they speak, as if they
> were coquettes and foolish comedians, lacking in self-control.]

The crucial lesson is that God can only be approached through love, which is an act of the will. We can reach an understanding ('fulheed of knowyng') of everything else in creation by thought, but since God is unknowable, 'by love may he be getyn and holden, bot bi þouʒt neiþer' (14.22–3). The author makes this same point in a number of different ways. All rational creatures, he argues, have two principal faculties, a 'knowable miʒt' and a 'lovyng miʒt'; to the former God will always be incomprehensible, to the latter he will make himself fully comprehensible (10.31–40). In this context imagination is worse than useless as a means to approach God, for, whether we are awake or asleep, the imagination presents to us unbidden images of the physical world as well as fantasies, and both are distracting to the contemplative (65.20–31).

The greatest of all dangers for the disciple is *coriousté*; the noun and its adjective are used repeatedly throughout the *Cloud*. It means inquisitiveness in a bad sense, an arrogant love of speculative enquiry, and it is allied to both imagination and intellect (*witte*). It will lead the novice astray from the very start, encouraging him to think of the cloud image in physical terms. 'Soche a derknes and soche a cloude maist þou ymagin wiþ coriousté of witte . . . Lat be soche falsheed; I mene not þus' (13.14–17). *Coriousté* is the very opposite of love, which is moved not by speculation but by a blind impulse (12.33–7). At its worst, *coriousté* leads to heresy, so that people

> for pride and coriousté of kyndely witte and letterly kunnyng ['natural intelligence and bookish learning'] leviþ þe comoun doctrine and þe counsel of Holy Chirche . . . At þe last þei brestyn up ['burst out'] and blasphemyn alle þe seyntes, sacramentes, statutes and ordenaunces of Holy Chirche. (58.1–2, 7–8)

The author's instructions are not meant for 'þees corious lettrid ne lewid men' (73.15–16), even though he deals with profound and difficult concepts. In the *Book of Privy Counselling* the writer acknowledges that he has been criticized for the complexity and obscurity of his earlier work:

> Softely, mornyngly and smylingly I merveyle me somtyme whan I here sum men sey (I mene not simple lewid men and wommen, bot clerkes and men of grete kunnyng) þat my writyng to þee and to oþer is so harde and so hei3, and so curious and so queinte, þat unneþes it may be conceivid of þe sotelist clerk or wittid man or womman in þis liif. (76.19–24)

> [With both sadness and amusement, I am secretly amazed sometimes when I hear some people say (I don't mean humble unlettered men and women, but scholars and men of great knowledge) that what I write to you and to others is so hard and so elevated, so strange and so intricate, that it can scarcely be comprehended by the most acute scholar or intelligent man or woman alive.]

His learned critics are blinded by their *coriousté* into regarding as complex a treatise that is 'bot a symple and a li3t lesson of a lewid man' (76.36–7).

Like Robert Manning before him, the *Cloud*-author chooses to write in English 'not for þe lerid bot for þe lewed' (Manning's *Chronicle* 6). For the authors of the pastoral guides in the vernacular, to be *lewed* was to be denied access to the treasury of the Latin learning of the universal church, so that the pastor had a duty to fill the gap as far as could be done. In the affective theology of the *Cloud*, writing in the vernacular is an advantage rather than a necessity, because learning is a potential hindrance to the work of contemplation, a distraction from the naked encounter with God (Watson 1999, 553–5). The *lewed* have been redefined as those who are prepared to approach God simply with a meek stirring of love (9.12). The ideal reader of the *Cloud* has an ardent desire for God, not a head stuffed with learning. In his characterization of those whose conceited *coriousté* leads them to question the authority of the church, the *Cloud*-author may be thinking of Wycliffe and his followers, but even so he shares with the Wycliffites the view that clerical learning obfuscates the way to God, and that it is the lewed soul that is more readily 'in lovely meeknes onyd ["united"] to God in parfite charité' (*Book of Privy Counselling* 76.31).

Retelling Biblical Stories

Long before the time of the Wycliffite translations of the Bible, there were Middle English translations and adaptations of those parts of the Old and New Testaments that were most important for lay people to know. The Psalms were a particular favourite, as the prescribed text for private prayer, with translations and commentaries in English from Old English times onwards (Muir 1970). Equally popular were versions of the Passion. *Patience*, based on the Old Testament Book of Jonah, and the York Crucifixion Play represent contrasting approaches to retelling the Bible story for lay audiences. What they have in common is a determination to show the relevance of the biblical message to their contemporaries.

In *Patience* the Book of Jonah is offered as an *exemplum* (ME *ensaumple*), that is, a demonstration of a truth universally acknowledged. Collections of *exempla* were gathered in handbooks for preachers to flesh out in their sermons, and such stories were promoted as particularly suitable for the delight and instruction of lay people (Welter 1927, 68–9; Burrow 1982, 82–4). The form was used to structure literary narrative by many fourteenth-century poets, from Robert Manning's *Handlyng Synne* early in the century, to some of Chaucer's *Canterbury Tales* at the end (Burrow 1982, 107–18; Scanlon 1994,

27–36). Gower's *Confessio Amantis* consists of a collection of *exempla* demonstrating the sins against love. For Chaucer's Pardoner the theme is 'love of money is the root of evils' (*CT* VI.334); for Gower's Confessor it may be 'boasting is despicable' (*CA* 1.2456) or 'there is danger when the will leads the heart in love' (*CA* 3.1326–8); for the narrator of *Patience* it is 'Patience is a virtue, though it may often displease' (1). Such general truths and proverbial utterances are then explored and enacted in the *exempla*, so the readers' pleasure derives not only from the interest in the narratives themselves, but also from the skill with which the stories give life and depth to the maxims that provoke them.

The first 60 lines of *Patience* constitute an investigation of the meaning of 'patience', and in the opening lines the narrator introduces a network of synonyms that will shape the concept in the *exemplum* to follow:

> Pacience is a poynt, þaȝ hit displese ofte:
> When hevy herttes ben hurt wyth heþyng oþer elles,
> Suffraunce may aswagen hem and þe swelme leþe,
> For ho quelles uche a qued and quenches malyce.
> For quoso suffer cowþe syt, sele wolde folȝe,
> And quo for þro may noȝt þole, þe þikker he sufferes.
> Þen is better to abyde þe bur umbestoundes
> Þen ay þrow forth my þro, þaȝ me þynk ylle.   (1–8)

[Patience is a virtue, though it may often displease: when heavy hearts are hurt by insult or anything else, endurance may comfort them and ease the pain, for that alleviates every injury and extinguishes malice. For if anyone were to put up with misfortune, happiness would follow, and anyone who through impatience is unable to endure, the more severely he suffers. Then it is better to endure the buffet sometimes, even if I resent it, than always give vent to my impatience.]

The noun *suffraunce* in this context means a patient acceptance of troubles (Putter 1996, 106–16). There is a play on the two senses of its verb *suffer* (5–6), 'endure' and 'feel pain', and the first of these meanings is repeated by *þole* (6) and *abyde* (7). All these words are used again in the *exemplum* so as to recall this opening discussion. From the start the narrator claims that willing endurance is the way to deal with pain and misfortune. The importance of this virtue is next demonstrated by recalling that Christ included patience among the eight Beatitudes in the Sermon on the Mount, and in glossing this biblical text the narrator gives a sharper definition of patience: it is the ability to steer one's heart (27), that is, to control and give direction to passions such as anger or fear. Indeed wrath is often seen as the opposite of patience, and so Chaucer's Parson gives 'pacience or suffraunce' as the remedy for anger, since it is the 'vertu that suffreth debonairely ["meekly"] alle the outrages of adversitee and every wikked word' (*CT* X.659). Patience is an active virtue rather than the passive endurance that we might suppose.

With the Sermon on the Mount, the narrator's argument seems to be leading towards a spiritual and ethical definition of patience, but now it takes a sudden turn towards everyday pragmatism. The narrator says he is poor; since he has to endure poverty, he might as well like it rather than resist it with anger and be still worse off (47–8). He offers a mini-*exemplum* that relates precisely to the major *exemplum* to follow: if his lord orders him to ride to Rome, he may as well obey and be rewarded with gratitude instead of being compelled to go in any case and incurring displeasure for his unwillingness. 'Of pacience comth obedience', as Chaucer's Parson says (*CT* X.673).

The medieval *exemplum* is characteristically used to address the laity in a sermon (as by Chaucer's Pardoner) or a confessional manual (so Gower's Confessor), but *Patience* is not a sermon and the narrator presents himself as a layman: a servant to a lord and a member of the congregation listening to the Gospel reading at high mass. His poverty is imposed, not adopted voluntarily (41–4), and his view of patience is essentially pragmatic: work co-operatively with what you are obliged to endure.

The narrative of the Book of Jonah is laconic, consisting of speech and action without commentary. It would have been familiar through artistic representations, which capture the drama of the moment when the sailors drop the prophet overboard into the mouth of the whale (see plate 8), and often manage to convey the New Testament interpretation of the whale's mouth as the mouth of Hell into which Christ entered for three days after his Crucifixion. The poet closely follows the biblical source, yet expanding it to explore the motives for Jonah's behaviour and the significance of the events. Thus the Bible story begins with God's instructions to Jonah to go to preach in Nineveh, 'for the wickedness thereof is come up before me. And Jonah rose up to flee into Tharsis from the face of the Lord' (Jonah 1.1–2). This

8 Jonah and the whale, wall-painting in Härkeberga church, Sweden. This wall-painting is the work of the fifteenth-century artist Albertus Pictor in a village church north of Stockholm. As in *Patience*, l. 251, Jonah enters the whale's mouth while the sailors are still holding him. On the left he is shown emerging from the whale, naked and cleansed. Photograph © Lennart Karlsson.

gives no explanation for Jonah's contrariness. The poet, in contrast, presents this as a lack of those virtues that the narrator has character-ized as *pacience*: his immediate reaction is anger and rebelliousness (74), his motive is fear rather than a patient acceptance of whatever his Lord ordains. He lets his fearful imagination run away with him, supposing that the Ninevites will imprison and shackle him, lock him in the stocks and put his eyes out (79–80). Since God has described the Ninevites' wickedness, Jonah's fear is understandable, but his stupidity in supposing that by going to sea he can escape God's power (109–12) cancels any sympathy we might have. The narrator comments:

> Lo, þe wytles wrechche! For he wolde noȝt suffer,
> Now hatz he put hym in plyt of peril wel more. *plyt* danger
>
> (113–14)

Jonah's character, as it is gradually revealed, combines childish intemperance with occasional moments of dignity. When he professes his faith in the God of Israel to the sailors (205–12), and in the belly of the whale utters a devout psalm of obedience to his Lord (305–36), he admirably demonstrates patience in adversity. Yet he is constantly grumbling (*janglande* 90, 433) about God, always ready to burst into anger (410–11, 481), and so filled with chagrin because his prophecy of the destruction of Nineveh is proved untrue that he petulantly asks for death (424–8).

The poet adds three major set-piece descriptions to the biblical account, in the style characteristic of alliterative poetry. The first is the embarkation from Joppa (97–108), itemizing the procedures of setting sail in the 'fayr schyp': the sailors weigh anchor, attach the reserve bowline to the bowsprit, tug at the guy ropes to release the mainsail, and set a course so as to catch the wind. (There is a similar scene in the alliterative *Morte Arthure* 736–45.) What the poet describes is a contemporary trading ship, as depicted in plate 8, encouraging us to admire its technological sophistication and then to reflect on Jonah's idiocy in thinking that he will be safe from God hidden under its strong hatches. The next scene, the storm at sea (137–64), is a favourite with the alliterative poets, and it gives them full rein to exploit the onomatopoeic effects of the verse-form (Jacobs 1972). The *Patience*-poet gives a particularly fine example of the topos. God commands the winds to blow, so that the violent storm batters the magnificent ship and smashes its gear. Not even the finest product of human skill can withstand the elements. The evidence of God's awesome power heightens the absurdity of Jonah's attempt to disobey. The third and most daring elaboration is the description of Jonah's passage into the guts of the whale (269–76), and naturally enough this has no parallel in alliterative verse. There can be no more conclusive demonstration of the necessity of patience than to be confined inside a whale, and the predicament finally inspires Jonah to utter a heartfelt prayer of submission. This is the high point of his reconciliation to the divine will, but it is only adversity that prompts his meekness: 'he knawez hym in care þat couþe not in sele' (296) – 'he recognizes him in trouble when he could not in happiness'.

After God has pardoned the Ninevites, Jonah falls again, angrily rebuking God and retiring 'al joyles and janglande' (433) to a vantage point, still hoping some disaster will befall the city. Now God teaches him a second lesson in patience, causing a fine ivy to grow to form a delightfully cool shelter, 'a hous as hit were' (450). Jonah is childishly pleased, and lies lolling beneath it all day, but during the night God sends a worm to destroy the root, and orders Zephyrus to blow his hot wind. The loss of his shelter is just the kind of minor misfortune that Jonah should have learnt to accept with patience, but instead he calls out passionately to God 'with hatel anger and hot' (481). God asks Jonah very reasonably:

> Is þis ryȝtwys, þou renk, alle þy ronk noyse,
> So wroth for a wodbynde to wax so sone?   (490–2)

[Is this just, my man, all your rebellious noise, to get so angry so quickly for an ivy?]

Jonah is incorrigible: in the belly of the whale he acknowledged that those who set their hopes on 'þink þat mountes to noȝt' – 'something that amounts to nothing' – forfeit God's mercy (330–2), but already he has forgotten. Briefly he is a model of patience, but his demonstration of impatience and its consequences is what we remember. Instead the virtue of patience is exemplified by God and his creation: the elements and the whale. The poet stresses the obedience of the winds, keen (*bayn*) to carry out God's command (136), and the whale which vomits Jonah onto dry land 'as bede hym oure Lorde' (340). As in Virgil, the winds are given names, Ewrus and Aquiloun, and are furthermore endowed with human characteristics: 'Þay wakened wel þe wroþeloker, for wroþely he cleped' (132) – 'they awoke so much the more angrily, for God called angrily'. As this line shows, God shares the same passions as Jonah: his anger is expressed by the word *wrath* (403, 518), and in his first word to Jonah he declares the wickedness of the Ninevites to be so great that 'I may not abide' (70; cf. *abyde* 7). Can even God his 'hert stere'? The poet's point is that if God did not feel impetuous anger he could hardly be a witness to the virtue of controlling anger, and so his patience could not act as a corrective to Jonah's lack of control. At the repentance of the Ninevites God held back his vengeance even though he had vowed otherwise (408), and in fury Jonah praises him sarcastically for just those qualities that he himself does not possess:

Wel knew I þi cortaysye, þy quoynt soffraunce,
Þy bounté of debonerté and þy bene grace,
Þy longe abydyng wyth lur, þy late vengaunce;
And ay þy mercy is mete, be mysse never so huge.   (417–20)

[I well knew your courtesy, your gracious patience, the generosity of
your kindness and your loving grace, your long sufferance with injury,
your slow vengeance; and your mercy is ever sufficient, however great
the sin.]

In his long speech to Jonah that ends the poem, God explains that
it is natural for him to care for his own creation, and directly contrasts
his own patience, his ability to *þole*, with Jonah's impetuosity:

Wer I as hastif as þou, heere, were harme lumpen;
Couþe I not þole bot as þou, þer þryved ful fewe.
I may not be so malicious and mylde be halden.   (520–3)

[If I were as hasty as you, sir, harm would be done. If I couldn't be
more patient than you, very few would survive. I couldn't be regarded
as merciful if I were so ill-willed.]

In the spare narrative of the Book of Jonah, God expresses no emotion of any kind, and Jonah's fury meets an impenetrable deity. Yet
other books of the Old Testament often present a God of anger, jealousy, love and generosity. The God of *Patience* stands in stark contrast
to the hidden God of *The Cloud of Unknowing*, and yet the God of
passion is entirely within the Judaeo-Christian tradition, looking forward to the Incarnation when Christ takes on human nature.

The traditional interpretation of Jonah, based on Christ's words in
the Gospels of Matthew and Luke, is that he was a precursor of
Christ, his three days in the whale prefiguring the time that Christ
spent in the heart of the earth after his Crucifixion (Matthew 12.40),
and a sign to the present generation of their need for the repentance
of the Ninevites (Luke 11.30–2). The poet alludes to this interpretation (96, 274–5), underlining that in most respects Jonah was everything Christ was not, in this sense the antithesis of Christ. Jonah
hides from the danger in fear that he might be cruelly torn apart on a
cross, 'on rode rwly torent' (96); Christ, by becoming man, willingly

accepts the dangers of his role as redeemer of sin. Ironically, Jonah redeems the Ninevites, despite all his efforts not to.

The religious plays offered an even more direct way of bringing the biblical stories to life, described in *A Tretise of Miraclis Pleyinge* as *quike bookis* – 'living books' – to instruct the unlearned (380). The four great cycles of mystery plays that survive, the York Plays, the Chester Plays, the Towneley Plays (perhaps from Wakefield), and the N-Town Plays from East Anglia, present the chief episodes of the Bible story from the Creation to the Last Judgement. In the surviving text of the York cycle some 47 plays are recorded. York civic and guild records provide the fullest evidence on staging, and moreover demonstrate the cultural prestige attached to the enterprise (Beadle 1994, 85–98). In York and other urban centres the plays were organized and performed by the powerful organizations of civic trades, the guilds (Tydeman 1994, 2–3). Plays were performed on separate pageant wagons that moved through the town in procession, stopping at a number of stations, usually 12 in York. The players would assemble at first light on the feast of Corpus Christi (which is close to the longest day) just inside the city walls opposite the modern railway station, and then the first pageant, the tanners' (*barkers*) Fall of the Angels, would begin outside Holy Trinity Priory (Beadle 1982, 30–9; Twycross 1994, 39–41). This would then move to the next station down Micklegate towards the river Ouse, and the second pageant, the plasterers' play of the Creation, would take its place. Soon the whole of the route would be occupied with performances. By the end of the day each play to be presented would have been performed at each of the stations.

Biblical scenes such as the Fall of Man, the Flood, Abraham and Isaac, the Birth of Christ, Herod's Massacre of the Innocents, the Last Supper, and above all the Crucifixion were played out by local towns-people on small stages in intimate contact with their audiences in the city streets. No other form of representation was as immediate or as moving. 'By siche miraclis pleyinge', said *A Tretise of Miraclis Pleyinge*, 'men and wymmen, seinge the passioun of Crist and of his seintis, ben movyd to compassion and devocion, wepinge bitere teris' (ll. 162–4). This writer condemned these expressions of sorrow because they were prompted by the sight of Christ's torments rather than by a recognition of sinfulness, yet we have seen in *Ancrene Wisse* and Richard Rolle that meditation on the physical torments of the Passion was a central element in a long tradition of affective piety. Its most wide-spread vernacular expression was in the religious lyrics, which were essentially private meditations focusing particularly on mortality and on the key events in the life of Christ and Mary. Their purpose was always to move the heart to devotion rather than to explore a doctrinal issue. As the best critic of the religious lyrics has written:

> In order that the reader of the poems may feel these emotions personally and keenly, he is persuaded by the lyric to imagine himself in a scene which will provoke them, and which is described often in minute visual detail. The reader is to imagine that he is present at the Nativity and overhears the Virgin comforting her Child, or that he is present at the Crucifixion and that Christ on the Cross appeals to him personally for compassion. (Woolf 1968, 19)

Lyrics on the Crucifixion may linger over the sufferings of Christ, and such verses would have been entirely suitable to aid the devotions prescribed by the author of *Ancrene Wisse*:

> Quanne hic se on rode
> Jesu mi lemman,
> An besiden him stonden
> Marie an Johan,
> And his rig iswongen,
> And his side istungen
> For þe luve of man,
> Wel ow hic to wepen
> And sinnes forleten
> Yif hic of luve kan,
> Yif hic of luve kan,
> Yif hic of luve kan.   (Brown 1932, no. 35b)

[When I see Jesus my beloved on the cross and Mary and John standing beside him, and his back lashed and his side pierced for the love of man, well ought I to weep and abandon sin if I know of love.]

Here we might suppose that the penitent is gazing at a picture of the Crucifixion, such as that reproduced as plate 7. Even more moving is the direct address by the crucified Christ to the penitent at the foot of the cross (which in reality might indeed be a crucifix). Here Christ lovingly reproaches the sorrower for not responding to his sufferings and matching his love. In his preaching book John of Grimestone records a touching example based on the Old Testament Lamentations:

> 3e þat pasen be þe wey3e,
>   Abidet a litel stounde.
> Beholdet, al mi felawes,
>   3ef ani me lik is founde.
> To þe tre with nailes þre
>   Wol fast I hange bounde.
> With a spere al þoru mi side
>   To min herte is mad a wounde.   (*BOME* 14m)

[You who pass by the way, wait a short moment. Behold, all my companions, if any is found like me. I hang fixed firmly to the wood with three nails. Through my side a wound to my heart is made by a spear.]

The dramatists draw directly on this tradition of affective piety, at times incorporating devotional lyrics within the plays. Thus this same motif of Christ's address from the cross is used by the York dramatist in this affecting speech at the most powerful moment in the Crucifixion play, when Christ has been brutally hammered to the cross by the soldiers (Woolf 1972, 261–2):

> Al men þat walkis by waye or strete,
> Takes tente 3e schalle no travayle tyne.
> Byholdes myn heede, myn handis and my feete,
> And fully feele nowe or 3e fyne
> Yf any mournyng may be meete
> Or myscheve mesured unto myne.
> My fadir, þat alle bales may bete,
> Forgiffis þes men þat dois me pyne;
> What þei wirke wotte þai noght;
> Therfore, my fadir, I crave
> Latte never þer synnys be sought,
> But see þer saules to save.   (253–64)

[All men who walk by way or street, pay attention so that you do not fail to see the suffering. Behold my head, my hands and my feet, and fully experience before you finish if any misery may be equal or suffering matched to mine. My Father, who may heal all evils, forgive these men who inflict pain on me: they know not what they do. Therefore, my Father, I beg you not to let their sins be examined, but ensure their souls are saved.]

Here the playwright has combined the words of Lamentations used in the Grimestone lyric with Christ's words of forgiveness in Luke 23.34, 'Father, forgive them, for they know not what they do.' The peculiar power of this moment will be appreciated when we realize that those who walk by way or street are the audience around the pageant wagon in Micklegate and Coney Street (Woolf 1968, 44).

This is the second of the two speeches that Christ utters in the play. Otherwise it is the soldiers who speak, and we see the Crucifixion through their eyes. Obviously this represents a radical shift from the Gospel accounts, in which the soldiers say no more than a few phrases. The dramatist imagines how the nailing of Christ on the cross might have been accomplished, incorporating literary meditations on the Passion as well as traditional accretions such as the Instruments of the Passion used to inflict pain on Christ (see Woolf 1968, 208–9) illustrated in plate 9. The York Crucifixion was performed by the pinners' guild so that in real life the actors were experts in metalwork and nails, and the tools of their trade, their hammers, nails, ropes and wedges, are prominently displayed like some grisly advertisement from the sponsors: 'here is a stubbe ["nail"] will stiffely stande' (102). Most horribly, these workmen have botched the initial preparations, so that the nail-holes on the cross have been bored too far apart, and therefore, causing Christ excruciating pain, they use ropes to drag his arms and legs to reach the holes before hammering the nails through his hands and feet.

The soldiers are craftsmen who take unjustifiable pride in their work, oblivious of the evil and cruelty of what they are doing. And we, the audience, become absorbed in it too, carried along by the rapid interchange of their conversation, so we are brought up short by Christ's dignified address to us. This is the most powerful of all the cycle plays in its depiction of the sufferings of Christ and the contrasting casual brutality of man. In the Middle Ages the crucifix was the central symbol of Christianity; it hung in front of the altar as the centrepiece of every church, and it was in all but the humblest of homes. This play is a living crucifix. The setting is simple – a central mound where the cross is to be placed; the only actors are Christ and the four soldiers chatting at the foot of the cross. Christ is nailed to the cross while it is on the

9 Christ's arms with the Instruments of the Passion, York Minster MS
XVI.K.6, f. 44v.
This is a woodcut attached to an early fifteenth-century Book of Hours. It
offers pardon to 'who sum ever devoutely behoildith thes armys of criste',
depicting the scourges, spear, crown of thorns, sponge, cords, pincers,
nails and hammer. Ker and Piper (1992, 727–30). Reproduced by kind
permission of the Dean and Chapter of York.

ground. Then the cross is raised on the mound with great suffering – ironically the dialogue is entirely concerned with the soldiers' sufferings, not Christ's. Visually Christ is the central figure in the action, and so it is remarkable that he hardly speaks at all. The attention of the audience is distracted by the busy activity and non-stop chatter of the soldiers. In the first of two majestic speeches Christ ignores the soldiers' everyday busyness and lovingly professes his obedience to God's plan of redemption; in other words, his 'patience':

> Almyghty God, my fadir free,
> Late þis materes be made in mynde.
> Þou badde þat I schulde buxsome be
> For Adam plyght for to be pyned.
> Here to dede I obblisshe me
> Fro þat synne for to save mankynde,
> And soveraynely beseke I þe
> That þai for me may favoure fynde
> And fro þe fende þame fende,
> So þat þer saules be saffe
> In welthe withouten ende;
> I kepe nought ellis to crave.   (49–60)

[Almighty God, my gracious Father, let these events be remembered. You ordered me to be obedient and to be tortured for Adam's sin. Here I submit myself to death to save mankind from that sin, and I ask you especially that they may find favour through me and defend themselves from the devil, so that their souls are safe in everlasting happiness. I ask for nothing else.]

In his second speech, as he hangs high above the soldiers and the audience in centre stage calling on all people to gaze at him on the cross, he again asks God that the soldiers may be redeemed. These generous and caring sentiments are in marked contrast to anything the soldiers have to say. Both Christ's speeches occupy a full, elaborate rhyming stanza, stately and measured in contrast to the soldiers' mundane, colloquial interchanges, which are barely contained within the tight stanzaic form:

> *2 Sold.*   We twoo schall see tille aythir side,
> For ellis þis werke wille wrie all wrang.

3 Sold.	We are redy.
4 Sold.	Gode sirs, abide,
	And late me first his fete up fang.
2 Sold.	Why tente ȝe so to tales þis tyde?
1 Sold.	Lifte uppe!
4 Sold.	Latte see!
2 Sold.	Owe, lifte alang!
3 Sold.	Fro all þis harme he schulde hym hyde
	And he war God.
4 Sold.	Þe devill hym hang.
1 Sold.	For grete harme have I hente!
	My schuldir is in soundre.
2 Sold.	And sertis I am nere schente,
	So lange have I borne undir. (181–92)

[*2 Sold.* The two of us will see to either side (of the body), otherwise this work will go all wrong. *3 Sold.* We're ready. *4 Sold.* Good sirs, wait, and let me first take up his feet. *2 Sold.* Why do you spend so much time chattering? *1 Sold.* Lift up! *4 Sold.* Let's see! *2 Sold.* Oh, lift it along! *3 Sold.* If he were God he would avoid all this pain. *4 Sold.* The devil hang him! *1 Sold.* I'm in real pain! My shoulder's in pieces. *2 Sold.* Certainly I'm about done in, I've been lifting for so long.]

In this play the Crucifixion is not just a historical event but something that takes place all around us. By our everyday actions, we, the audience, are the crucifiers. There's nothing exceptionally wicked about the soldiers, our friends and neighbours talking with familiar York-shire accents. For them the Crucifixion is just another job; it has no special significance. They make a few sarcastic comments on Christ's claim to be special, so when Christ says 'Forgive them, they know not what they do' it is all too evidently true. They are present at the Crucifixion but essentially miss it. The play ends with Christ hanging high above on the cross as the soldiers beneath him quarrel over who is to have his clothes: majesty and meanness. The soldiers represent us, and the playwright's purpose is to convey the common Christian message that we all contribute every day to the Crucifixion, not through any special evil in us but through ordinary and casual blind-ness and lack of concern, mixed with occasional brutality and the random desire to cause someone pain.

The Death of a Child

The only Gospel to mention the Virgin Mary at the Crucifixion is John's, in which she stands at the foot of the cross with the two other Marys. Nothing is said of her tears or grief. As the emphasis upon the sufferings of Christ increased from the twelfth century, so it was natural to dwell upon his mother's grief at his death (Woolf 1968, 239–73). Mary, the bereaved mother, weeps, wrings her hands and tears her face, like any mother who has lost a child. One lyric describes her distress as she recalls Christ as her infant son:

> My sone is go, my joy and my blys,   *is go* has gone
> Alas, y sawe my dere chylde blede,
> He may not speke to modur his.   *modur his* his mother
> I lullyd hym, y lapped hym, y wolde him fede,
>   [*lullyd* soothed; *lapped* fondled]
> So cruelly wes nevyr childe slayn ywys.   *ywys* indeed
>   (Brown 1939, no. 6, ll. 16–20)

Christ's blood can be tracked through the streets like a wounded animal's (33–4). Mary accuses the Jews of being uniquely pitiless:

> Cursyd Jues, why dude ye þusse?   *dude* did
> How durste ye sle youre savyoure?   (109–10)

Because Mary shares our human pain, we may appeal to her pity to act as intercessor for us with her son, arguing the case for mercy to outweigh justice.

The Prioress's Tale is an exploration of affective piety in its purest form, and Chaucer appropriately drew on a class of stories, the Miracles of the Virgin, which demonstrate Mary's compassion for the innocent, choosing a particular story that re-enacts the Virgin's grief for the loss of her son. The Prioress prefaces her tale with an elegant hymn of praise to the Virgin as both mother and intercessor, who so well understands our need that she gains for us her son's grace even before we think of praying for it. The tale is of the little boy killed by Jews for singing a hymn in honour of the Virgin; miraculously he continues singing even after he has been murdered, so that his body is discovered and the crime revealed. There are Latin versions of the story, and one in English in the Vernon manuscript, Bodley MS Eng. Poet. a.1, of about the same date as Chaucer's version (ed. Horstmann 1892, 141–5). In Vernon it is one of a set of Miracles of the Virgin, and is headed by a grisly illustration of scenes of the story (Scott 1996, i, col. pl. 3). Both versions of the story concentrate on its emotive power. In the Vernon poem the child is a beggar who earns his food by singing through the streets *Alma Redemptoris Mater*, 'Godus Moder, mylde and clene' (24). When he goes missing, his mother searches for him 'wiþ syk and serwe in everi strete' (61). Chaucer deepens the pathos by adding much more detail: the 'litel child', as he is called again and again, is just seven, and so he has started at 'a litel scole of Cristen folk' (*CT* VII.495) on the edge of the Jewish quarter of the city. His widowed mother has instilled in him such reverence for the Virgin that he falls to his knees to pray at the shrines to the Mother of Christ along the road. The loving relationship between little boy and widowed mother is painfully evoked by her fearful anxiety as she searches through the streets for him 'with face pale of drede and bisy thoght' (589), calling on Christ's mother all the while. Her devastation at finding his little dead body is implicitly a parallel to the Virgin's grief at the Crucifixion, and explicitly likened to the sorrow of the Old Testament Rachel weeping for her children (627).

Such uncomplicated goodness is countered by an equally straight-forward idea of evil. The sweet and pure innocence of the child is snuffed out by the malice of the Jews, in whose heart Satan has established 'his waspes nest' (559). The wanton cruelty of the murder is highlighted by the detail that the little body was thrown into a cesspit where, the Prioress adds gratuitously, 'thise Jewes purgen hire entraille' (573). Here, attracted by his sweet singing, his mother finds him. There can be no consolation for her in her terrible grief, but there can be judicial satisfaction in the equally terrible retribution meted out to the Jews. All those who know of the murder, not just those directly involved, are drawn by wild horses and hanged, on the principle that 'yvele shal have that yvele wol deserve' (632).

The piety of the tale is both genuine and moving, entirely of the heart. Christ praised such piety in words cited in *Pearl*: 'hys ryche no wyȝ myȝt wynne / Bot he com þyder ryȝt as a chylde' (722–3, from Luke 18.17) – 'no one might reach his kingdom unless he entered just as a child'. Inevitably, the little child's devotion is utterly unre-flective, as is emphasized in the circumstantial account of how he learnt by rote the hymn that so incensed the Jews, without any appreciation of its meaning:

> Noght wiste he what this Latyn was to seye,
> For he so yong and tendre was of age.   (523–4)

His older school-friend can teach him the notes, but even he only knows that *Alma Redemptoris* is a hymn in honour of the Virgin, since he understands only a little Latin: 'I lerne song; I kan but smal grammeere' (536).

By strengthening the impact of the tale, by setting sweet innocence side by side with harsh cruelty, the compassion of the Virgin with stern lack of compassion, by giving the story to a narrator whose own piety as described in the General Prologue is at best shallow, and placing it in a context of tales that deal more subtly in the shades of grey that lie between black and white, Chaucer allows the nature of this naive devotion to be seen as both admirable and questionable. Innocence is necessarily ignorance; Jews are necessarily evil, just as monks are always holy. Except that they are not, and the Prioress herself momentarily lifts the curtain onto a grown-up world of complex and compromised morality when she says:

> This abbot, which that was an hooly man
> As monkes been – or elles oghte be.   (642–3)

The Virgin's miracle serves to identify the killers but in other respects it resolves nothing. In some versions of the story she restores the child to life, but in Chaucer's story the bereaved mother, together with the abbot and his followers, are left weeping at his marble tomb.

Pearl is also concerned with the death of a small child, but in marked contrast to the Prioress, the author offers a theodicy of loss, an explanation of death and bereavement in terms of the divine order (Aers 1993). In both texts a leading theme is innocence, exemplified by the Maiden Mother whose symbols include 'the white lylye flour' (*CT* VII.461) and the 'bussh unbrent' (*CT* VII.468). Both symbols focus on her virginity, innocence in the sense of sexual purity: the spotless lily of the Song of Songs, and the burning bush that remains inviolate after the Incarnation. The pearl-maiden who died as a baby before she could know sin has become a little queen in the court of

Mary, Queen of Heaven, by virtue of her innocence, for 'þe innosent is ay saf by ry3t' (*Pearl* 684). Together with the little boy of the Prioress's Tale, the pearl-maiden has become one of the 144,000 virgin followers of the Lamb as described by 'the grete evaungelist, Seint John' (cf. *CT* VII.579–85 with *Pearl* 785–92). The argument of *Pearl* is that virgin innocents will secure the highest place in heaven.

The poem opens by describing the inconsolable grief of a father who flings himself on the grave of his spotless pearl. He characterizes his despair as a state of mind which is outside the control of reason:

> Bifore þat spot my honde I spennd,
> For care ful colde þat to me ca3t;
> A devely dele in my hert denned,
> Þa3 resoun sette myselven sa3t.
> I playned my perle þat þer watz penned
> Wyth fyrce skyllez þat faste fa3t;
> Þa3 kynde of Kryst me comfort kenned,
> My wreched wylle in wo ay wra3t.   (49–56)

[I clasped my hands by that spot because of chill sorrow that clutched me. A dismal sorrow took refuge in my heart, though reason offered me peace. With fierce arguments that struggled violently, I grieved for my pearl enclosed there. Though Christ's nature taught me comfort, my wretched will continually suffered in sorrow.]

There is here a recognition that Christ, who has shared our experience as suffering man, is ready as eternal Lord to offer us comfort if only we will take it; but the narrator is sunk so deep in misery that he is unable to grasp the proffered hand.

Is his grief reprehensible, a self-indulgence that cuts him off from grace? Influenced by the Stoic philosophers, the early church had been suspicious of the expression of grief, seeing it as an abnegation of reason and a loss of self-control, but St Bernard in a sermon on his brother's death had accepted grief as natural and proper (Woolf 1968, 241; Kean 1967, 234). The fittingness of grief could be demonstrated by a reminder that 'Jesus wept' at the death of his friend Lazarus (John 11.35). A range of views on grief is set out at the beginning of Chaucer's Tale of Melibee, where Dame Prudence quotes Seneca to her husband: 'The wise man shal nat take to greet disconfort for the deeth of his children but, certes, he sholde suffren it in pacience'

(*CT* VII.984–5). Melibee protests that Christ himself wept, and Prudence concedes that grief is proper in moderation: 'though attempree ["moderate"] wepyng be ygraunted ["allowed"], outrageous wepyng certes is deffended ["prohibited"]' (990).

In his dream the bereaved father meets his baby daughter, now miraculously transformed into a queen in heaven. Abashed at finding her so changed 'in so strange a place' (175), he ventures to tell her of the depth of his sense of loss:

> 'O Perle,' quoþ I, 'in perlez pyȝt,
> Art þou my perle þat I haf playned,
> Regretted by my one on nyȝte?
> Much longeyng haf I for þe layned
> Syþen into gresse þou me aglyȝte.' (241–5)

[‘O Pearl,’ I said, ‘adorned in pearls, are you my pearl that I’ve mourned for, wept about alone at night? I’ve concealed much sorrow for you since you slipped away from me into the grass.’]

Her reply is a cold reproof: 'Sir, ȝe haf your tale mysetente' (257) – 'Sir, you've spoken in error.' From her point of view her father's grief is merely foolish, a fixation on the past, since the rose he lost, fading as all things in nature do, has become a pearl of great price in a heavenly jewel-box:

> Bot, jueler gente, if þou schal lose
> Þy joy for a gemme þat þe watz lef,
> Me þynk þe put in a mad porpose
> And busyez þe aboute a raysoun bref.
> For þat þou lestez watz bot a rose
> Þat flowred and fayled as kynde hyt gef;
> Now þurȝ kynde of þe kyste þat hyt con close,
> To a perle of prys hit is put in pref. (265–72)

[But, noble jeweller, if you're going to lose your joy for a jewel that was precious to you, it seems to me you're set on a crazy course and you trouble yourself about an ephemeral matter. What you lost was merely a rose that flowered and died as nature intended; now through the nature of the jewel-case that encloses it, this has proved to be a pearl of great price.]

Expressing his reassurance that he can now be reunited with his pearl for ever, the dreamer is comprehensively snubbed for his foolishness (289–300). This conversation of mutual incomprehension continues, touching but at the same time comic. It is quite pointless, she tells him briskly, to argue with God, to struggle and bray like a deer in its death agonies; rather beg for his mercy, and perhaps God may ease your sorrow (337–60). The dreamer does his best to win his daughter's good graces, but every mention of his grief receives a contemptuous rebuke. He must 'forsake þe worlde' (743) and give up dwelling on his memories. The maiden is right, of course, as those in heaven must be, since they 'þurȝoutly haven cnawyng' (859) – 'have complete understanding'. From her perspective, the dreamer's grief is unreasonable, a self-indulgence and a rebellion against God's providence. How else could she see it? She can have had no experience of grief as a baby, and even if she had experienced sorrow in life, that 'mornyng' would have been erased by her heavenly state (262) (Putter 1996, 185). Yet as we acknowledge the rightness of the maiden's arguments, we must sympathize with the dreamer who so powerfully expresses those emotions that all humans share.

Eventually, though still complaining that she takes too little notice of his misery, he acknowledges that he is happy to find her prospering so well (385–96), and asks her to give him an account of the ways of heaven. This is a significant advance in the dreamer's position, to which his daughter responds with more conciliatory replies. Previously preoccupied with his loss, the dreamer now realizes that in order to come to terms with it he needs to understand the point and justice of it. Hence his brave persistence, polite but quite determined, in asking questions which he knows will seem ignorant to his know-all daughter. To us, earthbound as he is, the questions seem entirely reasonable. How can she be queen of heaven since that position is reserved for the Virgin Mary: 'may þys be trwe?' (421). She explains that all in heaven are kings or queens; but he raises the objection that gets to the heart of the issue: since she lived less than two years and was too young to serve God in any way, how could it be right for her to be made queen on her very first day in heaven (483–6)? She replies with the example of Christ's Parable of the Workers in the Vineyard, in which at the end of the day all received the same reward however long they had worked. The authority of Christ himself might have sufficed for anyone with less need to understand, yet the dreamer persists: 'Me þynk þy tale unresounable' (590). He knows his Bible too, and quotes the psalm-verse which says that all will be rewarded according to their just deserts (595–6). Her reply is that all alike may win grace: those who have sinned gain it through contrition and repentance, but the innocent receive the supreme pearl of great price 'by ry3t' (720).

The dreamer, questioning and objecting, sometimes abasing himself ('I am bot mokke and mul ["dust"]' 905), confusing the Heavenly Jerusalem with the city in Judea, mundanely envisaging its inhabitants as 'a pakke of joly juele' (929), is at the end entranced by the vision granted to him of his daughter (1147) in the procession following the Lamb through the heavenly city. Significantly, his gaze is only briefly held by the vision of the Lamb with wound wide and wet (1135), for he spots 'my lyttel quene' (1147). Once again his 'luf-longyng' (1152) overwhelms him, and driven by his human passion ('my manez mynde' 1154), he plunges madly into the river that separates him from the city. Even if he has acknowledged intellectually that he must remain separated from his beloved daughter until death, grief is not so quickly assuaged. The impetuous act wakes him from his glorious dream, and with dismay he says ruefully 'Now al be to þat Pryncez paye' (1176) – 'may all be as the Lord pleases'. He has accepted the truth of the Pearl's argument that it is madness to fight the will of God, but still he suffers 'a longeyng hevy' (1180). The knowledge that his baby daughter is so highly honoured in heaven leaves him with conflicting feelings that he expresses with precision: 'So wel is me in þys doel-doungoun' (1187) – 'I'm glad in this dungeon of sorrow.' He realizes he can only entrust his pearl to God's care, and does so in the formulaic words of benediction used by father to daughter: 'in Krystez dere blessyng and myn' (1208). The bereaved father, isolated by the depth of his misery (Aers 1993), at last expresses some sense of reintegration within the Christian community through Christ

> Þat in the forme of bred and wyn
> Þe preste us schewez uch a daye.
> He gef us to be his homly hyne
> Ande precious perlez unto his paye.   (1209–12)

[whom the priest shows us every day in the form of bread and wine. Christ grant that we might be servants of his household and precious pearls to please him.]

In these, his final words, the pronoun which had always been 'I' is now 'us'. This may represent an acceptance in some sense, but what remains is his misery at his final and indeed tragic separation from his daughter.

Pearl explores the conflict between grief and faith, emotion and reason, and recognizes the validity of grief, however illogical it is from the perspective of eternal bliss. The most devastating human emotion is mourning for the death of a child, and that cannot be dispelled even within the context of firm belief in the afterlife.

CHAPTER 6

Love and Marriage

Marriage and Love – and Sex

The plot of *Sir Orfeo* is driven by the deep love between Orfeo and his wife, which they express to one another in the most heartfelt terms. When Herodis realizes she will be snatched away by the fairy king, she says:

> Allas mi lord, Sir Orfeo,
> Seþþen we first togider were,
> Ones wroþ never we nere,
> Bot ever ich have yloved þe
> As mi liif, and so þou me.   (120–4)

[Alas my lord, Sir Orfeo, from the time that we were first together we were never once angry, but I've loved you always as my life, as you have loved me.]

Orfeo, having lost 'þe quen mi wiif' (178) apparently for ever, abandons his kingdom and wealth in his grief and retreats to the wilderness. When he sees Herodis there riding with the undead, they communicate their longing for one another by looks alone:

> ʒern he biheld hir, and sche him eke,
> Ac noiþer to oþer a word no speke.   (323–4)

[He looked at her longingly and she looked at him too, but neither spoke a word to the other.]

'Allas,' says Orfeo, 'whi nil min hert breke?' (338).

Though this is a romance, *Sir Orfeo*'s tender evocation of love within marriage presumably bears some relation to reality, if not to 'the actual practice of feudal society' as imagined by C. S. Lewis in an influential polemic at the beginning of *The Allegory of Love*: 'Marriages had nothing to do with love, and no "nonsense" about marriage was tolerated. All matches were matches of interest. . . . According to the medieval view passionate love itself was wicked, and did not cease to be wicked if the object of it were your wife' (Lewis 1936, 13–14). It would be perverse to suppose that some married couples did not love one another at least some of the time. It is true that first person accounts of married love are difficult to come by, and not necessarily trustworthy. Probably the most authentic is by Christine de Pizan, who married Étienne du Castel when she was about 16; the marriage was by her account a happy one, and when her husband died after 10 years of marriage, she expressed her profound grief in a variety of writings, including this poignant *ballade*:

> What can I do? It's not surprising that I weep and sigh, with my dear lover dead. For when I look deeply into my heart and see how sweetly and without hardship I lived from my childhood and first youth with him, I am assailed by such great pain that I will always weep for his death. (trans. Blumenfeld-Kosinski and Brownlee 1997, 6)

In fact, so far from demoting or condemning marital affection, the church encouraged couples to love one another, and so far from promoting marriage as merely an economic arrangement, the church defined the basis of marriage as consent (*consensus*) (Brooke 1989, 137–9). Without the consent of each of the partners, freely and validly given, a marriage did not exist; with consent given, nothing else needed to exist to establish marriage. There must be a verbal agreement 'through words or other clear signs', according to the theologian Peter Lombard, who continues: 'That pledge of words through which they consent, saying "I accept you as my husband, and I you as my wife", makes marriage' (trans. McCarthy 2004, 23). Therefore it was not necessary for marriage to take place in church, or in the presence of witnesses or even a priest, though such clandestine marriages were condemned by the authorities and the now-married couple would have to undergo penance. Inevitably clandestine marriages resulted in all kinds of problems and misunderstandings, deliberate or otherwise, and the ecclesiastical courts spent a great deal of time over matrimonial cases. Nevertheless, the church continued to teach that marriage was a sacrament between two people in the presence of God. One clear case of a clandestine marriage is this scene:

> John Beke, saddler, sitting down on a bench of that house, called in English 'le Sidebynke', called the said Marjory to him and said to her: 'Sit with me'. Acquiescing in this, she sat down. John said to her: 'Marjory, do you wish to be my wife?' And she replied: 'I will if you wish.' And taking at once the said Marjory's right hand, John said: 'Marjory, here I take you as my wife, for better or worse, to have and to hold until the end of my life, and of this I give you my faith.' The said Marjory replied to him: 'Here I take you, John, as my husband, to have and to hold until the end of my life, and of this I give you my faith.' And then the said John kissed the said Marjory through a wreath of flowers, in English 'Garland'. (trans. Helmholz 1974, 28–9)

The view of marriage as essentially a private contract between two people did indeed conflict with the other view of it as a social institution. Social and economic considerations have usually been the major factor in marriage in all societies (Stone 1979, 181–2). Only in modern western society has personal affection, 'romance', been elevated as the sole reason for two people to get married, often without taking full account of the more mundane role of marriage. It was essential for landowners to have legally recognized heirs so that they could pass on their estates smoothly, and to marry their children to partners who would form valuable alliances, consolidate their wealth and extend their power. Although 'consent' implies free choice, it can seldom have been truly free at any level of society, and it was least free in aristocratic society. Royal and noble children were sometimes 'married' as babies in order to secure an alliance between two families, although the marriage had to be confirmed when the children reached the age of consent (at least 14 for a boy, about 12 for a girl) (Brooke 1989, 137–8). The financial and legal arrangements had to be carefully negotiated: the bridegroom's family would expect to receive a substantial cash sum, and land had to be settled on the young couple as a 'jointure'. In extreme cases women who were irresistibly attractive in terms of their wealth and status were abducted and forcibly married, though technically (and sometimes actually) such forced marriages could be annulled. Even peasant marriages were tightly regulated, not only by families themselves anxious to ensure the descent of land they held, but also in the interest of the lord, who demanded clearly defined and secure arrangements to ensure the efficient and long-term cultivation of his estates, and who was entitled to levy various taxes on the marriages of his bondmen (Dyer 2002, 156–9; Schofield 2003, 90–9). The Reeve's Tale gives a cynical view of marriage arrangements in rural society, as the parish priest settles the marriage of his illegitimate daughter with the miller:

> With hire he yaf ful many a panne of bras   *yaf* gave
> For that Symkyn sholde in his blood allye.
>> [*in his blood allye* ally with his family]
> She was yfostred in a nonnerye,   *yfostred* brought up
> For Symkyn wolde no wyf, as he sayde,
> But she were wel ynorissed and a mayde,   *ynorissed* educated
> To saven his estaat of yomanrye.   (*CT* I. 3944–9)
>> [*To saven . . . yomanrye* To preserve his standing as a freeholder.]

All of these considerations meant that a simple love-match was very much the exception, and that love might more often be expected as the fruit of marriage rather than its motive. Even so, some women were stubborn enough to resist every pressure and to marry their heart's desire, whatever the consequences. In 1469 Margery Paston secretly married the family bailiff, Richard Calle, so the family called in the bishop to see if their clandestine arrangement constituted a binding marriage. The interview is described by Margery's mother:

> The bysschop . . . seyd þat he had hard ['heard'] sey þat sche loved seche on ['such a man'] þat here frend ['family'] were not plesyd wyth þat sche xuld ['should'] have, and therefore he bad here be ryth wel avysyd how sche ded ['consider very carefully how she behaved'], and seyd þat he woold ['wanted to'] undyrstond þe worddys þat sche had seyd to hym, wheythere ['(to decide) whether'] yt mad matramony ore not. And sche rehersyd ['repeated'] wat sche had seyd, and seyd yf thoo worddys mad yt not suhere ['sure'], sche seyd boldly þat sche wold make yt suerhere ['more sure'] ore þan ['before'] sche went thens, fore sche seyde sche thowthe ['thought'] in here conschens sche was bownd, watsoevere the worddys wern. Thes leud ['rude'] worddys gereve ['grieve'] me and here grandam as myche as all þe remnawnte ['rest']. (*Paston Letters*, I.342)

Margery got her Richard, but the family disowned her.

Margery's relationship with Calle is captured in the phrase *derne love*, 'secret love', used in the lyrics to suggest an affair that is unreliable and inherently unstable (Donaldson 1970, 19–20):

> Lutel wot hit any mon
> Hou derne love may stonde.   (Brook 1968, 32.1–2)

[Little does anyone know how long secret love will last.]

In his secret affair this disappointed lover concludes 'þe love of hire ne lesteþ nowyht ["at all"] longe' (32.5). The problems caused by *derne love* in the social world is the subject matter of several of these love-lyrics in MS Harley 2253, which describe the lover isolated by the intensity of his passion, but always surrounded by a bustling and intrusive world (Turville-Petre 1996, 206–11). One lyric describes the helter-skelter of spring, the sweet love-song of the nightingale, flowers blooming, birds courting, the whole of nature busy with wooing, but the lover standing outside all of this alone in misery:

> ʒef me shal wonte wille of on,
> Þis wunne weole y wole forgon
> Ant wyht in wode be fleme.   (*BOME* 14h, 34–6)

[If I should fail to have my way with a certain woman, I'll abandon this joyful happiness and become a fugitive in the wood.]

Another lyric records the intimate conversation between a would-be lover and a briefly resistant woman, who is well aware of the risks of being caught with a man of whom her family disapprove:

> Þou art wayted day ant nyht   *wayted* watched
> Wiþ fader ant al my kynne.   *Wiþ* By
> Be þou in mi bour ytake,
>   Lete þey for no synne
> Me to holde ant þe to slon;
>   Þe deþ so þou maht wynne.   (*BOME* 14j, 35–40)

[*Be ... wynne* If you are caught in my bedroom they won't hesitate, however wicked it might be, to imprison me and slay you, and so you might earn your death.]

The moral dangers for those who *luvie derne*, 'love secretly', are traced earlier than this in the *Owl and the Nightingale*, where there is a remarkable exploration of the personal/social aspects of love. The Nightingale, as presented in the Harley Lyrics and *Troilus and Criseyde*, is associated with springtime, love and youth, and in the *Owl and the Nightingale* she speaks up for young love before marriage. The Owl, bird of the night, watches over married women as they lie sleepless with worry or misery. In their debate, the Owl accuses the Nightingale of encouraging adultery, but the Nightingale responds that she sings not for married women, who should be faithful to their husbands, but for fair maidens discovering the joys of love, to teach them how to love honourably:

> An luvie mid rihte luve
> Þane þe schal beon hire buve;
> Swiche luve ich itache and lere.   (1345–7)

[And to love with proper love the one who will be lord over her; such is the love I teach and instruct.]

She concedes that her song may indeed be misused by women who love *derne* (1357). Love, she asserts boldly, is essentially good, though it may be corrupted (1378–86). Women are by their nature easily persuaded to love (1387), but if they stumble they may then recover themselves. Sin is of two kinds, physical and spiritual, and surely the latter is worse? For there are many people who are sexually pure and yet they are companions of the Devil. The Nightingale will support unmarried women in love, even if they love *dernliche*:

> ʒef maide luveþ dernliche,
> Heo stumpeþ and falþ icundeliche,
> For þah heo sumhwile pleie
> Heo nis nout feor ut of þe weie.
> Heo mai hire guld atwende
> A rihte weie þurþ chirche bende,
> An mai eft habbe to make
> Hire leofmon wiþute sake
> An go to him bi daies lihte,
> Þat er stal to bi þeostre nihte.   (1423–32)

[If a maiden loves secretly, she stumbles and falls in a way that is natural, for though she plays around for a time she doesn't stray far from the path. She may turn aside from her sin to follow the right path by means of the bonds of the church, and may afterwards have her lover as her mate without blame, and go to him by the light of day, when she used to steal to him in the dark night.]

Such love is according to the laws of Nature because it works in co-operation with Nature to fulfil God's purpose on earth. This is an idea that we shall explore in more detail in relation to Gower's *Confessio Amantis* and Chaucer's *Parliament of Fowls*. Since love is essentially good, the maiden's clandestine affair may easily be regularized by the church. When this is done, her secret lover will become her husband, and she can love him openly rather than under cover of darkness.

The Nightingale's brief song, which begins on a high note and ends on a low, teaches the youngster (*ȝunglinge*) that giddy (*dusy*) love doesn't last long (1455–66). Because she never sings when she is breeding, she reminds married women that gadding about (*utschute* 1468) is not for them, even if they find the bonds of marriage (*spusingbendes* 1472) harsh. In final rebuttal of the Owl's accusations, she gives this unlovely picture of the adulterer going where the woman's wretched husband has been before:

> Hu miȝte þar beo eni luve
> Wanne a cheorles buc hire ley buve?
> Hu mai þar eni luve beo
> War swuch man gropeþ hire þeo? (1493–6)

[How could there be any love when a churl's gut has been lying on top of her? How could there be any love where such a man gropes her thigh?]

We might judge that the Nightingale takes an amazingly relaxed attitude for the times towards teenage intimacies; certainly Chaucer's Parson takes a much sterner line, and specifically contradicts the bird's assertion that premarital sex is in accord with natural law:

> Fornicacioun, that is bitwixe man and womman that been nat maried,
> ... is deedly synne and agayns nature. Al that is enemy and destruccioun
> to nature is agayns nature. (*CT* X.865–6)

But then the Parson also views ardent sex within marriage as sinful (*CT* X.859–60), reflecting the Augustinian position (McCarthy 2004, 108–9). There was not one monolithic view of sex; we must take into account that the Parson's Tale is a manual of sin and that the Nightingale is a bird, well aware that whatever parsons preach, things frequently happen that have to be dealt with in the most practical and sympathetic way.

When her turn comes to speak, the Owl replies that she supports married women in their tribulations. First she gives a picture of a truly wretched marriage in which the wife is powerless to improve her position. The husband spends his money on a mistress while the wife remains at home with bare walls, deprived of food and clothes. When the husband comes home, he shouts and complains like a madman, and she may get a fist in her teeth even when she has done nothing wrong (1538). Is it surprising if his wife, 'wel nesche and softe' (1546), looks elsewhere to satisfy her needs?

> He deþ þat heo nadde ear iþoht.
> Dahet þat to swuþe hit bispeke
> Þah swucche wives heom awreke. (1560–2)

[She does what she hadn't considered previously. Shame on anyone who condemns that too harshly, even if such wives get their own back.]

The Parson takes a much more severe view:

> Certes, this is the fouleste thefte that may be, whan a womman steleth hir body from hir housbonde and yeveth it to hire holour to defoulen hire ['gives it to her lover to defile herself'], and steleth hir soule fro Christ and yeveth it to the devel. (*CT* X.877)

Is Nicholas of Guildford writing to shock his readers? The Owl's argument leads us step by step to the conclusion that a wife so horribly abused cannot be greatly criticized for adultery. Have we been taken in by specious logic, or is the Owl's sympathy for the wife as justifiable as the Nightingale's sympathy for the young girl who goes astray?

The Owl finishes her disquisition with a touching portrait of a loving marriage in which the husband, whether he is a *chapmon* ('merchant'), *cniht* or *bondeman*, treats his wife tenderly (1575–7). The good wife responds by serving her husband 'to bedde and to borde / Mid faire dede and faire worde' (1579–80). When the husband has to leave on a journey, the wife sits at home worrying and mourning 'Al for hire loverdes ["lord's"] sake' (1589). As she lies counting the hours of the night, the Owl calls out in sympathy for her grief;

> An mine gode song for hire þinge
> Ich turne sundel to murninge;
> Of hire seorhe ich bere sume,
> Forþan ich am hire wel welcume;
> Ich hire helpe hwat I mai
> For ho geþ þane rihte wai.   (1597–602)

[And for her benefit I turn my good song partly to mourning; I bear some of her sorrow. Therefore I am welcome to her; I help her as best I can because she travels the right path.]

Even though the speakers are just birds, who exaggerate and distort in order to score points in a debate, they give a recognizable picture of love and marriage experienced in the everyday world of knights and churls, wives and lovers. It is a picture to cling on to as we turn to more complex and philosophical explorations of love.

A Lover's Confession

Entering a wood in May, Amans, the narrator of John Gower's *Confessio Amantis*, falls to the ground and wishes for death. He begs Venus for grace, having loyally served in her court for so long. She instructs him to make his confession to her priest, Genius. Over the eight books of the poem the confessor takes Amans through the sins against love: a book each for pride, envy, wrath, sloth, avarice and gluttony, a seventh book on the qualities of a good ruler, and a final book on incest. The sins together with their branches are exemplified by many stories set in ancient and classical times. This structure allows Gower to reflect on different kinds and aspects of love, and sets the subject within the most traditional moral framework of all, the seven deadly sins. The same scheme is used in *Ancrene Wisse*, where the spiritual advisor explains the nature of the sins and warns the anchoresses of their consequences, and in *Piers Plowman*, where the sins themselves describe their evil activities in their confessions to Reason. The closest parallel is with Robert Manning's *Handlyng Synne*, for here, too, sins against the laws of Christ and his church are illustrated by a series of *exempla*. A sin against Venus might seem to be of a very different character but, when all is said and done, pride is still pride and envy is still envy, and so traditional Christian morality is never far away. C. S. Lewis remarked that 'except on certain obviously untractable points, the virtues of a good lover were indistinguishable from those of a good man' (Lewis 1936, 199). Indeed, Genius explains to Amans that he has a dual allegiance and a two-fold office, so that as priest he must describe each sin in general, while as priest of Venus he will demonstrate its application to love (1.237–62). After Genius has explained the sin, Amans confesses that he has committed it or would have done if given the opportunity, or else never had the inclination, and then the confessor narrates stories to reveal the consequences of such sin (Burrow 1983, 9–10).

As an example, we may follow the priest's examination of sloth, specifically idleness in love. Amans gives an account of his devotion to a disdainful lady whose heart never softens towards him despite his long service. Sometimes he asks her if he may lead her by the arm to chapel, and this encourages his imagination to run away with him:

> And seie, 'Ha Lord, hou sche is softe,
> How sche is round, hou sche is smal!   *smal* slender
> Now wolde God I hadde hire al
> Withoute danger at mi wille!'   *danger* resistance
> (4.1146–9)

Nothing ever comes of it, and yet he is always ready to do whatever she asks:

> What thing sche bit me don, I do,   *bit* bids
> And wher sche bidt me gon, I go.   *bidt* bids
> (4.1161–2)

When she stands he stands too; when she takes out her embroidery he gazes at her long fingers; he sings her an Ovidian love-song and looks for excuses to spend the entire day at her side: 'I serve, I bowe, I loke, I loute' (4.1169). But all is in vain. The priest concludes that

Amans has no cause to accuse himself of idleness in love, and continues with the story of Rosiphelee, who was warned by a vision of a woeful lady on a black horse not to leave love until too late. This leads the confessor to comment that although his lady Venus encourages 'love of paramours', the best end of love is marriage (Bennett 1966), and delay in this may mean that there are no children born, without which the world will fail:

> For thus a yer or tuo or thre
> She lest, er that sche wedded be,
> Whyl sche the charge myhte bere
> Of children, whiche the world forbere
> Ne mai bot if it scholde faile.   (4.1493–7)

[For thus she loses a year or two or three before she gets married, during which time she might take on the responsibility of children, which the world cannot do without if it is not to collapse.]

Even though Amans is far from idle, it becomes clear that his busy devotion shows no prospect of ever being requited. The love he worships is not going to develop into a relationship, still less produce offspring; since it is entirely concerned with itself, it is fruitless and sterile.

In order to avoid idleness, Genius enquires, does Amans ride abroad and perform heroic deeds in honour of his lady? Well no, Amans replies, because he might lose her while away, and in any case killing Saracens is wrong. So Genius is prompted to tell him the story of Ulysses, who was shamed into abandoning home comforts to go and fight at Troy.

There is another branch of sloth, *sompnolence*, 'sleepiness', which Genius says a lover must avoid at all costs. Not guilty, replies Amans; when my lady chooses to stay up dancing, 'with such gladnesse I daunce and skippe, / Me thenkth I touche noght the flor' (4.2784–5). If she wants to play dice instead, or debate some question of love, or read of Troilus, I'm all ready. I stay all night, and taking my leave I kneel and kiss her; then I turn back pretending I've lost a ring, so that I can try to kiss her again, though seldom do I succeed. So I go to bed and torment myself with dreams, 'Bot that I dreme is noght of schep, / For I ne thenke noght on wulle' (4.2894–5).

In *Handlyng Synne* Manning presents *exempla* designed to reflect the experiences of his penitents, so that they involve local and often recent events, such as the Norfolk knight who allowed his cattle to wander in the churchyard or the Lincolnshire executors who stole a dead man's property. By contrast, in *Confessio Amantis* there is a comic mismatch between the big world events, the wars and deaths of celebrated men and women that are a consequence of passion and sin, the heroic deeds of Ulysses on the one hand, and on the other the unrequited and rather creepy obsession of Amans, stalking his lady, gazing at her fingers, touching her in chapel, hoping to catch her off guard for a kiss. And yet Genius, as priest of Venus, is sympathetic to the lover's trivial concerns, because, as he points out so often, love is an overmastering force:

> Thou dost, my sone, ayein the riht,
> > [*ayein the riht* contrary to what is right]
> Bot love is of so gret a miht
> His lawe mai no man refuse;
> So miht thou thee the betre excuse.   (3.1193–6)

Responding to the lover's request that he might learn of something new and take his mind off his pain, the confessor devotes the seventh book to the virtues that kings must possess, but the strategy fails and in the end Amans admits that 'The tales sounen in myn ere, / Bot yit myn herte is elleswhere' (7.5411–12).

What Gower is saying about love comes through most clearly in the eighth book, the subject of which, oddly at first sight, is incest rather than the expected lust of the seven sins scheme. Much earlier in *Confessio Amantis* Genius had related the touching story from Ovid of young Canace and Machaire, brother and sister who grew up together and fell in love. Canace bore a child and her father, in a frenzy of anger, 'for he was to love strange' (3.213) – 'a stranger to love' – ignored her pleas for mercy and ordered her to kill herself with a sword. Before dying she wrote a heartrending love-letter to her brother, her 'dedly frend', begging that her son should be buried beside her if he also died. The baby, covered with her blood, was instead taken out to the forest to be devoured by wild beasts. This disturbing story is told as an *exemplum* of the sin of wrath. The father's lack of love is condemned in the strongest terms, while the love of brother and sister is described as inevitable, overmastering and, above all, natural. It is *kinde* (3.154), here 'natural instinct', that impels them. Genius contrasts the law of nature with the *lawe positif* (3.172), 'human legislation', and makes his favourite point that love is an irresistible power (3.212), and within this context incest is excusable (White 2000, 195–8).

In the eighth book, however, Genius deals with incest to make a very different point. The reason that the subject of this final book is specifically the sin of incest and not lust in general is that the traditional remedy for the vice of lust is the virtue of chastity, and this would not be a viable ideal for a priest of love; whereas the vice of incest can be set against the virtue of lawful marriage. Genius begins with the church's laws of consanguinity, explaining that the prohibition against incest is not part of the natural law but a law established by the church over time. Nature taught Adam and Eve to love, so that they did 'that is to kinde due' (8.57), what is consonant with natural instinct (White 2000, 190). It was no sin for their children to have sex together, and until Abraham's time brothers and sisters were stimulated by nature to love without sin. As available partners multiplied, siblings were not permitted to marry but cousins could, and gradually the prohibition was widened until the church in the Christian era proscribed marriage up to the fourth degree of kinship. It is clear from the confessor's account that the prohibition of incest had nothing at all to do with the natural law, but is imposed by the church for the regulation of marriage (Scanlon 1998, 107–12). The prime purpose of the institution of matrimony is to obey God's command to 'cresce and multiplie' (8.29). The story of Apollonius of Tyre, the last and longest in *Confessio Amantis*, is a demonstration of the need for the all-mastering natural urge of love to be contained within the framework of marriage. The story was well known and retold many times, and reappeared as Shakespeare's *Pericles*, where it is introduced by 'ancient Gower'.

The widowed king Antiochus, blinded by disordered passion, rapes his daughter, not restrained by her weeping. The father's unnatural cruelty is defined as *unkinde* (312). The daughter's old nurse asks her why she is distressed, and she can scarcely reply for the shame of it. The nurse says sadly that she must just put up with it, and so Antiochus continues his secret molestations at will. Gower gives this authentic and moving account of child abuse so that the girl's cries of distress will reverberate throughout the long story as the extreme example of disordered love. The many examples of lawful and wholesome love will stand as a corrective.

In order to rebuff the suitors for his beautiful daughter's hand, Antiochus devises a riddle referring to his guilty secret, and soon the heads of those who have attempted to answer it are impaled on the castle gate. Only Apollonius can solve it and, realizing that this knowledge puts his life in danger, he leaves hurriedly. In Pentapolis the king's daughter is sent to cheer him out of his depression by playing the harp. He plays in response, singing like an angel, and they fall in love. Her father and Apollonius agree a marriage settlement, and the wedding takes place with great ceremony. The couple leave for Tyre, but during a violent storm the queen gives birth and apparently dies. In great distress Apollonius commits his wife's body to the sea and takes his baby daughter to Tarsus. The body is washed ashore at Ephesus, where a skilled physician eventually restores the queen to health. Supposing her husband and baby to have drowned in the storm, she devotes herself to a life of chastity at the temple of Diana. Meanwhile Apollonius leaves his daughter, Taise, with friends in Tarsus, but when she reaches the age of 14 they treacherously try to kill her. Rescued by pirates who sell her to a brothel-keeper in Mytilene, she resists all her clients and even a servant sent to rape her, and sets up as a teacher for gentlewomen. Apollonius sails to Tarsus to fetch his daughter and is shown her elaborate tomb.

Through the pattern of actions repeated with variations, Gower draws out a contrast between wicked and honourable love. The crucial episode of repeated action follows Apollonius' arrival at Mytilene, stunned by grief at his daughter's death. He lies in the pitch-dark ship's cabin, refusing to say who he is. Young Taise is asked to do what she can and she plays her harp, but Apollonius is inconsolable and orders her to leave. She persists and touches him gently, at which he strikes her, and she mildly rebukes him for being 'so salvage' (1699). Taise's harping and singing for Apollonius repeat the scene in which her mother had similarly been sent 'to glade with that sory man' (759). This raises the terrible possibility that irresistible love, stirred a second time by the power of music, will lead father and daughter unwittingly into an incestuous relationship:

Non wiste of other hou it stod,
[Neither knew what the other's
circumstances were]
And yit the fader ate laste
His herte upon this maide caste,
That he hire loveth kindely,
And yit he wiste nevere why.   *wiste* knew
(1704–8)

Is the disordered love of Antiochus for his daughter, still reverberating through the tale, about to be repeated? Will it result in tragedy? The ambiguous word *kindely* does not resolve the question immediately, since we have seen that incest, though criminal in the Christian era, is not unnatural. But we find out that *kindely* here describes that instinctive love between those who are blood-relatives (1703), even though they do not know one another (Scanlon 1998, 122–3). And so the tragedy is averted through the power of virtuous love. All ends happily: Taise marries the widower king of Mytilene and they rule Tyre as king and queen. Apollonius sails to Ephesus, where he discovers his wife in the temple, and they rule as king and queen of Pentapolis.

So this eventful story presents two widowed kings driven by a need to love, one to criminal passion and the other to marriage. Antiochus 'sette his love unkindely' (2005), and the king of Mytilene also feels 'the lusti wo, the glade peine of love' (1763–4). There are two marriages, and in both instances the fathers do everything which is *honeste* (958, 1756) – 'proper' – for their daughters. With the single exception of Antiochus' incestuous relationship, sex outside marriage is steadily resisted; so Apollonius' wife, even though she supposes she is a widow, determines 'to kepe and holde hir chasteté' (1244), as does Taise in the brothel. The confessor draws this moral from Apollonius' virtuous attitudes to love:

Lo, what it is to be wel grounded:
For he hath ferst his love founded
Honesteliche as for to wedde,
Honesteliche his love he spedde
And hadde children with his wif.   (1993–7)

[See what it is to be set on a firm foundation: because he first established his love with virtue by getting married, his love prospered in virtue, and he had children by his wife.]

On the other side is Antiochus, whose lusts contravened the law of *kinde* (2007), and from this Amans may learn 'What is to love in good manere, / And what to love in other wise' (2010–11). The love that ends in the fruitful relationship of marriage is the corrective to the taboo passion that subverts the social order by crossing the bounds of kinship.

Many of the *exempla* in *Confessio Amantis* concern love leading to marriage or the relationship (loving or hating) in marriage, and they affirm that the end of marriage is reproduction, so that Jephtha's daughter, about to be killed by her father in fulfilment of his vow, regrets only 'That sche no children hadde bore' (4.1587). This is an important element in the confessor's dual role: Genius, the guardian spirit of generation in Roman times, is Nature's priest in Alain de Lille's *De planctu Naturae* ('The Complaint of Nature') and Jean de Meun's *Roman de la Rose*, always insisting on the need for reproduction (White 2000, 84–138; Baker 1976). In terms of this fundamental purpose of *honeste* love, Genius condemns the love of Amans, because, as has become obvious to us, his love exists only in his mind and nothing will ever come of it:

> Tak love where it mai noght faile
> For as of this which thou art inne,   *as of* as for
> Be that thou seist it is a sinne *Be . . . seist* By your own account
> And sinne mai no pris deserve.   *pris* reward
> (8.2086–9)

Gower devotes his French balade sequence written about the same date to married love, the *Traitié pour essampler les amantz marietz* (Bennett 1966, 113–14), and at this date too he himself married, in his sixties, apparently for the first time.

Genius advises Amans to be governed by reason rather than passion. Amans sharply objects that his suffering is just a game to the priest, who feels nothing of what he feels (2152–3). He is permitted to write a letter of appeal to Venus for her help. Venus appears, addressing him now as John Gower, assuring him:

> Mi medicine is noght to sieke
> For thee and for suche olde sieke.   (2367–8)

[My medicine is readily available for you and sick oldies like you.]

To here my confession...

Confessus Gemo si sit medicina salutis
Exprimat morbis quos tulit ipsa ...
...qui... ferro medicant... salut...

10 The lover and Genius the priest in *Confessio Amantis*.
A miniature by Herman Scheerre. The lover, shown as a young man,
kneels in front of the confessor. Griffiths (1983); Scott (1996, 86–8).
Photograph: Bodleian Library, University of Oxford, MS. Bodl. 294, fol. 9.

This is the moment when we are shocked to learn that the lover is an
old man (Burrow 1983, 12–17). Most of the illustrations of the lover
with the confessor conspire with the poet by depicting a youthful
man, such as that painted by Herman Scheerre in MS Bodley 294
(plate 10). He is finally unmasked as a stock figure in medieval satire,
the *senex amans* or elderly lover (Burrow 1986, 156–62). Chaucer
gives several memorable examples in the *Canterbury Tales*, especially
the foul old lecher January who marries the tender May in the
Merchant's Tale. The Reeve's self-portrait is from the same tradition;
the ridiculous old man still burning with youthful lusts:

> We hoppen alwey whil that the world wol pype,
> For in oure wyl ther stiketh evere a nayl

To have an hoor heed and a grene tayl   *hoor* white
As hath a leek; for thogh oure myght be goon, *myght* strength
Oure wyl desireth folie evere in oon.   *evere in oon* all the time
(*CT* I.3876–80)

Like the Reeve, Amans is wasting his time, for Venus points out to
him that in the unlikely event that he were to find love, he is too
feeble to consummate it (2417–20). At this, Amans swoons with deadly
sorrow, and in his swoon Cupid removes his dart and Amans wakes
to find that love has vanished 'riht as it hadde nevere be' (2877).
Venus hands him a mirror in which to see his wrinkled face and grey
locks, and laughs at him:

And axeth as it were in game   *And . . . game* And asked playfully
What love was, and I for schame
Ne wiste what I scholde ansuere,   *ne wiste* didn't know
And natheles I gan to swere   *natheles* nevertheless
That be my trouthe I knew him noght. (2872–5)

The extraordinary revelation of his age cannot cancel the amused
sympathy we have developed for him, notwithstanding the *senex amans*
tradition, and indeed he is treated by both Venus and her priest with
friendly gentleness. Forced to confront the reality that he is old, Amans
can finally be released by Venus and turn away from his obsession
with love. He receives absolution from Genius, and Venus gives him a
set of black rosary beads on which are written in gold the words *por
reposer*. At the very end of the poem, old, sick, feeble and impotent,
Gower commits his book to his readers, and, like his *alter ego* Amans,
takes his farewell of love, for his muse has instructed that he write no
more of love: 'that y no more of love make' (3143).

Love's Craft

Troilus and Criseyde is Chaucer's deepest exploration of the manners,
effects and consequences of love. Like the priest Genius, the narrator
of *Troilus and Criseyde* understands love to be an inescapable force, but
also recognizes that it is a force for good:

Now sith it may nat goodly ben withstonde,
And is a thing so vertuous in kynde,

Refuseth nat to love for to ben bonde,
Syn as hymselven liste he may yow bynde. (1.253–6)

[Now since love cannot well be resisted, and is a thing so good of itself,
do not refuse to be bound to love, since he has power to bind you at
will.]

The opening book establishes love as an ideal, with Troilus as the
faithful lover devastated by his emotions. He is first seen, however,
leading his young knights around the temple to eye the ladies, and
pouring scorn on anyone who is smitten. By the end of Book 1 love
has transformed him from an arrogant prig to a generous and caring
friend, with all those virtues characteristic of an elevated sensibility:

For he bicom the frendieste wight,
The gentilest, and ek the mooste fre,
The thriftiest, and oon the beste knyght
That in his tyme was or myghte be;
Dede were his japes and his cruelté
His heighe port and his manere estraunge,
And ecch of tho gan for a vertu chaunge. (1.1079–85)

[For he became the friendliest person, the noblest and also the most
gracious, the worthiest and the very best that existed or could have
existed in his time. His jokes and his cruelty, his arrogant bearing and
distant manner were at an end, and he swapped each of these vices for
a virtue.]

Love has two highly admirable effects on Troilus, and both are
described at the end of the third book when his relationship with
Criseyde is at its most fulfilled. In order to win his lady's admiration
he becomes a stronger and bolder warrior (3.1776–7), and at the
same time his new sensitivity leads him to feel sorrow for those who
are not in love, and to act graciously to everyone:

Thus wolde love, yheried be his grace,   *wolde* granted; *yheried* praised
That pride, envye, ire and avarice
He gan to fle, and everich other vice. (3.1804–6)

But to begin with, immobilized by love, Troilus seems to have no
prospect of ever meeting Criseyde to tell her of his devotion. His
friend Pandarus finds him lying on his bed, longing for death to

relieve his suffering. Pandarus, an experienced (if unsuccessful) lover, takes it upon himself to guide the untutored young man and to redress the situation.

The concept of love that is explored here is shared by many works centring on the courtly and chivalric life. Love is 'the crafte so longe to lerne', as the first line of the *Parliament of Fowls* puts it. It is an *art* that the narrator of *Troilus and Criseyde* knows so much less about than his courtly audience (3.1333), and Gawain so much less well than his seductress (*Gawain* 1543). It is, in a phrase Chaucer uses several times, 'the olde daunce', of which Pandarus knows every step (3.695), and which he struggles to teach Troilus. So Pandarus explains to the prostrate Troilus the virtue fundamental to this *art*, that of *service*: many a man has suffered for love for 20 years without being granted so much as a kiss, but what of that?

> What sholde he therfore fallen in dispayr,
> Or be recreant for his owne tene,
> Or slen hymself al be his lady fair?
> Nay, nay, but evere in oon be fressh and grene
> To serve and love his deere hertes queene,
> And thynke it is a guerdon hire to serve
> A thousand fold moore than he kan deserve.   (1.813–19)

[Why should he fall into despair as a result, or be cowardly in consequence of his own grief, or kill himself, even if his lady is lovely? No, he should always be keen and eager to serve and love his dear heart's queen, and think to serve her a reward a thousand times greater than he deserves.]

The lover as humble servant of the imperious lady is an essential character in the world of romantic love, in part, at least, because this relationship is so clearly distinct from that of marriage, where the woman loses her independence in law. When Criseyde eventually accepts Troilus as 'my knyght', she insists on a formal acknowledgement of his obeisance, even though he is a prince:

> A kynges sone although ye be, ywys,
> Ye shal namore han sovereigneté
> Of me in love than right in that cas is.
> N'y nyl forbere, if that ye don amys   *N'y nyl forbere* Nor will I refrain
> To wratthe yow; and whil that ye me serve,   *wratthe* be angry with

Chericen you right after ye disserve.

[*Chericen* Care for; *right after* just as]

(3.170–5)

The knight as devoted servant has no cause to complain if in return his lady is *daungerous*, meaning 'standoffish, haughty, unbending', although Pandarus advises his niece Criseyde to sweeten her standoffishness: 'so lat youre daunger sucred ben a lite' (2.384), and later reproves her more severely for her *daungerous* behaviour:

> But ye han played tirant neigh to longe,   *neigh* almost
> And hard was it youre herte for to grave.   *grave* impress
> Now stynte, that ye no lenger on it honge,
> Al wolde ye the forme of daunger save.   (2.1240–3)

[*Now . . . save* Stop now, so you don't dally on it any longer, even if you want to preserve the appearance of reserve.]

Pandarus comforts Troilus by assuring him that a virtuous lady will possess *pitee* among her other virtues (1.899).

Many elements of the craft of love come naturally to a *gentil* heart. In Chaucer's earliest poem, the *Book of the Duchess*, the Black Knight gives a full account of how from his youth, long before he had an object for his affections, he 'ches love to my firste craft' (791), and this came to him 'kyndely' (778), from nature, though it required application and study like any other branch of learning (Aers 1988, 121–5). Similarly, even before Pandarus' tutorials, Troilus has the inborn instincts of a courtly lover, and longs for the grace to serve Criseyde or even to pass as one of her servants (1.369–71). He has much to learn from Pandarus, though, especially on practical matters. Pandarus' role is clearly expressed in his advice on the letter he instructs Troilus to write. Though he leaves the actual contents to Troilus, he gives guidance on general aspects of style: Troilus should not write *craftyly*, 'artfully', or repeat himself too often, or use vocabulary from the wrong register, and should blot the letter a bit with his tears (2.1023–43). Doubting his ability, Troilus composes a simple and humble letter using the traditional *termes* of lovers:

> First he gan hire his righte lady calle,
> His hertes lif, his lust, his sorwes leche,   *lust* desire; *leche* healer

His blisse, and ek thise other termes alle   *ek* also
That in swich cas thise loveres alle seche;   *seche* seek
And in ful humble wise, as in his speche,

    [*wise . . . speche* manner with regard to his language]

He gan him recomaunde unto hire grace;

    [*gan him recomaunde* commended himself]

To telle al how, it axeth muchel space.   *axeth* would require

                      (2.1065–71)

It is through the use of the 'termes of talkyng noble', as the *Gawain*-poet puts it (917), that the courtly lover is to be recognized as a master of the art of love. The first question that Criseyde asks Pandarus about Troilus is 'Kan he wel speke of love?' (2.503). It seems an odd question, asking not 'Did he say he loved me?' but (to gloss it laboriously) 'Is he able to use the appropriate rhetorical conventions to express a sophisticated concept of love's craft?' If Pandarus can assure her of this, then she, herself at ease with the conventions, can prepare herself for their first meeting (2.504). Instead of admitting that his pupil still has much to learn, Pandarus recounts an episode of overhearing Troilus that is perhaps pure invention; at least we can safely assume that he gives a much improved version of Troilus' words in order to impress Criseyde. According to Pandarus, Troilus framed his overheard complaint in the traditional conceit of the religion of love, as in *Confessio Amantis*. Troilus is reported as having made his confession to the God of Love, 'Now *mea culpa*, Lord, I me repente' (2.525). The confession is couched in the French-derived vocabulary proper to such elevated religious discourse:

O God, that at thi disposicioun
Ledest the fyn by juste purveiaunce
Of every wight, my lowe confessioun
Accepte in gree, and sende me swich penaunce
As liketh the, but from disesperaunce
That may my goost departe awey fro the,
Thow be my sheld, for thi benignité.   (2.526–32)

[O God, you who at your disposal direct the end of everyone by just providence, accept my humble confession with good will, and send me what penance you wish, but in your beneficence be my defence against the despair that may sever my spirit from you.]

Here *disesperaunce* is the 'unforgivable sin' that separates the soul from God. The use of *sheld* as an inner metaphor within the outer metaphor of confession is followed by further conventional images, where love is a wound that must lead to death, and the need for a lover to conceal his passion is figured as burning coals covered with cold ashes (533–9). This speech constructed by Pandarus is expressed in a rhetorical discourse that is itself a fictional representation of reality. Is Troilus actually about to die of lovesickness? Pandarus has the best of motives (so he would say) for his fictions, to bring happiness to his friend and benefits to his niece, and so he produces the appropriate *termes* to express the misery that Troilus suffers. At the same time it is a signal that language can be used unscrupulously in the game of love, and Troilus' supposed confession is an emblem of the series of tricks, manipulations and evasions that Pandarus (with Troilus' connivance) will carry out in order to bring Criseyde to bed.

If Troilus had been a better pupil in the art, the audience might be more critical of his role. As he awaits his first meeting with Criseyde, he practises his love-talking: 'thus wol I sey, and thus' (3.52), but face to face with his beloved, fear drives out all his eloquence. In this passage the jerky syntax mirrors Troilus' anguished hesitation:

> In chaunged vois, right for his verray drede,
> Which vois ek quook, and therto his manere   *ek quook* also trembled
> Goodly abaist, and now his hewes rede,
> > [*Goodly abaist* attractively timid]
> Now pale, unto Criseyde, his lady dere,
> With look down cast and humble iyolden chere,
> > [*iyolden chere* submissive expression]
> Lo! the alderfirste word that hym asterte
> > [*alderfirste* very first; *hym asterte* passed his lips]
> Was twyes: 'Mercy, mercy, swete herte!'   (3.92–8)

As a player in the game of love, Troilus is handicapped by his sincerity and unmanned by his *trouthe* (Green 1979, 216–17). So much more skilful and successful is his rival Diomede, for whom love is nothing but game and whose emotions are untouched.

Diomede is as false as Troilus is true, as self-assured as Troilus is hesitant (Windeatt 1992, 294–8). He is a skilled exponent of the craft of love, who 'koude more than the crede ["the basics"] / In swich a craft' (5.89–90). Grasping Criseyde's bridle (literally and metaphorically) and leading her away from Troilus, he reflects that he may at the moment be wasting his time 'if that I speke of love' (5.101), but seizing his opportunity, he begs her nevertheless to treat him as a brother (5.134), then, as their journey nears its end, regrets that he has no time to tell all his *entente*, but asks her to give him her hand, for he will be her own (5.150–4). Growing still more pressing, he tells her (no doubt truly) that he has never loved a woman before, and that he has so much to learn before he can 'compleyne aright' (5.161). She is not to be surprised, he adds, that he should speak of love so early, for the God of Love must be obeyed, and he begs 'that ye me for youre servant wolde calle' (5.173). Criseyde has the choice of taking this seriously or just as love-talk to pass the journey pleasantly (5.96). In fact we are told that she was so preoccupied with her thoughts that she heard only a word here and there (5.176–82).

It is clear that Diomede is not in love with Criseyde but rather that he is aroused by the challenge, and 'to fisshen hire he leyde out hook and lyne' (5.777). What a 'conquerour' he would appear if he won her; after all he has nothing to lose 'but my speche' (5.792–8). After 10 days he makes his play for her. A master of the calculated gesture as well as of love-talking, he tells Criseyde of his desire to serve her, with a blush and a meaning look:

> And with that word he gan to waxen red,   *waxen* grow
> And in his speche a litel wight he quok,   *wight* bit; *quok* trembled
> And caste asyde a litel wight his hed,
> And stynte a while; and afterward he wok,
>   [*stynte* hesitated; *wok* stirred]
> And sobreliche on hire he threw his lok   *sobreliche* meaningfully
> And seyde, 'I am, al be it yow no joie,   *al* although
> As gentil man as any wight in Troie.'   *wight* man
>   (5.925–9)

The repetition of *And* conveys the impression of a mechanical series of well-rehearsed gestures (Burrow 2002, 132–3). The word *quok* takes us back to Troilus' trembling voice as he addresses Criseyde (3.93 above), and furthermore there is a direct contrast with the unaffected blushing of Troilus cheered by the Trojans as the conqueror returning bloody from battle (2.645–6).

Sir Gawain and the Green Knight gives the clearest display of 'þe lel layk of luf' (1513) – 'the true game of love'. We are introduced to

Gawain as the pious knight of the Pentangle, whose 'clannes ["purity"] and his cortaysye croked ["distorted"] were never' (653), but the courtiers of Hautdesert are in awe of Gawain's reputation for *luftalkyng* (927), which they recognize as a product of his noble upbringing, his *nurture* (919). They envisage this as a skill to be displayed as part of the Christmas celebrations, and indeed at the Christmas dinner they are able to observe Gawain and his host's wife very properly entertaining one another with 'dere dalyaunce of her derne wordez / Wyth clene cortays carp' (1012–13) – 'the refined conversation of their intimate words, with unsullied courteous talk'. However, the game is played out in a private space, when the lady comes to call on Gawain as he lies asleep in bed. A close reading of the first of the three bedroom scenes will provide a sharp demonstration of two experts playing the game of love (Burrow 1965, 78–86).

The lady's first words on surprising Gawain asleep are couched in one of the most traditional of all courtly-love metaphors: the imprisoned lover (Green 1979, 203). Unless the two of them can establish a truce, she says as she leans over him, she will bind him in his bed; with laughter the lady uttered these pleasantries (*bourdez* 1212). Keeping up the game of metaphors, Gawain yields himself and sues for mercy, asking her to release her prisoner for the practical purpose of getting dressed. 'And þus he bourded aȝayn ["returned the jest"]' (1217). Using the same metaphor, in earnest not in jest, Troilus embraced Criseyde for the first time and said to her:

> Now be ye kaughte; now is ther but we tweyne.
>> [*but we tweyne* just the two of us]
> Now yeldeth you, for other bote is non.
>> [*yeldeth you* yield yourself up; *bote* deliverance]
>>> (3.1207–8)

Pinning Gawain to his bed, the lady's game takes on much more serious overtones. Her husband, she points out, has gone hunting, the servants are asleep, the door is bolted, and she intends to make good use of her time with this knight so famous for his courtesy:

> Ȝe are welcum to my cors
> Yowre awen won to wale;
> Me behovez of fyne force
> Your servaunt be, and schale. (1236–9)

[You're welcome to my body to do what you want; of sheer necessity I
must be your servant, and I shall be.]

Though this appears to be a shameless invitation to sex, it is still
possible for Gawain to interpret it as a game. '3e are welcum to my
cors' may involve a French idiom and mean no more than a polite
'I'm happy to have you here.' The term *servaunt* is ubiquitous in
elegant conversation, where it can simply be an expression of politeness, as when Gawain asks the lady and her elderly companion on
first meeting if he may be their *servaunt* (976). The reverse usage by a
woman to address a man, however, has much more obvious sexual
promise.

As a delicate way of drawing back from this proposition, Gawain
denies that he is 'he þat 3e of speken' (1242) and worthy of such
praise; the lady persists in her flattery, yet Gawain always has a
faultless response (1261–2). She says extravagantly that if she were
worth the sum total of all women in the world, even so she would
choose Gawain. Brilliantly – here is the art of love-talking at its most
skilful – Gawain reminds her that she has already chosen a better
man in her husband, then thanks her for her compliments, and
concludes:

> And soberly your servaunt, my soverayn I holde yow,
> And yowre kny3t I becom, and Kryst you for3elde.   (1278–9)

[And absolutely as your servant I look on you as my sovereign, and I
am your knight, and may Christ reward you.]

Again there is the word *servaunt*, now in the traditional man-to-
woman usage, in this case to distance the relationship by formalizing
it. The narrator's own comment on this action is that the lady behaved as if she loved Gawain, and he acted defensively (1281–2).
Finally she prepares to leave, but turns back at the door, saying that if
he were really the knight so famed for courteous behaviour he would
have asked her for a kiss 'by his courtaysye' (1300). For once Gawain
is caught off guard and replies rather grudgingly that he will kiss
her if she commands him to. As with everything else in this scene,
the kiss has ambiguous significance (Burrow 2002, 150–1), either as
farewell or as foreplay, the former standard in company, the latter

reserved for the bedroom. Having kissed him in farewell, the lady leaves the bedroom for that occasion.

'All this Mean I by Love'

At the height of his affair with Criseyde, Troilus sings a song in praise of the love that governs earth and sea and binds the discordant elements of the world so that they remain in perpetual union (3.1744–71). The source for this song is a poem by Boethius (c. 480–524) at the end of Book 2 of *The Consolation of Philosophy*, the most popular philosophical work throughout the Middle Ages, translated by both Alfred the Great and Chaucer. The counsel that Boethius puts in the mouth of Lady Philosophy is that men should turn from the empty joys of the world to the true goodness of the Father of Creation, and they can escape the fickleness of Fortune by cleaving to the enduring power of love that holds all in balance:

> The world in constant change
> Maintains a harmony. . . .
> And all this chain of things
> In earth and sea and sky
> One ruler holds in hand:
> If Love relaxed the reins
> All things that now keep peace
> Would wage continual war
> The fabric to destroy
> Which unity has formed
> With motions beautiful.   (trans. Watts 1969, 77)

Yet *Troilus and Criseyde* ends with Troilus' spirit, taken up into the heavens, looking down at the earth so tiny below and laughing contemptuously at the preoccupations of the world:

> And in hymself he lough right at the wo   *lough* laughed
> Of hem that wepten for his deth so faste,
> And dampned al oure werk that foloweth so
> The blynde lust, the which that may nat laste,
> And sholden al oure herte on heven caste.   *sholden* we should
> (5.1821–5)

Though this passage is based directly on Boccaccio's *Teseide*, behind that lies Lady Philosophy's image of the soul, freed from its earthly prison, rising to heaven from where it despises earthly things (see Chaucer's translation, *Boece* Book 2, the end of prosa 7).

What are we to think of Troilus' recantation? Was he so besotted with Criseyde that he mistook his moment of supreme passion for the great chain of love that holds the world in its eternal embrace? Or is his soul's final contempt of the world insufficiently generous in acknowledging the value of human love, even though it expresses a valid perspective? The ending of *Troilus and Criseyde* is unsettling in that it moves from enraptured praise of love to contempt for all transitory concerns. By contrast, the *Parliament of Fowls* starts with *contemptus mundi* and ends with a celebration of love and the coming of spring on St Valentine's Day (Minnis 1995, 253).

As his source for the first movement of the *Parliament of Fowls*, Chaucer acknowledges Cicero's *Somnium Scipionis* ('The Dream of Scipio'), which passed down to the Middle Ages with a Neoplatonist commentary by Macrobius, written in around 400 (ed. Stahl 1952). In his dream Scipio finds himself in the stars, where his ancestor, the great conqueror Africanus, appears to him as guide and instructor. As Scipio looks down at the insignificant earth below, Africanus explains to him the revolution of the spheres and the music they create with their movement. This music of the spheres is the origin of harmony (in both its senses) in the universe. Chaucer paraphrases:

> And aftir shewed he hym the nyne speres,   *speres* spheres
> And aftir that the melodye herd he
> That cometh of thilke speres thries thre,   *thilke* these
> That welle ys of musyke and melodye   *welle* source
> In this worlde here, and cause of armonye. (59–63)

The lowest of the nine spheres is the earth, subject to ceaseless change so that nothing can last. Chaucer summarizes the instruction of Africanus:

> Than bad he hym, syn the erthe was so lite,
>
>   [*bad* told; *syn* since; *lite* little]
> And was somedel fulle of harde grace,
> That he ne shuld hym in the worlde delyte. (64–6)

During his earthly life Scipio should work 'to comune profyte' (75). Chaucer's phrase, meaning 'the general good', is much more comprehensive than Cicero's concept of working for the benefit of the Roman republic, and it leaves open the question of what actually constitutes 'comune profyte'. The souls of those who do good work, says Africanus, pass swiftly to heaven, but others will have to suffer for endless ages. Chaucer adds to his pagan source the Christian sentiment that finally the sinful will be forgiven:

> But brekers of the lawe, soth to seyne,
> And lecherous folke, after that they be dede
> Shul alwey whirle aboute th'erthe in peyne
> Til many a worlde be passed, out of drede,
>> [*out of drede* without a doubt]
> And than, foryeven al hir wikked dede,
>> [*foryeven* having been forgiven]
> Than shul they come unto that blysful place
> To which to come God sende ech lover grace!   (77–84)

Somnium Scipionis is the first of many authorities that Chaucer invokes in the *Parliament of Fowls* for a puzzled meditation on the nature and significance of love. Macrobius judged that 'there is nothing more complete than this work, which embraces the entire body of philosophy' (Stahl 1952). Even so, as the *Parliament of Fowls* makes clear immediately, Cicero's ascetic philosophy leaves many questions unanswered.

The context of Chaucer's retelling of *Somnium Scipionis* is a search for some unspecified information. The narrator introduces himself as a naif in matters of love, the 'dredeful joy' (3) that appears to him to be complex, difficult and contradictory. He has read in books of love's wonder and cruelties without in any way relieving his perpetual astonishment (1–14). He turns to the *Dreme of Scipion* (31) and spends the whole day reading this old book 'a certeyn thing to lerne' (20). As the light fades he puts the book away and goes to sleep, much troubled by his thoughts:

> Fulfilled of thought and besy hevenesse,
> For bothe I had thinge which that I nolde,
> And eke I ne had thynge that I wolde.   (89–91)

[Consumed with anxiety and troubled uneasiness, for I both had the thing I didn't want, and also didn't have the thing I did want.]

This is a glancing allusion to a passage in Boethius (3, prosa 3) where Philosophy explains that possessions do not free men from dissatisfaction, since they still feel that they have what they do not want and lack what they do not have. Whatever it is that the narrator lacks, it may be that his dream will offer him a different and perhaps valid perspective. As Macrobius explains, dreams can be profound or trivial, misleading or instructive (Spearing 1976, 8–11).

The dreamer meets Africanus, no longer the stern figure who had instructed Scipio, but a more genial guide who implicitly acknowledges that the dreamer has found nothing to his purpose in 'myn olde booke al totorne' (110), and promises to reward him for his labour. He brings the dreamer to the gates of a walled park with contradictory inscriptions, very troubling after the firm certainties of *Somnium Scipionis*. On one side the inscription promises entry to 'that blysful place / Of hertes hele and dedely woundes cure' (127–8); the other leads to 'the mortale strokes of the spere' (135). Though Cicero had said nothing of it, this is the garden of love, familiar to Chaucer's readers from the *Roman de la Rose* (Bennett 1957, 70–8). The dreamer stands rooted to the spot in fear, but Africanus shoves him through the gates, saying that the inscriptions apply to love's servants, not to a mere observer of love: 'That thou canst not do, yet thou maist hyt se' (163).

The dreamer find himself, as the dreamer does in *Pearl*, in a paradisiacal landscape of trees, rivers, fish, birds, charming animals, sweet music and a climate never too hot or too cold, where no one ever grows old or falls ill. Cicero's world-view had no room for this idealized scene of natural beauty and, most significantly, harmony, not the music of the spheres in this case but the song of birds 'with voys of aungel in her armony' (191), and of stringed instruments 'in acorde' (197) (Kean 1972, 1, 77–8).

This is modelled on Boccaccio's *Teseide*, with the addition of the references to harmony. Also based on the *Teseide* is the description of the Temple of Brass that next appears to the dreamer. Outside the temple he sees Cupid, forging his arrows, and his daughter Will, who tempers them in the water of a spring. Nearby is a group that includes Plesaunce ('pleasure, delight'), Array ('adornment'), Lust ('desire') and Curtesye; and also Crafte – 'dysfigured was she' – who has power to force a man to act foolishly (218–22). These figures of ambivalent moral status seem to represent the worldly preoccupations that Africanus condemned, and they apparently confirm the dangers of submitting to their sway. Of the remaining figures, some are pretty and innocently sensual (naked Beauté, cheerful Yowthe), but others are disturbing (Flatery and Mede, 'reward').

Inside the temple the sound is of hot sighs of sorrow, born of desire, fanned by jealousy. In a prime position stands (in two senses) Priapus, while men attempt to set garlands on his head. Over in a dark corner, with her doorkeeper Rychesse ('wealth'), reclines Venus, her hair lying loose on the bed, naked to her breast, the rest of her body covered with a diaphanous scarf. The aspects of the goddess that are represented here are clear enough, and they are confirmed for the dreamer as he passes deeper into the temple. There he sees painted on the wall the stories of virgins who had wasted their time (since they were raped), and a group of tragic lovers, including Dido, Helen, Cleopatra and Troilus.

The church has always had problems with Venus. However reprehensible the passion that she provokes, there would be no increasing and multiplying without it. We have seen how Gower reveals the contradictions and inconsistencies of conventional morality very sensitively in *Confessio Amantis*. In the twelfth century Bernard Silvestris tried to solve the problem by positing 'two Venuses, one lawful and the other the goddess of wantonness' (Windeatt 1992, 224), and this is repeated by Boccaccio in his gloss to his *Teseide*, which Chaucer probably had not read (Minnis 1995, 283–5). The proem to Book 3 of *Troilus and Criseyde* gives the finest expression of the 'lawful' Venus as the planetary influence controlling harmonious love in all creatures, and there is a brief reference to this aspect of her in *Parliament of Fowls* 113–19, where the narrator prays to her, under her title of Cytheria, to help him relate the dream which she gave to him. In the temple, though, we see the 'goddess of wantonness'. Yet as we shall learn, she, too, has a vital part to play in the complexities of creation.

Without commenting, the dreamer steps outside to the place 'so swoote and grene' (296), and walking along idly comes across a queen lovelier than any other being: the goddess Nature sitting on a flowery hill. The source he explicitly acknowledges for the description of Nature is Alain de Lille's *De planctu Naturae* (316), a work to which

Gower was indebted for his account of Nature and her priest. As in Alain, Nature is seen as God's agent on earth:

> Nature, the vyker of th'almyghty lorde,   *vyker* deputy
> That hoot, colde, hevy, lyght, moiste and drye
> Hath knyt be evene noumbre of accorde.
>
>   [*be . . . accorde* in due proportions]
>
>   (379–81)

The wording here again reflects the influence of the *Consolation*; Boethius (in Chaucer's own translation) says of the Creator:

> Thow byndest the elementis by nombres proporcionables ['proportional'],
> that the coolde thinges mowen ['may'] accorde with the hote thinges,
> and the drye thinges with the moyste. (*Boece* 3, metrum 9, 18–21)

God, acting through Nature, binds together the elements of a universe full of variety (Bennett 1957, 194–212). In the earlier description of the paradisiacal park, the dreamer observed the plenitude of the natural world in an idealized state, and now 38 kinds of bird are enumerated together with their natural characteristics. One is *gentil*, another is fierce, one a thief, another false; one is an enemy of the eel, another of the quail, a third a murderer of small birds. They demonstrate not only the fullness of the earth but also its discordant elements, which so much need binding into one harmonious whole, were that possible. Such variety as well as discordancy is emphasized by the artist of the Pepysian model book (plate 11). It is St Valentine's Day, and Nature is set on imposing her order on this variety of creatures so that they can fulfil her purpose in creation: the propagation of the species, 'in furtherynge of youre nede' (384), as she puts it. Her vocabulary, *statute, governaunce* (387) and *ordenaunce* (390), expresses her determination to legislate and impose control.

Nature's difficulty is that she has to work in co-operation with Venus; the birds must be allowed to choose: the verb *chese* and the noun *choys* are repeated seven times in this passage. Accepting the necessity of this freedom, she nevertheless sets up an avian hierarchy that mockingly mirrors that of human society, starting with royalty and proceeding downwards to the churl. Dearest to Nature is the female eagle (*formel*) sitting on her hand, the most lovely and noble

11 Birds in Magdalene College, Cambridge, MS Pepys 1916, f. 12r.
The paintings of birds of about 1400 were apparently intended to serve as
models for miniaturists. On the top row are four falcons, three on gloved
hands and one on a perch; in the middle a hawk kills a mallard; beneath
stand a moorhen and a bullfinch (labelled 'bwollfinch'). Scott (1996,
no. 8). Photograph: Pepys Library, Magadelene College, Cambridge.

of all her works, whom she gazes at fondly and whose beak she kisses. The formel's three eagle suitors (*tercels*) all make their claims in terms of their *service*. The first two stress how long they have served her, while the third, who has to admit that he cannot boast of 'longe servise' (470), feels the necessity of emphasizing the concept all the more:

> A man may serven bette, and more to pay,   *to pay* satisfactorily
> In halfe a yere, although hyt were no more,
> Than somme man dooth that hath served ful yore.
>
> [*ful yore* a very long time]
>
> (474–6)

Such are the classic expressions of the courtly attitude to love, though somehow less appropriate from an eagle's beak than from Troilus' mouth. The dreamer comments that he never heard 'so gentil plee in love' (485). The other birds, however, having spent the whole day listening to these professions of love with rising impatience, break out in anger at the delay to their own pairings:

> 'Come of!' they cride, 'Allas, ye wol us shende!   *shende* ruin
> Whan shal youre cursed pledynge have an ende?'   (494–5)

Nature, always on the watch for disharmony, calls out sharply 'Holde your tonges there!' (521), and demands that a representative of each kind should be appointed. The result is yet more discord, expressing a set of mutually incompatible attitudes to love. The goose thinks the rejected suitors should choose another partner, as Pandarus had advised Troilus in an attempt to cheer him up; the turtle-dove urges the tercels to *serve* unrewarded until death, as Pandarus had also advised Troilus on an earlier occasion. The merlin, previously characterized as a killer of larks (339–40), abuses the cuckoo as a murderer of hedge-sparrows (612–13). Nature, despairing of making progress, commands 'pes!' (617), and hands the choice to her formel, while urging her to follow reason in choosing the royal eagle. The shy and modest formel is surprisingly stubborn in asking for a year's respite before making her choice, because:

> I wol noght serven Venus ne Cupide
> Forsoth as yet, by no maner wey.   (652–3)

Nature's purpose has been frustrated by her favourite, and she can only advise the eagles to *serve* for another year. Quickly the other birds choose their mates 'by evene acorde' (668), mutual agreement, and a Boethian harmony is restored with their embraces, sealed by the harmony of their final roundel of love and the unchanging change of the annual cycle.

Nature and Venus are both inhabitants of the garden of love, and it becomes clear that Nature relies on her fellow for her purpose to be fulfilled, for choice of a partner is driven by desire. In *De planctu Naturae* Venus is Nature's deputy acting to promote the continuance of the race, but she is corrupted by man's perversity (Minnis 1995, 271–6). The formel's rejection of Venus and Cupid comes as an unexpected obstacle to Nature's plan. Love, with all its destructive and conflicting passions, is still a necessary part of the scheme of things, of a creation that is essentially disharmonious and held in precarious balance by Nature as God's vice-regent. Cicero's vision of the harmony of the spheres involves a rejection of the created world, and the only chink in his austere philosophy is the notion of 'comune profyte'. The general good needs to find a place for love. The old book has not satisfied the dreamer, for its view of the world makes no contact with the dream of the lovely garden of Venus and Nature. But then, like all dreams, the dream is of dubious authority and uncertain significance, and so the dreamer must turn back to his library:

> I hope, ywyse, to rede so sommday
> That I shal mete somme thyng for to fare
> The bet; and thus to rede I wol not spare.   (697–9)

Bibliography

Aers, David, 1979. 'Criseyde: Woman in Medieval Society', *Chaucer Review* 13, 177–200; reprinted in *Critical Essays on Chaucer's 'Troilus and Criseyde' and his Major Early Poems*, ed. Benson, C. David (Milton Keynes, 1991), 128–48

Aers, David, 1988. *Community, Gender, and Individual Identity* (London)

Aers, David, 1993. 'The Self Mourning: Reflections on *Pearl*', *Speculum* 68, 54–73

Allen, Dorena, 1964. 'Orpheus and Orfeo: The Dead and the *Taken*', *Medium Ævum* 33, 102–11

Allen, Hope Emily, ed., 1931. *English Writings of Richard Rolle* (Oxford)

Ancrene Riwle, ed. Day, M., 1952; *Ancrene Wisse*, ed. Millett, Bella, 2006; trans. White, Hugh, 1993

Andrew, Malcolm, and Ronald Waldron, eds., 2002. *The Poems of the Pearl Manuscript* (3rd edn., Exeter)

Anglo-Saxon Chronicle, eds. Plummer, Charles, and John Earle, 1892–9; trans. Swanton, Michael, 2000

Arnould, E. J., ed., 1940. *Le Livre de Seyntz Medicines*, ANTS 2

Assumption of our Lady, ed. Lumby, J. Rawson, 1866

Audelay, John, ed. Whiting, Ella Keats, 1931

Ayenbite of Inwyt, ed. Morris, Richard, 1866

Baker, Denise N., 1976. 'The Priesthood of Genius: A Study of the Medieval Tradition', *Speculum* 51, 277–91

Barker, Juliet R. V., 1986. *The Tournament in England 1100–1400* (Woodbridge)

Barron, W. R. J., 1983. 'The Ambivalence of Adventure: Verbal Ambiguity in *Sir Gawain and the Green Knight*, Fitt I', in *The Legend of Arthur in the Middle Ages*, eds. Grout, P. B., R. A. Lodge, C. E. Pickford and E. K. C. Varty (Cambridge), 28–40

Bartlett, Robert, 2000. *England under the Norman and Angevin Kings 1075–1225* (Oxford)

Baugh, Albert C., and Thomas Cable, 2002. *A History of the English Language* (5th edn., Upper Saddle River, NJ)

Beadle, Richard, ed., 1982. *The York Plays* (London)

Beadle, Richard, 1994. 'The York Cycle', in *The Cambridge Companion to Medieval English Theatre*, ed. Beadle, Richard (Cambridge), 85–108

Bede, *A History of the English Church and People*, trans. Sherley-Price, Leo, rev. Latham, R. E., 1968

Bennett, J. A. W., 1957. *The Parlement of Foules: An Interpretation* (Oxford)

Bennett, J. A. W., 1966. 'Gower's "Honeste Love"', in *Patterns of Love and Courtesy*, ed. Lawlor, John (London), 107–21

Bennett, J. A. W., 1974. *Chaucer at Oxford and Cambridge* (Toronto)

Bennett, J. A. W., and G. V. Smithers, eds., 1968. *Early Middle English Verse and Prose* (Oxford)

Benson, Larry D., ed., 1987. *The Riverside Chaucer* (Boston and Oxford)

Bergen, Henry, ed., 1924–7. *Lydgate's Fall of Princes*, i–iv, EETS e.s. 121–5

Blumenfeld-Kosinski, Renate, and Kevin Brownlee, trans., 1997. *The Selected Writings of Christine de Pizan* (New York)

Boethius, *The Consolation of Philosophy*, trans. Watts, V. E., 1969

Book of Privy Counselling, ed. Hodgson, Phyllis, 1982

Brehe, S. K., 1990. 'Reassembling the First Worcester Fragment', *Speculum* 65, 521–36

Brereton, Geoffrey, trans., 1968. *Froissart: Chronicles* (Harmondsworth)

Brewer, Elisabeth, 1992. *Sir Gawain and the Green Knight: Sources and Analogues* (Woodbridge)

Brewer, Elisabeth, 1997. 'Sources I: The Sources of *Sir Gawain and the Green Knight*', in *A Companion to the Gawain-Poet*, eds. Brewer, Derek, and Jonathan Gibson (Cambridge), 243–55

Brook, G. L., ed., 1968. *The Harley Lyrics* (4th edn., Manchester)

Brook, G. L., and R. F. Leslie, eds., 1963, 1978. *Laȝamon: Brut*, EETS 250, 277

Brooke, Christopher N. L., 1989. *The Medieval Idea of Marriage* (Oxford)

Brown, Carleton, ed., 1932. *English Lyrics of the XIIIth Century* (Oxford)

Brown, Carleton, ed., 1939. *Religious Lyrics of the XVth Century* (Oxford)

Burgess, Glyn S., and Keith Busby, trans., 1986. *The Lais of Marie de France* (Harmondsworth)

Burnley, David, 1989. *The Language of Chaucer* (Basingstoke)

Burnley, David, 1998. *Courtliness and Literature in Medieval England* (London)

Burnley, David, 2000. 'Language', in *A Companion to Chaucer*, ed. Brown, Peter (Oxford), 235–50

Burrow, J. A., 1965. *A Reading of Sir Gawain and the Green Knight* (London)

Burrow, J. A., 1982. *Medieval Writers and their Work* (Oxford)

Burrow, J. A., 1983. 'The Portrayal of Amans in *Confessio Amantis'*, in *Gower's Confessio Amantis: Responses and Reassessments*, ed. Minnis, A. J. (Cambridge), 5–24

Burrow, J. A., 1984. *Essays on Medieval Literature* (Oxford)

Burrow, J. A., 1986. *The Ages of Man* (Oxford)

Burrow, J. A., 1993. *Thinking in Poetry: Three Medieval Examples* (London)

Burrow, J. A., 1994. *Thomas Hoccleve*, Authors of the Middle Ages 4 (Aldershot)

Burrow, J. A., ed., 1999. *Thomas Hoccleve's Complaint and Dialogue*, EETS 313

Burrow, J. A., 2002. *Gestures and Looks in Medieval Narrative* (Cambridge)

Camille, Michael, 1987. 'Labouring for the Lord: The Ploughman and Social Order in the Luttrell Psalter', *Art History* 10, 423–54

Cannon, Christopher, 1993. 'The Style and Authorship of the Otho Revision of Laʒamon's *Brut*', *Medium Ævum* 62, 187–209

Cannon, Christopher, 2004. *The Grounds of English Literature* (Oxford)

Cartlidge, Neil, ed., 2001. *The Owl and the Nightingale* (Exeter)

Cawley, A. C., ed., 1958. *The Wakefield Pageants in the Towneley Cycle* (Manchester)

Chaucer, Geoffrey, *Works*, ed. Benson, Larry D., 1987; *The Parliament of Fowls*, ed. *BOME*

Christine de Pizan, trans. Blumenfeld-Kosinski, Renate, and Kevin Brownlee, 1997

Clanchy, M. T., 1983. *England and its Rulers 1066–1272* (London)

Clanchy, M. T., 1993. *From Memory to Written Record* (2nd edn., Oxford)

Clark, Cecily, ed., 1970. *The Peterborough Chronicle 1070–1154* (2nd edn., Oxford)

Cleanness, eds. Andrew, Malcolm, and Ronald Waldron, 2002

Cloud of Unknowing, ed. Hodgson, Phyllis, 1982

Collins, Hugh E. L., 2000. *The Order of the Garter 1348–1461* (Oxford)

Crane, Susan, 1986. *Insular Romance: Politics, Faith, and Culture in Anglo-Norman and Middle English Literature* (Berkeley)

Crane, Susan, 1999. 'Anglo-Norman Cultures in England, 1066–1460', in *The Cambridge History of Medieval English Literature*, ed. Wallace, David (Cambridge), 35–60

Cursor Mundi, ed. Morris, Richard, 1879–93

Davidson, Clifford, ed., 1993. *A Tretise of Miraclis Pleyinge* (Kalamazoo, MI)

Davis, Norman, ed., 2004. *Paston Letters and Papers of the Fifteenth Century*, i–ii, EETS s.s. 20, 21 (1st pub. Oxford, 1971)

Day, M., ed., 1952. *The English Text of the Ancrene Riwle: Edited from Cotton Nero MS. A.XIV*, EETS 225

de Hamel, Christopher, 1992. *Medieval Craftsmen: Scribes and Illuminators* (London)

Dean, Ruth, J., 1999. *Anglo-Norman Literature: A Guide to Texts and Manuscripts*, ANTS Occasional Publications Series 3

Dialogus de Scaccario, ed. Johnson, Charles, 1983

Dickins, Bruce, and R. M. Wilson, eds., 1951. *Early Middle English Texts* (London)

Dillon, Janette, 1998. *Language and Stage in Medieval and Renaissance England* (Cambridge)

Dobson, R. B., ed., 1983. *The Peasants' Revolt of 1381* (2nd edn., London)

Donaldson, E. Talbot, 1970. *Speaking of Chaucer* (London)

Doyle, A. I., 1983. 'English Books In and Out of Court from Edward III to Henry VII', in *English Court Culture in the Later Middle Ages*, eds. Scattergood, V. J., and J. W. Sherborne (London), 163–81

Doyle, A. I., 1989. 'Publication by Members of the Religious Orders', in *Book Production and Publishing in Britain 1375–1475*, eds. Griffiths, Jeremy, and Derek Pearsall (Cambridge), 109–23

Doyle, A. I., and M. B. Parkes, 1978. 'The Production of Copies of the *Canterbury Tales* and the *Confessio Amantis* in the Early Fifteenth Century', in *Medieval Scribes, Manuscripts and Libraries*, eds. Parkes, M. B., and Andrew G. Watson (London), 163–210

Dyer, Christopher, 1994. 'Piers Plowman and Plowmen: A Historical Perspective', *Yearbook of Langland Studies* 8, 155–76

Dyer, Christopher, 2002. *Making a Living in the Middle Ages* (New Haven, CT)

Eccles, Mark, ed., 1969. *The Macro Plays*, EETS 262

Edwards, A. S. G., 1997. 'The Manuscript: British Library MS Cotton Nero A.x', in *A Companion to the Gawain-Poet*, eds. Brewer, Derek, and Jonathan Gibson (Cambridge), 197–219

Ellis, Roger, ed., 2001. *'My Compleinte' and Other Poems: Thomas Hoccleve* (Exeter)

First Worcester Fragment, eds. Dickins, Bruce, and R. M. Wilson, 1951

Fox and the Wolf, eds. Bennett, J. A. W., and G. V. Smithers, 1968

Franzen, Christine, 1991. *The Tremulous Hand of Worcester: A Study of Old English in the Thirteenth Century* (Oxford)

Froissart, Jean, *Chronicles*, trans. Brereton, Geoffrey, 1968

Furnivall, Frederick J., ed., 1897. *Hoccleve's Works: The Regiment of Princes*, EETS e.s. 72

Geoffrey of Monmouth, *The History of the Kings of Britain*, trans. Thorpe, Lewis, 1966

Gillespie, Vincent, 1989. 'Vernacular Books of Religion', in *Book Production and Publishing in Britain 1375–1475*, eds. Griffiths, Jeremy, and Derek Pearsall (Cambridge), 317–44

Gower, John, *Confessio Amantis*, ed. Macaulay, G. C., 1899–1902

Green, Richard Firth, 1979. 'Troilus and the Game of Love', *Chaucer Review* 13, 201–20

Green, Richard Firth, 1999. *A Crisis of Truth: Literature and Law in Ricardian England* (Philadelphia, PA)

Griffiths, Jeremy, 1983. '"Confessio Amantis": The Poem and its Pictures', in *Gower's Confessio Amantis: Responses and Reassessments*, ed. Minnis, A. J. (Cambridge), 163–78

Hall, Joseph, ed., 1920. *Selections From Early Middle English 1130–1250* (Oxford)

Hanna, Ralph, 1989. 'Sir Thomas Berkeley and his Patronage', *Speculum* 64, 878–916

Hanna, Ralph, 1993. *William Langland*, Authors of the Middle Ages 3 (Aldershot)

Hanna, Ralph, 1996. *Pursuing History: Middle English Manuscripts and their Texts* (Stanford, CA)

Hanna, Ralph, 2000. 'Reconsidering the Auchinleck Manuscript', in *New Directions in Later Medieval Manuscript Studies*, ed. Pearsall, Derek (Woodbridge), 91–102

Hanna, Ralph, 2004. 'Rolle and Related Works', in *A Companion to Middle English Prose*, ed. Edwards, A. S. G. (Cambridge), 19–31

Hanna, Ralph, 2005. *London Literature, 1300–1380* (Cambridge)

Harley Lyrics, ed. Brook, G. L., 1968

Havelok, ed. Smithers, G. V., 1987

Helmholz, R. H., 1974. *Marriage Litigation in Medieval England* (Cambridge)

Henry of Lancaster, *Livre de Seyntz Medicines*, ed. Arnould, E. J., 1940

Hoccleve, Thomas, *The Regiment of Princes*, ed. Furnivall, Frederick J., 1897; *Complaint and Dialogue*, ed. Burrow, J. A., 1999; *Balade to H. Somer*, ed. Ellis, Roger, 2001

Hodgson, Phyllis, ed., 1982. *The Cloud of Unknowing and Related Treatises* (Salzburg)

Horstmann, Carl, ed., 1892. *The Minor Poems of the Vernon MS*, i, EETS 98

Horstmann, Carl, ed., 1895–6. *Yorkshire Writers* (London)

Hudson, Anne, 1985. *Lollards and their Books* (London)

Hudson, Anne, 1988. *The Premature Reformation* (Oxford)

Jacobs, Nicolas, 1972. 'Alliterative Storms: A Topos in Middle English', *Speculum* 47, 695–719

Johnson, Charles, ed., 1983. *Dialogus de Scaccario: The Course of the Exchequer* (Oxford)

Justice, Steven, 1994. *Writing and Rebellion: England in 1381* (Berkeley)

Kean, P. M., 1967. *The Pearl: An Interpretation* (London)

Kean, P. M., 1972. *Chaucer and the Making of English Poetry* (London)

Keen, Maurice, 1990. *English Society in the Later Middle Ages* (London)

Ker, N. R., and A. J. Piper, 1992. *Medieval Manuscripts in British Libraries*, IV (Oxford)

King, Edmund, ed., 1994. *The Anarchy of King Stephen's Reign* (Oxford)

Laȝamon's *Brut*, eds. Brook, G. L., and R. F. Leslie, 1963, 1978

Laing, Margaret, 1993. *Catalogue of Sources for a Linguistic Atlas of Early Medieval English* (Cambridge)

Langland, William, *Piers Plowman*, (B-Text) ed. Schmidt, A. V. C., 1995; (C-Text) ed. Pearsall, Derek, 1994

Legge, M. Dominica, 1963. *Anglo-Norman Literature and its Background* (Oxford)

Lewis, C. S., 1936. *The Allegory of Love* (Oxford)

Lumby, J. Rawson, ed., 1866. *King Horn, Floriz and Blauncheflur, The Assumption of our Lady*, EETS 14 (rev. McKnight, G. H., 1901)

Lyall, R. J., 1989. 'Materials: The Paper Revolution', in *Book Production and Publishing in Britain 1375–1475*, eds. Griffiths, Jeremy, and Derek Pearsall (Cambridge), 11–29

Lydgate, John, *The Churl and the Bird*, ed. MacCracken, H. N., 1934; *Fall of Princes*, ed. Bergen, Henry, 1924–7

Macaulay, G. C., ed., 1899–1902. *The Complete Works of John Gower*, 4 vols. (Oxford)

McCarthy, Conor, 2004. *Marriage in Medieval England* (Woodbridge)

MacCracken, H. N., ed., 1934. *John Lydgate: The Minor Poems*, vol. 2, EETS 192

Mankind, ed. Eccles, Mark, 1969

Manning, Robert, *The Chronicle*, ed. Sullens, Idelle, 1996

Marie de France, *Lais*, trans. Burgess, Glyn S., and Keith Busby, 1986

Mathew, Gervase, 1968. *The Court of Richard II* (London)

Meditacioun of þe Fyve Woundes, ed. Horstmann, Carl, 1895–6, vol. 2, 440–1

Merrilees, Brian S., ed., 1970. *Le Petit Plet*, ANTS 20

Middleton, Anne, 1997. 'Acts of Vagrancy: The C Version "Autobiography" and the Statute of 1388', in *Written Work: Langland, Labor, and Authorship*, eds. Justice, Steven, and Kathryn Kerby-Fulton (Philadelphia, PA), 208–317

Millett, Bella, 1996. 'Women in No Man's Land', in *Women and Literature in Britain, 1150–1500*, ed. Meale, Carol M. (2nd edn., Cambridge)

Millett, Bella, ed., 2006. *Ancrene Wisse*, i, EETS 325

Millett, Bella, and Jocelyn Wogan-Browne, eds., 1990. *Medieval English Prose for Women* (Oxford)

Minnis, A. J., 1995. *Oxford Guides to Chaucer: The Shorter Poems* (Oxford)

Mooney, Linne R., 2006. 'Chaucer's Scribe', *Speculum* 81, 97–138

Morgan, Nigel, 1982. *Early Gothic Manuscripts (I) 1190–1250* (London)

Morris, Richard, ed., 1866. *Dan Michel's Ayenbite of Inwyt*, EETS 23

Morris, Richard, ed., 1879–93. *Cursor Mundi*, EETS 57, 59, 62, 66, 68, 99, 101

Muir, Laurence, 1970. 'Translations and Paraphrases of the Bible, and Commentaries', in *A Manual of the Writings in Middle English 1050–1500*, ed. Severs, J. Burke (Hamden, CT), vol. 2, 381–409

Nicholls, J. W., 1985. *The Matter of Courtesy: Medieval Courtesy Books and the Gawain Poet* (Woodbridge)

Owl and the Nightingale, ed. Cartlidge, Neil, 2001

Parkes, M. B., 1979. *English Cursive Book Hands 1250–1500* (2nd edn., London)

Parkes, M. B., 1992. *Pause and Effect: An Introduction to the History of Punctuation in the West* (Aldershot)

Paston Letters, ed. Davis, Norman, 2004

Patch, Howard Rollin, 1950. *The Other World* (Cambridge, MA)

Patience, ed. BOME

Pearl, eds. Andrew, Malcolm, and Ronald Waldron, 2002

Pearsall, Derek, 1985. *The Canterbury Tales* (London)

Pearsall, Derek, 1992. *The Life of Geoffrey Chaucer* (Oxford)

Pearsall, Derek, ed., 1994. *Piers Plowman: An Edition of the C-Text* (2nd edn., Exeter)

Pearsall, Derek, 1996. 'Madness in *Sir Orfeo*', in *Romance Reading on the Book*, eds. Fellows, Jennifer, Rosalind Field, Gillian Rogers and Judith Weiss (Cardiff), 51–63

Peterborough Chronicle, ed. Clark, Cecily, 1970

Petit Plet, ed. Merrilees, Brian S., 1970

Plummer, Charles, and John Earle, eds., 1892–9. *Two of the Saxon Chronicles Parallel*, 2 vols. (Oxford)

Proverbs of Alfred, ed. Hall, Joseph, 1920

Putter, Ad, 1995. *Sir Gawain and the Green Knight and French Arthurian Romance* (Oxford)

Putter, Ad, 1996. *An Introduction to the Gawain-Poet* (London)

Revard, Carter, 2000. 'Scribe and Provenance', in *Studies in the Harley Manuscript*, ed. Fein, Susanna (Kalamazoo, MI), 21–109

Richmond, Colin, 1990. *The Paston Family in the Fifteenth Century: The First Phase* (Cambridge)

Rigg, A. G., 1992. *A History of Anglo-Latin Literature 1066–1422* (Cambridge)

Robertson, Elizabeth, 2003. '"This Living Hand": Thirteenth-Century Female Literacy, Materialist Immanence, and the Reader of the *Ancrene Wisse*', *Speculum* 78, 1–36

Rolle, Richard, *English Psalter*, ed. Allen, Hope Emily, 1931

Rothwell, William, 1976. 'The Role of French in Thirteenth-Century England', *Bulletin of the John Rylands Library* 58, 445–66

Rothwell, William, ed., 1990. *Walter de Bibbesworth, Le Tretiz*, ANTS Plain Texts Series 6

Rouse, Robert Allen, 2005. *The Idea of Anglo-Saxon England in Middle English Romance* (Cambridge)

St Erkenwald, ed. BOME

Salter, Elizabeth, 1988. *English and International: Studies in the Literature, Art and Patronage of Medieval England*, eds. Pearsall, Derek, and Nicolette Zeeman (Cambridge)

Sandler, Lucy Freeman, 1986. *Gothic Manuscripts 1285–1385*, 2 vols. (London)

Saul, Nigel, 1997. *Richard II* (New Haven, CT)

Scanlon, Larry, 1994. *Narrative, Authority and Power: The Medieval Exemplum and the Chaucerian Tradition* (Cambridge)

Scanlon, Larry, 1998. 'The Riddle of Incest: John Gower and the Problem of Medieval Sexuality', in *Re-Visioning Gower*, ed. Yeager, R. F. (Asheville, NC), 93–127

Scase, Wendy, 1992. 'Reginald Pecock, John Carpenter and John Colop's Common-Profit Books', *Medium Ævum* 61, 261–74

Schmidt, A. V. C., ed., 1995. *The Vision of Piers Plowman: A Critical Edition of the B-Text* (2nd edn., London)

Schofield, Phillipp R., 2003. *Peasant and Community in Medieval England, 1200–1500* (Basingstoke)

Schramm, Wilbur Lang, 1933. 'The Cost of Books in Chaucer's Time', *Modern Language Notes* 48, 139–45

Scott, Kathleen L., 1996. *Later Gothic Manuscripts*, 2 vols. (London)

Second Shepherds' Play, ed. Cawley, A. C., 1958

Severs, J. Burke, 1967. *A Manual of the Writings in Middle English 1050–1500*, vol. 1 (New Haven, CT)

Shepherd, Geoffrey, ed., 1959. *Ancrene Wisse: Parts Six and Seven* (London)

Sherley-Price, Leo, rev., Latham, R. E., trans., 1968. *Bede: A History of the English Church and People* (Harmondsworth)

Shonk, Timothy A., 1985. 'A Study of the Auchinleck Manuscript: Bookmen and Bookmaking in the Early Fourteenth Century', *Speculum* 60, 71–91

Short, Ian, 1991. 'Patrons and Polyglots: French Literature in Twelfth-Century England', *Anglo-Norman Studies* 14, 229–49

Sir Gawain and the Green Knight, eds. Andrew, Malcolm, and Ronald Waldron, 2002

Sir Orfeo, ed. BOME

Sisam, Kenneth, ed., 1921. *Fourteenth Century Verse and Prose* (Oxford)

Smith, J. J., 1996. *An Historical Study of English* (London)

Smithers, G. V., ed., 1987. *Havelok* (Oxford)

Spearing, A. C., 1976. *Medieval Dream-Poetry* (Cambridge)

Stahl, William, trans., 1952. *Macrobius: Commentary on the Dream of Scipio* (New York)

Stanley, E. G., 1969. 'Laȝamon's Antiquarian Sentiments', *Medium Ævum* 38, 23–37

Stone, Lawrence, 1979. *The Family, Sex and Marriage in England, 1500–1800* (London)

Strohm, Paul, 1971. '*Storie, Spelle, Geste, Romaunce, Tragedie*: Generic Distinctions in the Middle English Troy Narratives', *Speculum* 46, 348–59

Sullens, Idelle, ed., 1996. *Robert Mannyng of Brunne: The Chronicle* (Binghampton)

Swanson, R. N., 1989. *Church and Society in Late Medieval England* (Oxford)

Swanton, Michael, trans., 2000. *The Anglo-Saxon Chronicles* (2nd edn., London)

Thomas, Hugh M., 2003. *The English and the Normans: Ethnic Hostility, Assimilation, and Identity 1066–c.1220* (Oxford)

Thompson, John J., 1987. *Robert Thornton and the London Thornton Manuscript* (Cambridge)

Thorpe, Lewis, trans., 1966. *Geoffrey of Monmouth: The History of the Kings of Britain* (Harmondsworth)

Tolkien, J. R. R., 1929. '*Ancrene Wisse* and *Hali Meiðhad*', *Essays and Studies* 14, 104–26

Tolkien, J. R. R., 1934. 'Chaucer as a Philologist: *The Reeve's Tale*', *Transactions of the Philological Society*, 1–70

Tretise of Miraclis Pleyinge, ed. Davidson, Clifford, 1993

Trevisa, John, *Dialogue between a Lord and a Clerk*, ed. BOME

Turville-Petre, Thorlac, 1990. 'The Relationship of the Vernon and Clopton Manuscripts', in *Studies in the Vernon Manuscript*, ed. Pearsall, Derek (Cambridge), 29–44

Turville-Petre, Thorlac, 1996. *England the Nation: Language, Literature, and National Identity, 1290–1340* (Oxford)

Turville-Petre, Thorlac, 2003. 'Oxford, Bodleian Library, MS Digby 86: A Thirteenth-Century Commonplace Book in its Social Context', in *Family and Dynasty in Late Medieval England*, eds. Eales, Richard, and Shaun Tyas (Donington), 56–66

Twycross, Meg, 1994. 'The Theatricality of Medieval English Plays', in *The Cambridge Companion to Medieval English Theatre*, ed. Beadle, Richard (Cambridge), 37–84

Tydeman, William, 1994. 'An Introduction to Medieval English Theatre', in *The Cambridge Companion to Medieval English Theatre*, ed. Beadle, Richard (Cambridge), 1–36

Vale, Juliet, 1982. *Edward III and Chivalry* (Woodbridge)

Vale, Juliet, 2001. 'Arthur in English Society', in *The Arthur of the English*, ed. Barron, W. R. J. (Cardiff), 185–96

Vale, Malcolm, 2001. *The Princely Court: Medieval Courts and Culture in North-West Europe, 1270–1380* (Oxford)

Wace's *Roman de Brut*, ed. and trans. Weiss, Judith, 2002

Walter de Bibbesworth's *Tretiz*, ed. Rothwell, William, 1990

Ward, Jennifer C., 1992. *English Noblewomen in the Later Middle Ages* (London)

Watson, Nicholas, 1995. 'Censorship and Cultural Change in Late-Medieval England: Vernacular Theology, the Oxford Translation Debate, and Arundel's Constitutions of 1409', *Speculum* 70, 822–64

Watson, Nicholas, 1999. 'The Middle English Mystics', in *The Cambridge History of Medieval English Literature*, ed. Wallace, David (Cambridge), 539–65

Watts, V. E., trans., 1969. *Boethius, The Consolation of Philosophy* (Harmondsworth)

Weiss, Judith, ed. and trans., 2002. *Wace's Roman de Brut: A History of the British* (2nd edn., Exeter)

Welter, Jean-Thiébaut, 1927. *L'Exemplum dans la Littérature Religieuse et Didactique du Moyen Âge* (Paris)

Whatley, Gordon, 1986. 'Heathens and Saints: *St. Erkenwald* in its Legendary Context', *Speculum* 61, 330–63

White, Hugh, trans., 1993. *Ancrene Wisse: Guide for Anchoresses* (London)

White, Hugh, 2000. *Nature, Sex, and Goodness in a Medieval Literary Tradition* (Oxford)

Whiting, Ella Keats, ed., 1931. *The Poems of John Audelay*, EETS 184

Wilson, R. M., 1970. *The Lost Literature of Medieval England* (2nd edn., London)

Windeatt, Barry, 1992. *Oxford Guides to Chaucer: Troilus and Criseyde* (Oxford)

Woolf, Rosemary, 1968. *The English Religious Lyric in the Middle Ages* (Oxford)

Woolf, Rosemary, 1972. *The English Mystery Plays* (London)

Woolf, Rosemary, 1986. *Art and Doctrine: Essays on Medieval Literature*, ed. O'Donoghue, Heather (London)

Yeager, R. F., 2000. 'Politics and the French Language in England during the Hundred Years' War: The Case of John Gower', in *Inscribing the Hundred Years' War in French and English Cultures*, ed. Baker, Denise N. (Albany, NY), 127–57

York Plays, ed. Beadle, Richard, 1982

Index

References to major discussions of texts are in **bold** type.

.

Printed and bound by CPI Group (UK) Ltd, Croydon, CR0 4YY
12/04/2022

03119976-0001